Foundations of Atlas

Rapid Ajax Development with ASP.NET 2.0

Laurence Moroney

Apress®

Foundations of Atlas: Rapid Ajax Development with ASP.NET 2.0

Copyright © 2006 by Laurence Moroney

ISBN-13 (pbk): 978-1-59059-647-0

ISBN-10 (pbk): 1-59059-647-1

Printed and bound in the United States of America 9 8 7 6 5 4 3 2

Lead Editor: Ewan Buckingham
Technical Reviewer: Keith Smith
Editorial Board: Steve Anglin, Ewan Buckingham, Gary Cornell, Jason Gilmore, Jonathan Gennick, Jonathan Hassell, James Huddleston, Chris Mills, Matthew Moodie, Dominic Shakeshaft, Jim Sumser, Keir Thomas, Matt Wade
Project Manager: Kylie Johnston
Copy Edit Manager: Nicole LeClerc
Copy Editor: Kim Wimpsett
Assistant Production Director: Kari Brooks-Copony
Production Editor: Laura Esterman
Compositor: Linda Weidemann, Wolf Creek Press
Proofreader: Nancy Sixsmith
Indexer: Michael Brinkman
Artist: Kinetic Publishing Services, LLC
Cover Designer: Kurt Krames
Manufacturing Director: Tom Debolski

Distributed to the book trade worldwide by Springer-Verlag New York, Inc., 233 Spring Street, 6th Floor, New York, NY 10013. Phone 1-800-SPRINGER, fax 201-348-4505, e-mail orders-ny@springer-sbm.com, or visit http://www.springeronline.com.

For information on translations, please contact Apress directly at 2560 Ninth Street, Suite 219, Berkeley, CA 94710. Phone 510-549-5930, fax 510-549-5939, e-mail info@apress.com, or visit http://www.apress.com.

The source code for this book is available to readers at http://www.apress.com in the Source Code section.

This book is dedicated to my brother, Niall, all-round cool guy and great big brother, as well as provider of free accommodation whenever I visit Ireland; to his wife, Sandra, among the warmest and most loving people I have ever met; to his son, Sean, the local guitar god; and to his daughter, Aideen, the sweetest girl in Ireland.

Contents at a Glance

Contents

Foreword

The last year has seen a series of incredible advances in user experiences on the Web. As the Web continues to grow as a marketplace for web applications and services, the user experience has become a key differentiator in attracting and retaining users and in driving revenue and productivity. This has led to an explosion of richer, more personalized, more interactive sites that fully exploit the capabilities of the browser platform.

What is all the more remarkable about this trend is that it is built on a technology foundation that has been around for a long time and has only recently acquired the name Ajax. Microsoft pioneered both Dynamic HTML and CSS in Internet Explorer nearly a decade ago, and the current edition of the JavaScript language is several years old. And the cornerstone of Ajax—the XMLHttpRequest object, which enables more flexible communication between the browser and server—was built into Internet Explorer in 1998 to support pioneering applications such as Outlook Web Access.

So why has Ajax suddenly started to catch on now? Clearly, the technology has matured and standardized; Ajax's capabilities are available on more platforms and browsers than ever before and can now be found on the vast majority of desktop computers. The computing power of the desktop computer has also grown significantly. And, finally, the Web itself has evolved into a rich platform. These trends have, in turn, driven the need to invest in better, more differentiated experiences.

With these experiences, however, come greater challenges for the developer. It is no secret that developers often lack the frameworks, tools, and skills to be effective with DHTML and JavaScript. Differences in browsers are also a frequent cause for trouble. Finally, these applications are also harder to develop because the Ajax model is inherently asynchronous in nature. To try to address these kinds of challenges, Ajax libraries have become commonplace, but few provide a rich framework and the tools that are integrated with today's web programming models and tools.

When we began building Atlas in the summer of 2005, we set out to build an end-to-end framework and the tools that would bring unparalleled productivity to web application development and make it easy for anyone to build a rich web experience on the standards-based web client platform. At a high level, we designed Atlas with the following goals in mind:

A rich framework for web experiences: Allow anyone to develop an interactive, personalized web experience by easily wiring together controls and components. Provide a rich toolbox of built-in components, and allow developers to easily develop their own. Even developers who are familiar with scripting should benefit from patterns that enable easier manageability and reuse.

Seamless integration with the .NET programming model: Deliver an end-to-end experience that allows Atlas applications to have easy access to the richness of the programming model of ASP.NET and the .NET Framework on the server.

Choice of server-centric or client-centric application models: Allow developers who use server-centric models such as ASP.NET to easily enrich their applications with Atlas, without learning scripting or asynchronous client communications. At the same time, allow anyone to use the richness of Atlas to take full advantage of the browser.

Fully cross-platform and standards-based: We expect that developers using Atlas will want to build applications that can run on any browser. Atlas is designed to work on a wide variety of modern browsers and platforms and includes functionality that takes much of the worry out of browser compatibility. The Atlas Script framework also works with any web server.

No installation footprint: Atlas doesn't require any new client installation; it works on the browser you have on your desktop computer today. The Atlas "client" consists of a set of JavaScript files that are downloaded by the browser like any other web content.

In trying to achieve these goals, we built a free, cross-platform, standards-based framework that lets you easily build richer, more interactive, more personalized experiences on the Web.

In developing Atlas, we also took an open approach that sets a new example for how we hope to build developer tools and frameworks at Microsoft. From early in the product cycle, we began making Atlas available to the developer community as a Community Technology Preview (CTP) release—the first release was less than eight weeks after the start of the project—and have continued to release previews every four to six weeks since then. Through these CTPs, we have gathered an incredible amount of early feedback that has helped shape the product profoundly, and we are indebted to our developer community for their participation. As we continue to work toward the full release of Atlas, we have started to invite community partnership in new ways, such as by releasing the Atlas Control Toolkit, a collection of samples that we will develop in collaboration with the developer community.

Such an open development model has not come without its growing pains. In the first preview releases of Atlas, we had a raw product with little documentation and few samples. The small number of early adopters and partners who used Atlas in these early days had to dig deep to understand it and have stood by us over the months as we developed it into what it is today.

As an author, Laurence was one of those early partners, and his knowledge of the product clearly shows in this definitive guide to Atlas. This book gives you everything you need to get started building rich web experiences with Atlas. It covers all the concepts, starting with a clear explanation of the Ajax model and of ASP.NET. It then guides you through the Atlas framework in great breadth, exploring the client script framework, the Atlas server controls for ASP.NET, and the rich toolbox of built-in controls and components.

He covers each topic with a straightforward, step-by-step narrative, accompanied by code examples and illustrations that present concepts in a clear and practical way. A special feature is Chapter 11, which illustrates how to apply Atlas effectively to develop a rich real-world application.

I am very excited about Atlas and the potential it delivers for building rich web experiences. If you are looking for tools to unleash your creativity and help you build new, differentiated experiences on the Web, you will find Atlas and this book invaluable. I sincerely hope you have as much fun working with Atlas as we had building it.

Shanku Niyogi
Product Unit Manager, UI Framework and Services Team
Microsoft Corporation

About the Author

 **LAURENCE MORONEY** is the director for technology evangelism at Mainsoft, the cross-platform company. He specializes in evangelizing the power of ASP.NET and Visual Studio .NET through Mainsoft technology for the development and maintenance of J2EE applications. Prior to Mainsoft, he worked as an architect for Reuters developing financial and communications applications for the Wall Street community. An experienced developer and architect, he has designed and implemented software for a variety of applications spanning the spectrum from casinos to banks to jails to airports. He's a big fan of professional sports, particularly soccer, and is still waiting for Bruce Arena to call him up for the U.S. World Cup squad.

About the Technical Reviewer

■**KEITH SMITH** is a senior product manager at Microsoft Corporation in Redmond, Washington. Keith joined Microsoft in 1998 as a software engineer on Microsoft Visual J++ where he was responsible for the Windows Foundation Class's DHTML controls. Today he focuses on ASP.NET, Atlas, and the web development technologies and components of Visual Studio (VS) and Visual Web Developer Express Edition (VWD). Keith's ASP.NET involvement dates back to version 1.0 when he was a member of the engineering team responsible for the core ASP.NET controls and when he led the team responsible for ASP.NET performance and stress testing. More recently, Keith managed the entire VWD quality assurance engineering team. Following the release of VS 2005 and ASP.NET 2.0, Keith moved to his current product management role, in developer marketing, where he owns the overall marketing strategy and execution of creative programs that drive the adoption of Microsoft's web platform and tools.

Acknowledgments

I'd like to take this time to acknowledge some people who were amazing in helping to construct this book:

- Scott Guthrie owns the Atlas technology at Microsoft and was a terrific supporter in writing it and in getting access to the technology.

- Shanku Niyogi, the ASP.NET group program manager at Microsoft, was there to meet with me when I was shaping ideas for the construction of the book, to listen to my feedback on where the technology should be going, and to help fix bugs in my code when Atlas was at an early stage.

- Keith Smith, the product manager for ASP.NET and Atlas at Microsoft, was hands down the best technical reviewer I have ever worked with. Straight to the point, factual, and extraordinarily pleasant, he helped hone this book into what it is today.

- Simon Calvert, a developer on the Atlas project, was there to help me navigate the undocumented sections. I thanked him profusely for being the technical reviewer before realizing I had mixed him up with Keith! (Sorry, guys.)

- Wilco Bauwer is the joint-best Atlas blogger there is (`http://www.wilcob.net`).

- Nikhil Kothari is also the joint-best Atlas blogger there is (`http://www.nikhilk.net`).

- Joel Bonette, a researcher at Lousiana State University, discovered the book through my blog and, through being the first purchaser of it, strongly encouraged me through the dark and frustrating days when I couldn't make head or tail of the undocumented features.

- Ewan Buckingham, editor at Apress, is the perfect editor—hands-off and completely trusting.

- Kylie Johnston, project manager at Apress, kept me sane and having fun as I wrote.

- Kim Wimpsett, the copy editor, made me feel really good by not making too many corrections to the text.

Thank goodness this isn't the Oscars, because I just have too many people to thank; it is a book, so I can take my time to name them all!

Introduction

Ajax is fast becoming *the* buzzword in web development for 2006. It's also becoming a de facto standard for developing user-centric web applications. It's an evolutionary step in the user experience and is being used in more and more web applications from Google Local maps to Live.com to Amazon and beyond.

But how do you write Ajax applications? You've got to be a JavaScript expert and use tools that are not as sophisticated as those your C# or Java friends use. As such, it can be difficult and time-consuming to develop, debug, and maintain Ajax applications despite their innate user friendliness.

Microsoft is contributing to the solution for this problem with its Atlas framework. This builds on top of the best-of-breed ASP.NET technology and Visual Studio 2005 integrated development environment (IDE) to bring major productivity leaps to Ajax development.

With Atlas you can easily convert your existing ASP.NET applications to Ajax ones, and you can add sophisticated user interface elements such as drag and drop, networking, and browser compatibility layers with simple declarative programming (or, if you prefer to use JavaScript, you can do that too).

This book is a primer on this technology. It will take you through the evolution of web applications to where they are today, introduce you to Ajax, put it in context, and then take you into how to build Ajax applications quickly and simply, taking advantage of the IDE productivity and full debugging offered by Visual Studio 2005.

It's going to be a fun ride, and by the end of it, you'll be an expert in Web 2.0 and hungry to start developing for it. And who knows? You may even start shaping Web 3.0!

Who This Book Is For

This book is for anybody who is interested in developing next-generation web application interfaces that make the most of Ajax-style asynchronous functionality. Anybody who has ever coded a web page will understand the latency problems associated with postbacks and maintaining state and will be able to gain valuable new tools for their programming arsenal by reading this book.

Even if you don't know ASP.NET, C#, or Visual Basic .NET, you should still be able to understand and follow along with this book, but it would be helpful to get a good grounding in these technologies first.

How This Book Is Structured

This book starts by describing the evolution of user interface software from the earliest punch cards to the modern Ajax applications. It describes how the thin client model can be used to cut costs and complexity and tells the true story of how a thin client, Ajax-style application got the Wall Street community up and running quickly after September 11, 2001.

It then dives into what Ajax is and how it works so that if you aren't familiar with it, you can see what all the fuss is about.

Next, it introduces Atlas and how it works in the context of ASP.NET. It describes the client-side and server-side functionality of Atlas, showing each of the libraries and controls and describing how you can use them.

It is packed with sample code and figures, so you'll learn by example. The final chapter is devoted to a single example of a large-scale application that brings all the concepts together. It's very much a hands-on book.

Prerequisites

You'll need Visual Studio 2005; any edition is fine. You'll also need the Atlas binaries and add-ins to Visual Studio 2005, which can be downloaded from `http://atlas.asp.net`.

Downloading the Code

You will be able to download chapter-by-chapter source code from the Apress web site at `http://www.apress.com`. This is compressed in a single zip file for your convenience.

Contacting the Author

You can reach Laurence Moroney via `ljpm@philotic.com` or at `http://www.philotic.com/blog`.

■ ■ ■

CHAPTER 1

Introducing Ajax

Welcome to *Foundations of Atlas*. This book is intended to get you up and running with the new framework from Microsoft that allows you to build web 2.0 applications that implement Ajax functionality. If you've been working in the web field at all, you will have found Ajax hard to avoid—and even harder to implement. Microsoft has thrown its hat into the Ajax arena by doing what it does best—giving you, the developer, tools that allow you to be productive and solve your business needs.

This chapter will bring you up-to-date on web application technology from the dawn of computing history to today, putting Ajax and Atlas in context. It's the beginning of what I hope will be a fun and informative ride. This book is based on the July 2006 Community technical preview of the Atlas SDK, available on `http://atlas.asp.net`.

Delving into the History of Web Application Technology

The user interface has evolved along a cyclical path from a light footprint to a heavy footprint and back again. Users' requirements and demands for extra functionality drive the heavier footprint, and users' requirements and demands for an easy installation, upgrade, and maintenance drive the lighter footprint. With each iteration, the "lighter" user interfaces gain rich functionality, and the "heavier" user interfaces become easier to install, upgrade, and maintain.

The original user interfaces were probably the lightest clients of all—punch cards that were fed into a central server that in turn printed results, resulting in a simple request/response architecture (see Figure 1-1).

As computers became more sophisticated, the punch card and printer were replaced by a terminal that fed results into and rendered results from the central server (see Figure 1-2). For basic processing this was useful, but as computers' needs increased—for example, to handle the new requirements of email or network news—the terminals had to get smarter. If you remember the old terminal-based email programs such as elm or the network news-readers, you'll remember needing three or four extra fingers to do anything useful! Architecturally, this wasn't much different from the punch card request/response architecture, but it unified the point of contact with the mainframe and changed the medium from paper to electrons. So, although the architecture did not change, the implementation did—and it was this change in implementation that was a driving factor in improving the overall user experience of applications, a fact that is still true today.

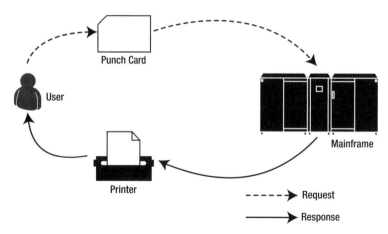

Figure 1-1. *Punch card request/response architecture*

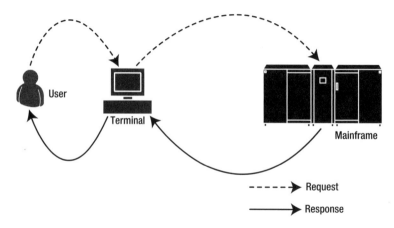

Figure 1-2. *Terminal-based request/response architecture*

With the advent of the personal computer, much of the old server functionality wasn't necessary anymore. This was because the main use of servers at that time was for functions that could easily take place on a personal computer, such as calculations or analyses (see Figure 1-3). Functionality that required connectivity, such as email and network newsreaders, could still be achieved on a personal computer through terminal emulation.

Then someone had the bright idea of using the power of the personal computer to enhance the online experience, taking it away from the green-and-black terminal and allowing features such as email, news, and graphics to appear in full four-color glory (see Figure 1-4). The personal computer flourished in power, and the early personal computers gave way to much more powerful machines with better graphics, faster processing chips, more memory, and persistent storage through hard drives.

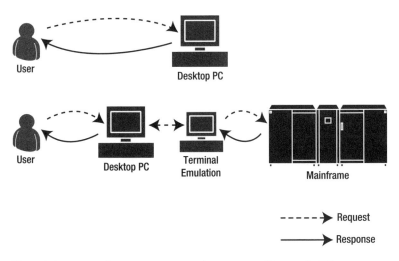

Request

Response

Figure 1-3. *Personal computer request/response online and offline*

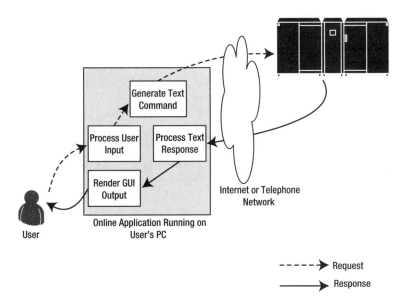

Request

Response

Figure 1-4. *Request/response architecture of graphical user interface (GUI) application talking to mainframe*

With this steadily exponential increase in computing power at the desktop, applications became more sophisticated, complex, and functional than anything before on centralized mainframe supercomputers. Full GUIs soon became the norm. Microsoft Windows appeared, following Apple, Atari, and other GUI-focused computers. Soon after, office productivity applications exploded onto the scene; and as people began using these applications daily, they required even faster and more sophisticated platforms, and the client continued to evolve exponentially.

It's important to note that the more sophisticated applications were *disconnected* applications. Office productivity suites, desktop-publishing applications, games, and the like, were
all distributed, installed, and run on the client via a fixed medium such as a floppy disk or CD.
In other words, they weren't connected in any way.

The other breed of application, which was evolving much more slowly, was the *connected* application, where a graphical front end wrapped a basic, text-based communication
back end for online applications such as email. CompuServe was one of the largest online
providers, and despite the innovative abstraction of its simple back end to make for a more
user-centric, graphical experience along the lines of the heavy desktop applications, its
underlying old-school model was still apparent. Remember the old Go commands? Despite
the buttons on the screen that allowed a user to enter communities, these simply issued a
Go *<communityname>* command behind the scenes on your behalf.

Although this approach was excellent and provided a rich online experience, it had to be
written and maintained specifically for each platform, so for a multiplatform experience, the
vendor had to write a client application for Windows, Unix, Apple, and all other operating
systems and variants.

But in the early 1990s, a huge innovation happened: the web browser.

This innovation began the slow merger of these two application types (connected and
disconnected)—a merger that still continues today. We all know the web browser by now, and
it is arguably the most ubiquitous application used on modern computers, displacing solitaire
and the word processor for this storied achievement!

But the web browser ultimately became much more than just a new means for abstract-
ing the textual nature of the client/server network. It became an abstraction on top of the
operating system on which applications could be written and executed (see Figure 1-5). This
was, and is, important. As long as applications are written to the specification defined by that
abstraction, they should be able to run anywhere without further intervention or installation
on behalf of the application developer. Of course, the browser would have to be present on the
system, but the value proposition of having a web browser available to the operating system
was extremely important and ultimately launched many well-known legal battles.

The problem, of course, with this abstraction was that it was relatively simple and not
originally designed or implemented for anything more complex than laying out and formatting text and graphics. I am, of course, referring to Hypertext Markup Language (HTML). This
specification, implemented by a browser, meant that simple text could be placed on a server,
transferred from a server, interpreted by a browser, and laid out in a far more pleasing way
than simple green-on-black on a page, giving the user a better experience. More important,
however, it could generate a whole new breed of application developers; all a developer had
to do for an online, connected application to have a graphical experience was to generate it as
HTML, and the browser would do the rest. You wouldn't need the resources of a CompuServe
or an America Online to build an application that rendered the text for you! All you had to do
was generate HTML, either by coding it directly or writing a server-side application (in C) that
would generate it for you. Although the Internet had been around for a long time, only at this
point was it really being born.

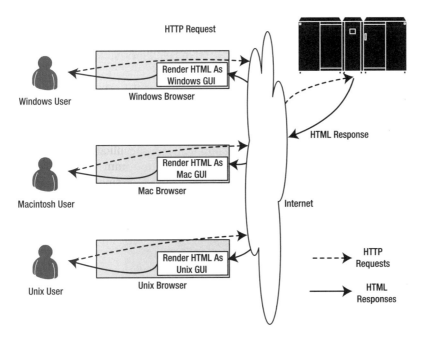

Figure 1-5. *Web browser–based request/response architecture*

And guess what happened? The cycle began again.

Everybody jumped on the browser bandwagon, and Common Gateway Interface (CGI) applications, written on a server and delivered to a browser, were hot. The user experience, with the only interaction being postbacks to the server (in much a similar vein to terminals, only prettier), soon became too limiting, and new technologies began to emerge to improve the user experience.

Enter Java and the applet. Java, a virtual machine on top of a virtual machine (the browser) on top of a virtual machine (the operating system) on top of a real machine (the underlying hardware), gave a greater abstraction, and it introduced a new platform that developers could code to and have even richer applications running within the browser. This was important, because it accelerated what could be done within a browser, delivered using the simple transport mechanisms of the Internet but again without requiring the resources of a huge company writing your own GUI platform on which to do it. Of course, it suffered from constraints; namely, to achieve a cross-platform experience, developers had to follow a lowest common denominator approach. The clearest example of this was in its support for the mouse. The Apple operating systems supported one button, the Microsoft Windows–based ones supported two, and many Unix platforms supported three. As such, Java applets could support only one button, and many Unix users found themselves two buttons short!

The Java virtual machine and language evolved to become a server-side implementation and a great replacement for C on the server. In addition to this, HTML continued to evolve, allowing for more flexibility, and its big brother, Dynamic HTML (DHTML), was born. In addition, scripting was added to the platform (at the browser level), with JavaScript (unrelated to Java despite the name) and VBScript being born. To handle these scripting languages, parsers were bolted onto the browser, and the extensible browser architecture proved to be a powerful addition.

Thanks to extensibility, applications such as Macromedia Flash added a new virtual machine on top of the browser, allowing for even more flexible and intense applications. The extensible browser then brought about ActiveX technology on the Windows platform, whereby native application functionality could be run within the browser when using Microsoft browsers (or alternative ones with a plug-in that supported ActiveX). This was a powerful solution, because it enabled native functionality to be accessible from networked applications (see Figure 1-6). This got around the restrictions imposed by the security sandbox and lowest common denominator approach of the Java virtual machine, but this ultimately led to problems in the same vein as distributing client-only applications; specifically, a heavy configuration of the desktop was necessary to get them to work. Although this configuration could be automated to a certain degree, it gave two show-stopping points for many.

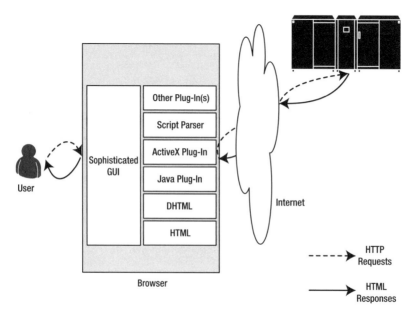

Figure 1-6. *Sophisticated browser architecture*

First, it didn't always work, and the nature of configuration, changing the Windows registry, often failed—or worse, broke other applications. ActiveX controls were rarely self-contained and usually installed runtime support files. Different versions of these support files could easily be installed on top of each other, a common occurrence leading to broken applications (called DLL Hell).

The second problem was security. A user's computer, when connected to the Internet, could effectively allow code to run, written by anybody, and the ActiveX technology was fully native, not restricted by the Java or HTML sandboxes (more about these in a moment); therefore, a user could innocently go to a web page that downloaded an ActiveX control that wrought havoc or stole vital information from their system. As such, many users refused to use them, and many corporate administrators even disallowed them from use within the enterprise. The virtual nature of Java and HTML—where applications and pages were coded to work on a specific virtual machine—offered better security; these machines couldn't do anything malicious, and therefore applications written to run on them also couldn't. The user was effectively safe, though limited in the scope of what they could do.

At the end of the 1990s, Microsoft unveiled the successor to ActiveX (among others) in its Java-like .NET Framework. This framework would form Microsoft's strategic positioning for many years. Like Java, it provided a virtual machine (the common language runtime [CLR]) on which applications would run. These applications could do only what the CLR allowed and were called *managed* applications. The .NET Framework was much more sophisticated than the Java virtual machine, allowing for desktop and web applications with differing levels of functionality (depending on which was used). This was part of "managing" the code. With the .NET Framework came a new language, C#, but this wasn't the only language that could be used with .NET—it was a multilanguage, single-runtime platform that provided great flexibility.

The .NET Framework was revolutionary because it united the client-application experience and connected-application experience across a unified runtime, which ActiveX tried but ultimately failed to do. Because the same platform could be written for both, the result was that the user experience would be similar across both (see Figure 1-7). Coupled with the emergence of Extensible Markup Language (XML), a language similar to HTML but specialized for handling data instead of presentation, web application development was finally coming of age.

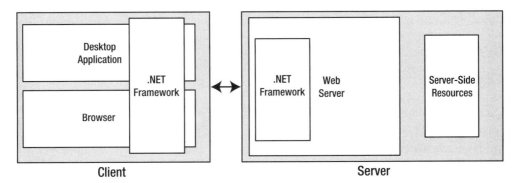

Figure 1-7. *The .NET Framework provides consistent browser, desktop, and server application programming interfaces (APIs).*

Thus, the pendulum has swung back toward the thin client/fat server approach. Ironically, the thin client is probably fatter than the original servers, because it's an operating system that can support a browser that is extended to support XML (through parsers), scripting (through interpreters), and other plug-ins, as well as Java or .NET virtual machines! With all these runtime elements available to developers and a consistent server-side API (through the .NET Framework or Java server side), rich, high-performing applications built on a client/server model are now fully possible.

Thin Client Applications Arriving to Save the Day

It was in the summer of 2001 that I had my first "wow" experience with the power of what could be done with a browser-based interface using asynchronous XML, DHTML, and scripting. I was working for a product development group in a large financial services company in New York and was invited by one of their chief technical officer (CTO) teams to take a look at their new prototype of zero-footprint technology for delivering financial information, both streaming and static. They claimed they could stream news, quotes, and charts to a browser with no installation necessary at the desktop, and they could do it in such a manner that it met all the requirements of a typical client. In those days, the biggest support problems were in the installation, maintenance, and support of heavy Component Object Model (COM) desktop applications, and this would wipe them all out in a single blow.

Naturally I was skeptical, but I went to see it anyway. It was a prototype, but it worked. And it largely preserved the user experience that you'd expect from a heavier application with drag-and-drop functionality; streaming updates to news, quotes, and charts; and advanced visualization of data. If anything, it was almost superior to the heavy desktops we were using!

And it was all built in DHTML, JavaScript, DHTML behaviors, and a lot of server-side functionality using Microsoft-based server products. It was pretty revolutionary.

In fact, it was too revolutionary—and it was too hard for the development management to take a risk on it because it was so beyond their understanding of how applications *should* work and how the market would accept it. (To be fair, part of their decision was based on my report of concerns about how well the streaming part would scale, but that was nothing that couldn't be fixed!)

But then something terrible happened: September 11, 2001. On that fateful day, a group of individuals turned airliners into missiles, crashing into the World Trade Center and the Pentagon and killing thousands of people. Part of all this destruction was the loss of many data distribution centers that our company ran for the Wall Street community. With the country having a "get-up-and-running" attitude, wanting the attack to have as little impact on day-to-day affairs as possible, the pressure was on our company to start providing news, quotes, charts, and all the other information that traders needed to get the stock market up and running. The effort to build new data centers and switch the Wall Street users over to them by having staff reconfigure each desktop one by one would take weeks.

The CTO group, with its zero-footprint implementation, ran a T3 line into the machines in their lab that were hosting the application, opening them to the Internet; set up a Domain Name System (DNS) server; and were off and running in a matter of hours. Any trader—from anywhere—could open Internet Explorer, point it at a uniform resource locator (URL), and start working. No technical expertise required!

Thanks to an innovative use of technology, a business need was met. And that is what our business is all about. Thanks to this experience, and what that group did, I was hooked. I realized the future was again with the thin client and massive opportunities existed for developers and companies that could successfully exploit it.

Ajax Entering the Picture

Ajax, which once stood for Asynchronous Java and XML, is a technique that has received a lot of attention recently because it has been used to great success by companies such as Amazon and Google. The key word here is *asynchronous*, because, despite all the great technologies available in the browser for delivering and running applications, the ultimate model of the browser is still the synchronous request/response model. As such, the refreshing and updating of applications that the user is used to is hard to achieve. The typical web application involves a refresh cycle where a postback is sent to the server and the response from the server is rerendered. This is a drawback of this type of architecture, because the round-trip to and from the server is expensive in user time and bandwidth cost, particularly for applications that require intensive updates.

What is interesting about the Ajax approach is that nothing is really new about it. The core technology—the XMLHttpRequest object—has been around since 1999 with Microsoft Internet Explorer, when it was implemented as an ActiveX plug-in. More recently, it has been added to the Mozilla and Safari browsers, increasing its ubiquity, and has been covered in a World Wide Web Consortium (W3C) specification (DOM Load and Save). With the popularity of web applications that use XMLHttpRequest such as Google Local, Flickr, and Amazon A9, XMLHttpRequest is fast becoming a de facto standard.

The nice part about this is that it doesn't require any proprietary or additional software or hardware to enable richer applications. The functionality is built right into the browser. As such, it is server agnostic, and besides needing to make some minor browser security restrictions, you can use it straightaway, leveraging coding styles and languages you already know.

To see an example of how it works, refer to Google Local (see Figure 1-8). As you use the mouse to drag the map around the screen, the new sections of the map that were previously hidden come into view quickly; this is because they were cached on your first viewing of the map. Now, as you are looking at a new section (by having dragged the mouse), the sections bordering the current one are downloading in the background, as are the relevant satellite photographs for the section of map you are viewing.

It is this background downloading, using the XMLHttpRequest object, that makes using Google Local such a smooth and rewarding experience. Remember, nothing is *new* here; it's just that having an object built into the browser that can do this asynchronously makes it easier to develop applications like this. For full details on how to develop in Ajax, check out *Foundations of Ajax* (Apress, 2005).

You will be looking at Ajax from a high level in this book and delving more deeply into how Microsoft ASP.NET Atlas will allow you to quickly and easily build Ajax-type applications.

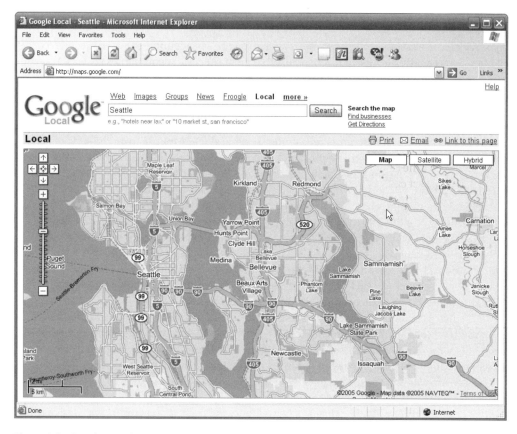

Figure 1-8. *Google Local uses Ajax extensively.*

Using the XMLHttpRequest Object

As mentioned, the XMLHttpRequest object is the heart of Ajax. This object sends requests to the server and processes the responses from it. In current versions of Internet Explorer, it is implemented using ActiveX, whereas in other browsers, such as Firefox, Safari, and Opera, it is a native JavaScript object. Unfortunately, because of these differences, your JavaScript code has to be coded to inspect the browser type and create an instance of it using the correct technology. (In Internet Explorer 7, Microsoft will be supporting XMLHttpRequest as a native JavaScript object.)

Thankfully, this process is a little simpler than the spaghetti code you may remember having to write when using JavaScript functions that heavily used the Document Object Model (DOM) that had to work across browsers:

```
var xmlHttp;
function createXMLHttpRequest() {
    if (window.ActiveXObject) {
        xmlHttp = new ActiveXObject("Microsoft.XMLHTTP");
    }
    else if (window.XMLHttpRequest) {
            xmlHttp = new XMLHttpRequest();
        }
}
```

In this case, the code is simple. If the browser doesn't support ActiveX objects, the window.ActiveXObject call will return null, and therefore the xmlHttp object will be set to a new instance of XMLHttpRequest (the native JavaScript object); otherwise, a new ActiveXObject of type Microsoft.XMLHTTP will be created.

Now that you have an XMLHttpRequest object at your beck and call, you can start playing with its methods and properties. I discuss some of the more common methods you can use in the next few paragraphs.

The open method sets up the call to your server to initialize your request. It takes two required arguments (the Http command of GET, POST, or PUT and the URL of the resource you are calling) and three optional arguments (a Boolean indicating whether you want the call to be asynchronous, which defaults to true, and strings for the username and password if the server requires these for security). It returns void.

```
xmlHttp.open("GET" , "theURL" , true , "MyUserName" , "MyPassword");
```

The send method makes the request to the server and passes it a single argument containing the relevant content. Had the original request been declared as asynchronous (using the boolean flag mentioned earlier), the method would immediately return; otherwise, this method would block until the synchronous response could be received. The content argument (which is optional) can be a DOM object, an input stream, or a string.

```
xmlHttp.send("Hello Server");
```

The setRequestHeader method takes two parameters: a string for the header and a string for the value. It sets the specified Hypertext Transfer Protocol (HTTP) header value with the supplied string.

```
xmlHttp.setRequestHeader("Referrer","AGreatBook");
```

The getAllResponseHeaders method returns a string containing the complete set of response headers from the XMLHttpRequest object. Examples of this include the HTTP headers of Content-Length and Date, with their appropriate values. This is accompanied by the getResponseHeader method, which takes a parameter representing the name of the header you want to query, and its value is returned as a string.

```
var strCL;
strCL = xmlHttp.getResponseHeader("Content-Length");
```

In addition to supporting these methods, the XMLHttpRequest object supports a number of properties, as listed in Table 1-1.

Table 1-1. *The Standard Set of Properties for XMLHttpRequest*

Property	Description
onreadystatechange	Specifies the name of the function to call whenever the state of the XMLHttpRequest object changes
readyState	The current state of the request (0=uninitialized, 1=loading, 2=loaded, 3=interactive, and 4=complete)
responseText	The current response from the server as a string
responseXML	The current response from the server in XML
status	The current HTTP status code from the server (for example, 404 for Not Found)
statusText	The text version of the HTTP status code (for example, Not Found)

Using Visual Studio 2005

Throughout this book you'll be using Visual Studio 2005 for developing Ajax applications using the Atlas extensions for ASP.NET 2.0. Several editions of this application are applicable to different tasks.

You can download the free edition, Visual Web Developer 2005 Express, from the Microsoft Developer Network (http://msdn.microsoft.com/vstudio/express/vwd/). From this page you can also navigate to the downloads for the other Express editions including ones for C#, VB .NET, and C++ development.

You may also use any of the other editions of Visual Studio 2005, including Standard, Professional, or Team System, to use and build the samples included in this book.

If you are following along with the figures in this book, you'll see these have been captured on a development system that uses the Team System edition of Visual Studio 2005.

Seeing a Simple Example in Action

Understanding how this technology all hangs together is best shown using a simple example. In this case, say you have a client application that uses JavaScript and an XMLHttpRequest object that calls a server to perform the simple addition of two integers. As the user types the values into the text boxes on the client, the page calls the server to have it to add the two values and return a result that it displays in a third text box. You can see the application in action in Figure 1-9.

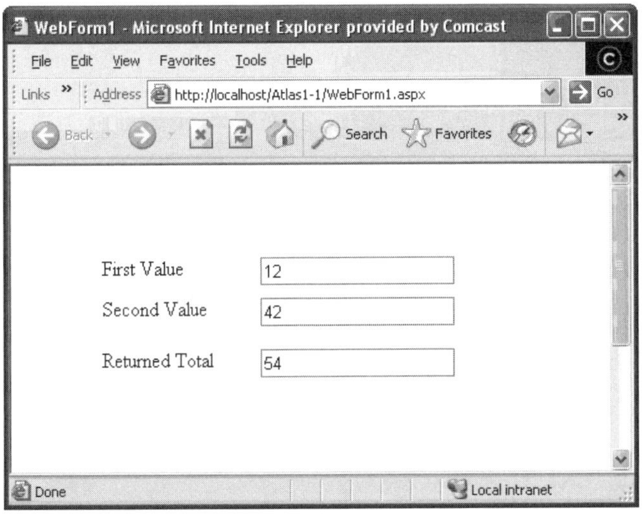

Figure 1-9. *The Ajax addition client*

To create this client, start a new Visual Studio 2005 web site, and edit the default
Default.aspx content to match Listing 1-1.

Listing 1-1. *Creating Your First Ajax Application*

```
<%@ Page language="c#" Codebehind="Default.aspx.cs" AutoEventWireup="false"
Inherits="Atlas1_1.Default" %>

<!DOCTYPE HTML PUBLIC "-//W3C//DTD HTML 4.0 Transitional//EN" >
<HTML>
  <HEAD>
  <title>WebForm1</title>
  <script language="javascript">
    var xmlHttp;

    function createXMLHttpRequest() {
        if (window.ActiveXObject) {
            xmlHttp = new ActiveXObject("Microsoft.XMLHTTP");
        }
        else if (window.XMLHttpRequest) {
                xmlHttp = new XMLHttpRequest();
        }
    }
```

```
        function updateTotal() {
            frm = document.forms[0];
            url="Default2.aspx?A=" + frm.elements['A'].value +
                    "&B=" + frm.elements['B'].value;
            xmlHttp.open("GET",url,true);
            xmlHttp.onreadystatechange=doUpdate;
            xmlHttp.send();
            return false;
        }

        function doUpdate() {
            if (xmlHttp.readyState==4) {
                    document.forms[0].elements['TOT'].value=xmlHttp.responseText;
            }
        }

    }
    </script>
    </HEAD>
    <body onload="createXMLHttpRequest();">
            <form>
            <TABLE height="143" cellSpacing="0" cellPadding="0"
                        width="300" border="0" >
                    <TR vAlign="top">
                            <TD height="32">First Value</TD>
                            <TD><INPUT type="text" id="A" value="0"
                                                    onkeyup="updateTotal();"></TD>
                    </TR>
                    <TR vAlign="top">
                            <TD height="32">Second Value</TD>
                            <TD><INPUT type="text" id="B" value="0"
                                                    onkeyup="updateTotal();"></TD>
                    </TR>
                    <TR vAlign="top">
                            <TD height="23">Returned Total</TD>
                            <TD><INPUT type="text" id="TOT" value="0"></TD>
                    </TR>
            </TABLE>
            </form>
    </body>
</HTML>
```

When the web page loads, the createXMLHttpRequest function is called (from onload= in the body tag) to initialize the object. After that, whenever a key is pressed in the A or B text boxes, the updateTOT function is called (by trapping the onkeyup event).

This function then takes the values of A and B from their form elements and uses them to build the URL to WebForm2.aspx, which will look something like Default2.aspx?A=8&B=3. It then calls the open method on XMLHttpRequest, passing it this URL and indicating that this will be an asynchronous transaction. Next, it specifies the dotheupdate function to handle the readystate changes on the XMLHttpRequest object.

The dotheupdate function checks to see whether the readyState is 4, indicating that the process is complete, and if it is, it updates the TOT field with the returned value from the XMLHttpRequest object.

To get this application to work, add a new C# web form to the project, and keep the default name of Default2.aspx. In the page designer, delete all the default HTML so that the page contains just the ASPX declaration:

```
<%@ Page language="c#" Codebehind="Default2.aspx.cs"
    AutoEventWireup="false" Inherits="Default2" %>
```

Then, add the following code to the C# code file:

```
private void Page_Load(object sender, System.EventArgs e)
{
        int a = 0;
        int b = 0;
        if (Request.QueryString["A"] != null)
        {
                a = Convert.ToInt16(Request.QueryString["A"].ToString());
        }
        if (Request.QueryString["B"] != null)
        {
                b = Convert.ToInt16(Request.QueryString["B"].ToString());
    }

        Response.Write(a+b);
}
```

This handles the request from Default.aspx, getting the values of A and B, and writes them back to the response buffer. The XMLHttpRequest object within Default.aspx then handles the communication and asynchronously updates the Returned Total box.

Summary

In this chapter, you got a brief history lesson on the methodologies for building user interfaces to servers that process your data and on the constantly swinging pendulum from thin client to fat client. You were brought up to date on what the newest trend in this development is—web-based thin clients with rich functionality thanks to the asynchrony delivered by the XMLHttpRequest object. This object is the core of Ajax, and in this chapter you built a simple demonstration that used it. This example was straightforward and barely scratched the surface of what you can do with Ajax; however, it demonstrated one of the drawbacks of using this methodology, namely, that it is heavy on the scripting. JavaScript, although powerful, is difficult and onerous to debug and manage when compared to languages such as C#, VB .NET, and Java. As such, the application benefits you receive by using an Ajax approach may be nullified by the application development getting bogged down in thousands (or more) lines of JavaScript.

It is with this problem in mind that Microsoft is attempting to bring the productivity of ASP.NET with Visual Studio 2005 to the Ajax space, and thus Atlas was born. In the next chapter, you'll be introduced to the wonderful world of Atlas, you will look at the architecture of it, you will learn how it allows you to use Visual Studio 2005 and ASP.NET 2.0 controls to generate client-side code from server-side controls, and you will see how this can give you the best of Ajax while avoiding the worst of it.

CHAPTER 2

Atlas: Taking Ajax to the Next Level

In Chapter 1 you were introduced to the methodology of using Ajax and saw a code example on how you can use Ajax to build a web page that responds to user input asynchronously. In this chapter, you will be introduced to Atlas, Microsoft's extension to ASP.NET 2.0 that allows you to build Ajax applications more easily and manage their development, deployment, and debugging through Visual Studio 2005.

ASP.NET Atlas is a package of technologies including some script libraries that get deployed to the client and that implement a number of common functions and programming features for you. You simply need to include them in your JavaScript scripts, and you are good to go. Perhaps more important, it also includes web server controls that, when used on a web page, generate HTML and JavaScript that run on the browser. Through the use of web server controls, the developer can orchestrate which JavaScript code gets delivered to the client without actually doing much hand-coding—the server-side ASP.NET controls generate the HTML and JavaScript. This is one of the fundamental underpinnings of ASP.NET and is essential to understanding Atlas. In this chapter, you will learn about the entire architecture of Atlas and how it all hangs together under ASP.NET 2.0.

Introducing ASP.NET 2.0 Server Controls

To better understand Atlas and its architecture, it's best to understand ASP.NET 2.0 server controls. These are a fundamental part of the ASP.NET framework. At their core, server controls are classes in the .NET Framework that represent visual elements on a web form. Some of them are straightforward and map closely to standard HTML tags, effectively providing server-side implementations of those tags. Others are larger-scale abstractions that encapsulate complex GUI tasks such as grids but represent them using HTML. It's important to note that applications using server controls are rendered in the browser. Specifically, the server, using the control, compiles its logic and representation in HTML and/or JavaScript that gets delivered to the browser to render.

Several types of server controls exist:

HTML server controls: These classes wrap standard HTML tags but are declared with the runat="server" attribute. An example is the HtmlAnchor control, which is a server-side representation of the <a>, or anchor, tag.

Web controls: These classes duplicate the functionality of basic HTML tags but have methods and properties that have been standardized across their entire range, making it easier for developers to use them. Many of them are analogous to HTML server controls (for example, the button), but their APIs have been designed to be used by C# and other .NET developers, as opposed to being an echo of the API used by the standard HTML controls. As such, they are more consistent to use when developing applications, particularly if you don't have much experience hand-coding HTML.

Rich controls: These are a special class of web controls that are complex in nature and generate large amounts of HTML and JavaScript. An example of this is the Calendar control.

Validation controls: These controls validate input against a predetermined criteria, such as a telephone number or a ZIP code. Should they fail validation, they encapsulate the logic to represent this on the web form.

Data controls: These encapsulate and display large amounts of data. They include controls such as grids and lists, and they support advanced features such as using templates, editing, sorting, paginating, and filtering.

Navigation controls: These display site maps and allow users to navigate a site.

Login controls: These have built-in logic for forms authentication, providing a turnkey solution for authentication in your web sites.

WebPart controls: These build components for web portals running under Windows SharePoint Services.

Mobile controls: These are for applications that render on portable devices such as personal digital assistants (PDAs) and smart phones.

The power of server controls is best demonstrated by example. Fire up Visual Studio 2005, and create a new ASP.NET web site called Atlas2. Drag a calendar from the Standard folder in the Toolbox to the design surface of the Default.aspx file that was created for you by Visual Studio. You should have something that resembles Figure 2-1.

If you look at the source for this page, you will see some pretty straightforward HTML, and there isn't a whole lot of it—certainly not enough to render the calendar you just saw, much less the interactivity of selecting dates and paging back and forward through the months. You can see the code in Figure 2-2.

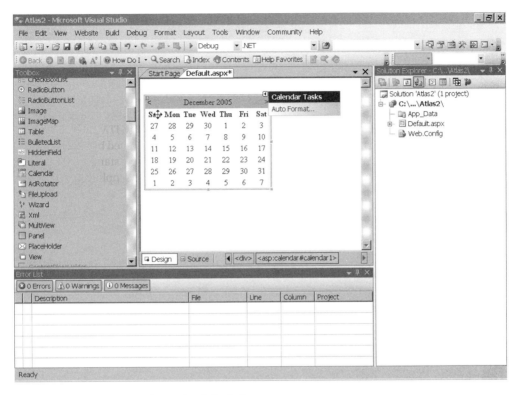

Figure 2-1. *Adding a calendar to the default form*

Figure 2-2. *Inspecting the server-side code behind the calendar page*

The workhorse line is this one:

```
<asp:Calendar ID="Calendar1" runat="Server"></asp:Calendar>
```

At runtime, the ASP.NET engine takes this and uses its built-in Calendar control to generate the HTML. Similarly, VS .NET uses the Calendar control within ASP.NET to create the visual representation within the integrated development environment (IDE). This HTML looks vastly different from what you saw in Figure 2-2, because it is the output of the rendering of the server control as HTML. Figure 2-3 shows the page being rendered in Internet Explorer.

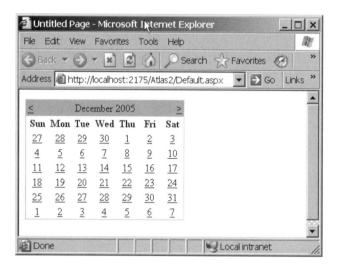

Figure 2-3. *Viewing the calendar page in a browser*

Using the Browser's View ➤ Source functionality, you can inspect the HTML and JavaScript (see Figure 2-4). You can see that it is vastly different from what was shown at design time in Figure 2-2. The `<asp:Calendar>` control has been replaced by an HTML `<div>` containing all the layout and information for the calendar; showing the days, dates, and month; and showing the JavaScript that handles the links to move forward and backward by month.

This is an example of the power of server-side controls, and it is with controls such as these that you will be able to deliver Ajax functionality to the browser without going through overly complex hand-coding, as demonstrated in Chapter 1. You will also be able to take advantage of using a professional IDE so that you can debug and manage your Atlas pages as easily as standard web forms or Windows applications.

This has been one of the premier design goals of Atlas. It is well understood that creating Ajax-based web applications can be complex and requires extensive knowledge of client-side script, which is slow to develop and debug. It is here where Microsoft is diverging its development of an Ajax API, which allows developers to continue using the great productivity characteristics that they are used to using in Visual Studio to build web applications for greater user flexibility.

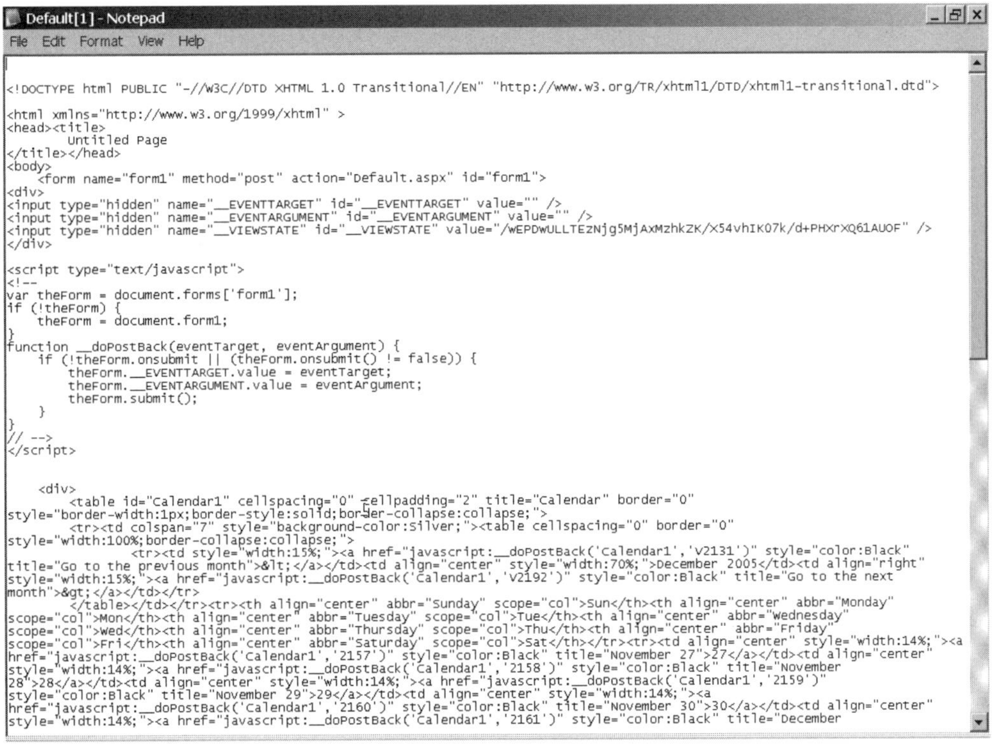


```
<!DOCTYPE html PUBLIC "-//W3C//DTD XHTML 1.0 Transitional//EN" "http://www.w3.org/TR/xhtml1/DTD/xhtml1-transitional.dtd">

<html xmlns="http://www.w3.org/1999/xhtml" >
<head><title>
        Untitled Page
</title></head>
<body>
    <form name="form1" method="post" action="Default.aspx" id="form1">
<div>
<input type="hidden" name="__EVENTTARGET" id="__EVENTTARGET" value="" />
<input type="hidden" name="__EVENTARGUMENT" id="__EVENTARGUMENT" value="" />
<input type="hidden" name="__VIEWSTATE" id="__VIEWSTATE" value="/wEPDwULLTEzNjg5MjAxMzhkZK/X54vhIK07k/d+PHXrXQ61AUOF" />
</div>

<script type="text/javascript">
<!--
var theForm = document.forms['form1'];
if (!theForm) {
    theForm = document.form1;
}
function __doPostBack(eventTarget, eventArgument) {
    if (!theForm.onsubmit || (theForm.onsubmit() != false)) {
        theForm.__EVENTTARGET.value = eventTarget;
        theForm.__EVENTARGUMENT.value = eventArgument;
        theForm.submit();
    }
}
// -->
</script>


    <div>
        <table id="Calendar1" cellspacing="0" cellpadding="2" title="Calendar" border="0"
style="border-width:1px;border-style:solid;border-collapse:collapse;">
        <tr><td colspan="7" style="background-color:Silver;"><table cellspacing="0" border="0"
style="width:100%;border-collapse:collapse;">
                <tr><td style="width:15%;"><a href="javascript:__doPostBack('Calendar1','V2131')" style="color:Black"
title="Go to the previous month">&lt;</a></td><td align="center" style="width:70%;">December 2005</td><td align="right"
style="width:15%;"><a href="javascript:__doPostBack('Calendar1','V2192')" style="color:Black" title="Go to the next
month">&gt;</a></td></tr>
        </table></td></tr><tr><th align="center" abbr="Sunday" scope="col">Sun</th><th align="center" abbr="Monday"
scope="col">Mon</th><th align="center" abbr="Tuesday" scope="col">Tue</th><th align="center" abbr="Wednesday"
scope="col">Wed</th><th align="center" abbr="Thursday" scope="col">Thu</th><th align="center" abbr="Friday"
scope="col">Fri</th><th align="center" abbr="Saturday" scope="col">Sat</th></tr><tr><td align="center" style="width:14%;"><a
href="javascript:__doPostBack('Calendar1','2157')" style="color:Black" title="November 27">27</a></td><td align="center"
style="width:14%;"><a href="javascript:__doPostBack('Calendar1','2158')" style="color:Black" title="November
28">28</a></td><td align="center" style="width:14%;"><a href="javascript:__doPostBack('Calendar1','2159')"
style="color:Black" title="November 29">29</a></td><td align="center" style="width:14%;"><a
href="javascript:__doPostBack('Calendar1','2160')" style="color:Black" title="November 30">30</a></td><td align="center"
style="width:14%;"><a href="javascript:__doPostBack('Calendar1','2161')" style="color:Black" title="December
```

Figure 2-4. *Viewing the client-side code behind the calendar page*

Atlas extends the Ajax concept in two significant ways. First, it encapsulates much of the commonly used JavaScript into client script libraries that simplify the task of creating rich user interfaces (UIs) and remote procedure calls as well as provides you with true object-oriented APIs that you can use in a JavaScript environment. You can use these libraries as they are to enhance web sites built on any platform via Ajax-style techniques. You'll be looking at these in more detail in Chapter 3. This client-side framework also introduces a new methodology for building your client-side applications—a declarative XML-based markup called Atlas Script.

Using this script, you map XML elements to underlying HTML ones. These XML elements can then be attributed, or have behaviors and actions associated with them, using child tags. The Atlas runtime will then parse this script and generate the appropriate runtime behavior.

Second, Atlas provides a server development platform, which is integrated with ASP.NET 2.0. When used with ASP.NET 2.0, Atlas provides a programming model that makes it simple to create rich Ajax user experiences on the Web, and it allows you to easily extend your existing ASP.NET applications to provide this functionality. This is the most important part of the server-side aspect of Atlas. It allows you to "wrap" your existing applications with server controls called UpdatePanels that empower that part of your page to be updated asynchronously and without a complete-page refresh. This is extremely important because it allows you to turn your existing ASP.NET web applications into Ajax applications with asynchronous, partial-page updates!

Introducing the Atlas Architecture

The Atlas architecture consists of two major pieces. First is the Atlas client script library, which makes it more productive for you to build the client-side functionality of your web applications. It has a rich component model and allows for object-oriented scripting. It provides many classes that add value to your applications, including network access, user interface enhancements, behaviors, actions, string manipulation, and more. It also provides an XML-based scripting platform with which you can declaratively put together client-side behavior. You can use it to map actions, behaviors, and data-binding functionality to your applications. Because it is based on XML and is declarative, it will provide the future basis for visual tools to generate Ajax UIs for Atlas.

Second is the set of server extensions; these extensions allow you to integrate the application model between the client and the server. You can use existing ASP.NET applications and target the Atlas runtime on the client.

You can see this architecture in Figure 2-5.

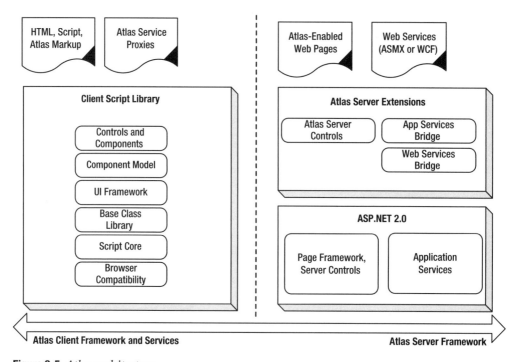

Figure 2-5. *Atlas architecture*

Thus, when building an application with Atlas, the process is similar to what you do today when building an ASP.NET web forms application. Server controls send the HTML UI as well as the declarative script, and the pages run on the client using the Atlas client framework. Your applications can then run richly on the client without doing a lot of postbacks. They can also connect directly to web services or Windows Communication Foundation (WCF) services using the Atlas service proxies and provide a richer experience on the client.

This architecture allows for increased productivity where you use fewer lines of code, with server controls generating much of the code for you. It allows for the clean separation of content, style, behavior, and code. A typical design pattern for an Atlas application may involve it consuming web services or WCF services directly from the client without requiring an intermediary web application layer that slows down communication and complicates the application design, implementation, and deployment. Finally, it is multibrowser compatible, being based on known standards and using a browser compatibility layer script library that supports all modern browsers including Mozilla/Firefox, Safari, and of course Internet Explorer. You'll learn more about this in Chapter 3.

Atlas Client Script Library

Atlas presents a rich client API that has a rich type system. JavaScript itself has a basic concept of classes but doesn't have a rich type system. To allow developers to build classes and components more easily, Atlas provides some libraries within JavaScript that give a richer set of libraries and types, which in turn allow you to use namespaces, classes, interfaces, inheritance, and other artifacts that are usually associated with modern high-level languages. The script libraries also include a base class library with helper classes that make it easier to write scripts. It includes string builder, serializers, debugging, and tracing classes as well as networking classes. Microsoft will be providing tools that integrate with the tracing and debugging classes to provide a better experience in debugging scripted applications. Chapter 3 will cover the script library in depth.

Atlas has a client-side networking stack built upon XMLHTTPRequest that allows you to access server functionality. For example, classes such as WebRequest, WebResponse, and MethodRequest are available within the client-side script libraries. These classes, built to work across different browsers, abstract the use of XMLHTTPRequest and provide a consistent programming layer that allows you to build Ajax applications that are protected from the different implementations of XMLHTTPRequest on different browsers.

Additionally, the framework provides a web services bridge to the server side, which allows services to be accessed directly from a browser. It does this by generating a JavaScript proxy that gets downloaded to the client when the service is invoked using a special URI.

These JavaScript proxies provide the interface layer, are automatically generated by the web services bridge, and are called by appending "/js" to the service URI like this: `http://servername/servicename/service.asmx/js`.

Adding the tag `<script src="http://servername/servicename/service.asmx/js" />` to your JavaScript will then include the proxy code within your application so that you can call the service via its proxies.

So if you have wrapped or exposed your middleware as a web service using the .NET Framework, when using Atlas, you can now access that web service directly from the browser. Previously you would have had to write a web application that consumed the web service and provided services to the browser.

Additionally, if you have an existing web application built on ASP.NET, you can expose methods on your page using attributes and expose them as web services. This allows you to take your existing non-service-oriented applications and expose atomic units of functionality from them to be consumed by Ajax applications on the browser! This provides an excellent alternative to using page callbacks, and you'll see more of this in Chapters 6 and 10.

JavaScript Object Notation (JSON)

To allow for a more efficient transfer of data and classes, Atlas supports the JavaScript Object Notation (JSON) format. This is lighter weight than XML and SOAP, and because of differences in the implementation of the XML/SOAP parsers on various browsers, these formats may not always give a consistent experience. JSON turns the object into the syntax you would use to create an instance of the object in JavaScript.

For example, the following code shows the object representing a person's name and age in typical class notation:

```
Public class MyDetails{
    Public string FirstName;
    Public string LastName;
    Public in Age;
}
```

You can represent an instance of this object in JSON like this:

```
{ FirstName : "Landon"
    LastName : "Donovan"
    Age : 22 }
```

Atlas Web User Interfaces

Ajax applications traditionally use HTML and its associated technologies such as DHTML and Cascading Style Sheets (CSS) to build user interfaces. Where the interfaces need to change dynamically, they typically call the server using XMLHTTPRequest, and the server delivers new markup language that gets inserted into the DOM and rerendered by the browser.

For example, consider the case of implementing a financial portal using Ajax. You will see a full example of this in Chapter 11. When you change the company you want to inspect, several areas of the page should update. Figure 2-6 shows the basic application with a basic quote and a couple of charts. Consider the scenario where you want the user to decide whether they want to see more detailed quotation information for the company; if they do, they click a button to get it. You want this information to appear on the same page but don't want to refresh the whole page to get it—you just want it to appear (see Figure 2-7). Even if your round-trip is fast, if you don't use an Ajax technique, your entire page will "blink" as the new data is rendered. The browser will clear and redraw the entire page, even though most of it doesn't need it.

Figure 2-6. *Loading extended quote details*

Figure 2-7. *Rendering the extended quote without a page blink*

Part of the problem with this approach is that it doesn't give a clean separation of the presentation from the business logic. The server that manages the chat also effectively manages the UI, and the presentation layer dumbly inserts what the server dispatched to it. Of course, the server doesn't have to send the markup and could simply send text, but it is generally more onerous to have a JavaScript program parse this text and generate the UI from it than it is to do it on the server side where you can make the most of Visual Studio and C# or VB .NET—or indeed Java and any Java IDE.

Atlas follows the model where the data stays on the server side, where it belongs, and the presentation, after the first rendering, remains on the client side. It has components and controls that run within the browser and take care of all the rendering on the page. They are higher-level classes that fall into two categories:

- *Components* are reusable building blocks that can be created declaratively or programmatically. They can easily be wired up to each other through bindings or events and manage their own lifetime.

- *Controls* are user interface elements that are associated with DHTML elements. They can manage and control all the rendering for that element.

You'll see the Atlas web UI in a lot more detail in Chapter 7.

Atlas Web UI Data Binding

Atlas provides a data-binding structure that allows you to wire components to each other and to data sources to allow them to integrate. It supports such features as two-way data binding that allows data sources to be edited and transforming that allows you to apply basic business logic to the data upon binding to change it from one value to another.

Figure 2-8 shows an example of a data-bound control in Atlas. This comes from an example in Chapter 5, where I discuss data binding in more detail.

Within Atlas, you can attribute your web services with the [DataObjectMethod()] attribute, which allows you to specify whether the connection is a select, insert, update, or delete operation.

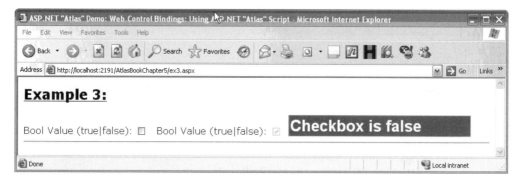

Figure 2-8. *Data binding a control in Atlas*

Here's an example that specifies a select operation:

```
[DataObjectMethod(DataObjectMethodType.Select)]
public SampleRow[] SelectRows() {
    return SampleDataService.Data.ToArray();
}
```

This will integrate with the client-side data binding to provide an end-to-end data experience. You would use it within an Atlas client using server-side controls and an Atlas script like this:

```
<atlas:ScriptManager runat="server" ID="scriptManager" />

    <h3>Data-Bound ListView</h3>

    <div id="dataContents"></div>

    <div style="visibility:hidden;display:none">
        <div id="masterTemplate">
            <div id="masterItemTemplate">
                <b><span id="masterName"></span></b><br />
                <asp:linkbutton id="LinkButton1" runat="server">
                <span id="masterDescription"></span>
                </asp:linkbutton><br />
            </div><br/>
        </div>
        <div id="masterNoDataTemplate">No data</div>
    </div>

    </form>
```

```xml
<script type="text/xml-script">
  <page xmlns:script="http://schemas.microsoft.com/xml-script/2005">
    <components>
      <dataSource id="dataSource" serviceURL="DataService.asmx"
        propertyChanged="onChange"/>

      <listView id="masterRepeater" targetElement="dataContents"
        itemTemplateParentElementId="masterTemplate"
        propertyChanged="onChange">
        <bindings>
          <binding dataContext="dataSource" dataPath="data"
            property="data"/>
        </bindings>
        <layoutTemplate>
          <template layoutElement="masterTemplate"/>
        </layoutTemplate>
        <itemTemplate>
          <template layoutElement="masterItemTemplate">
            <label targetElement="masterName">
              <bindings>
                  <binding dataPath="Name" property="text"/>
              </bindings>
            </label>
            <hyperLink targetElement="masterDescription">
              <bindings>
                  <binding dataPath="Description" property="text"/>
              </bindings>
            </hyperLink>
          </template>
        </itemTemplate>
        <emptyTemplate>
          <template layoutElement="masterNoDataTemplate"/>
        </emptyTemplate>
      </listView>

      <application>
        <load>
            <invokeMethod target="dataSource" method="select"/>
        </load>
      </application>
    </components>
  </page>
</script>
```

A lot of this may not make much sense right now, but don't worry; as you work through this book and see how elegantly Atlas Script matches to the underlying HTML and empowers it with GUI logic, and you see how the server-side controls mesh neatly with this, it will soon become second nature.

This code first sets up a ScriptManager called MyManager to make sure the correct scripts and script libraries are downloaded to the client. Next comes the HTML markup that defines the user interface, which is a simple list derived from the master template for the page. Following this you'll see your first example of Atlas Script.

The first step this script takes is to set up the data source. You do this with the <dataSource> tag like this:

```
<dataSource id="dataSource" serviceURL="DataService.asmx"
        propertyChanged="onChange"/>
```

This uses attribution to set up the data source's name and the URL of the web service that provides the data. Finally, it defines an event to call (called an *action* in Atlas parlance) when a property of the data source changes. It then sets up a listView control that is bound to this data source, which generates a list off of the response from the web service. You'll see a lot more of this in Chapters 5, 6, and 7.

The last part to notice is where the binding is actually triggered. This happens upon application loading and is defined in the Atlas script like this:

```
<application>
  <load>
    <invokeMethod target="dataSource" method="select"/>
  </load>
</application>
```

It's pretty straightforward and self-explanatory—invoke the select method on the data source when the page loads. This triggers the binding, and the list gets refreshed with the new data.

The data source control is very rich for handling client-side editing. It is effectively a disconnected data set, implemented in JavaScript, that has concepts of tables, columns, rows, and so on. It also supports batched updates that allow changes to be made locally to the client before a single batched update commit. It also provides optimistic concurrency, keeping track of the changes so they can be posted back to the server to resolve conflicts.

Chapter 7 discusses how Atlas handles data.

Creating Atlas Components

You have two ways to construct components on the client and connect them to each other using Atlas. You can build them *programmatically*, where you use JavaScript to create instances of these objects and connect them using a script. Or you can build them *declaratively* using an Atlas declarative script, an XML variant that describes an Atlas page.

On the server side you can turn your existing ASP.NET server-side controls into panes on the page that update asynchronously by wrapping them in UpdatePanel controls, which are provided by the Atlas server-side suite.

Here is an example of programmatically constructing Atlas elements using JavaScript:

```
Var myTextBox = new Sys.UI.TextBox(document.getElement('TextBox1'));
myTextBox.initialize();

var myLabel = new Sys.UI.Label(document.getElement('Label1'));

var myBinding = new Sys.Binding();
myBinding.set_dataContext(myTextBox);
myBinding.set_dataPath('text');
myBinding.set_property('text');
myBinding.set_direction(Web.BindingDirection.In);

myLabel.get_bindings().add(myBinding);

myLabel.Initialize();
```

This is suitable if you are a script developer who wants to develop new components or aggregations of existing components using code you already know how to use. The previous listing instantiates two Atlas components, one for an HTML text box and the other for an HTML label. The script then binds the contents of the text box to the label so any changes made to the text box will be updated on the label.

As you can see, the extensions to JavaScript that come with Atlas provide a consistent model for programming, which will look familiar to C# or VB .NET developers. It makes for scripts that are easier to maintain and debug, but it is still quite verbose in terms of the number of lines of code.

Using the declarative format, you can set up the same bindings and connect them using XML like this:

```
<script type="text/xml-script">
  <page xmlns := http://schemas.microsoft.com/xml-script/2005">
    <components>
      <script:label targetElement="MyLabel"/>
        <bindings>
          <binding dataContext="MyTextBox" dataPath="text"
                  property="text" direction="In" />
        </bindings>
      </script:label>
      <script:textbox targetElement="MyTextBox"/>
    </components>
  </page>
</script>
```

If you simply want to provide the asynchronous update functionality with the partial-page refreshes that are promised by the Ajax methodology, perhaps the easiest approach is to wrap your existing ASP.NET markup with UpdatePanel controls. Here's an example:

```
<atlas:UpdatePanel ID="THTextPanel" runat="server">
  <ContentTemplate>
    <asp:Panel ID="Panel1" runat="Server"
      ScrollBars="auto" Width="200px" Height="100px">
      <asp:Label ID="lblPH" runat="server" Text="">
      </asp:Label>
    </asp:Panel>
  </ContentTemplate>
</atlas:UpdatePanel>
<atlas:UpdateProgress runat="server" ID="Prog3">
  <ProgressTemplate>
    Loading...
  </ProgressTemplate>
</atlas:UpdateProgress>
```

In this example, a standard ASP.NET Panel control contains an ASP.NET Label control.

The Label control contains HTML markup that points to an image server (you'll see more of this in Chapter 11), and the Panel control provides scrollbars on this.

By placing these controls within the <ContentTemplate> element of the UpdatePanel, the Atlas runtime will provide partial-page refreshes whenever the contents change. So, if your application code generates new content for the Label control, only this part of the page will refresh, and you will not get a full-page "blink."

Additionally, you can present content while you are waiting for the asynchronous update. In this case, it shows "Loading…." Refer to Figures 2-6 and 2-7 to see this in action.

Atlas Behaviors

Beyond simple data access and updates, presentation layers generally present some more sophisticated UIs, intended to ease a user's workflow. One of the technologies to this end offered by Atlas is behaviors. These are similar to DHTML behaviors, but they are greatly improved because they are not limited to Internet Explorer. They work on all browsers because they are built using standard JavaScript. An Atlas behavior attaches itself to DHTML elements using controls. They dynamically change the behavior of the control based on this attachment.

So, for example, if you want to add drag-and-drop functionality to a control, you can do this by attaching the appropriate behavior. Other typical GUI enhancements such as tooltips, floating windows, autocomplete, and some animations and visual effects are implemented as Atlas behaviors for you to use.

So, for example, you can specify an area of the page, contained within a <div>, to be draggable and droppable around the page using a behavior like this:

```
<script type="text/xml-script">
<page xmlns:script="http://schemas.microsoft.com/xml-script/2005">
<references>
  <add src="AtlasUIDragDrop.js" />
</references>
```

```
<components>
  <control targetElement="popup">
    <behaviors>
      <popupBehavior id="popupBehavior"
                     parentElement="hoverLink"
                     positioningMode="BottomLeft"/>
      <floatingBehavior handle="popup" />
    </behaviors>
  </control>

  <hyperLink targetElement="hoverLink">
    <behaviors>
      <hoverBehavior unhoverDelay="1000" hoverElement="popup">
        <hover>
          <invokeMethod target="popupBehavior" method="show"/>
        </hover>
        <unhover>
          <invokeMethod target="popupBehavior" method="hide"/>
        </unhover>
      </hoverBehavior>
    </behaviors>
  </hyperLink>
</components>
</page>
</script>
```

You'll see many more demos and discussions of the various behaviors that come with Atlas in Chapter 5.

Summary

In this chapter, you were introduced to the overall architecture of Atlas, and you went on a tour of the various features of this architecture and how Atlas can empower your development of richer browser-based clients. Atlas is based on two pillars: the script library, which encapsulates many common functions as well as provides an object-oriented API layer for JavaScript developers and proxies to network services, and the server extensions, which provide server-based controls that can be used to implicitly generate JavaScript code that uses the libraries to implement your application on the client but that can also be debugged and maintained as server-side web applications.

I also introduced the concepts of components and controls.

In addition, I introduced data binding and gave a simple demonstration of how to connect client applications directly to web services or other middleware. In addition, I showed how to use Atlas behaviors—browser-independent, JavaScript-based enhancements to UI elements that are implemented on those elements using attribution.

In the next chapter, you'll see in more detail how Atlas makes JavaScript much easier. You'll be introduced to the various libraries and how they create and present a unified design and coding framework with ASP.NET server pages. You'll get an overview of the libraries and each of their functions and will learn about details such as the namespaces, inheritance, and various interfaces that these libraries offer you as a developer.

CHAPTER 3

Atlas: Making Client-Side JavaScript Easier

In the first two chapters, you began to get a sense for the power of Ajax and Altas and how they can help you build responsive web applications using asynchronous JavaScript and XML. Chapter 2 gave you an overview of ASP.NET 2.0 and in particular the server controls, including how you can use them to generate client-side JavaScript. This methodology is used throughout Atlas to make developing, deploying, and debugging rich client web applications as easy as possible. You also looked at some JavaScript code and how you can use this within Atlas. This chapter will go into more detail on the JavaScript libraries and APIs that Atlas provides. The chapter will start with a tour of the new features that have been added to JavaScript, such as namespaces and inheritance, so you can get a feel for how they work.

Using JavaScript in Atlas

In the following sections, you'll learn how to use JavaScript in Atlas by creating your first Atlas application.

Creating Your First Atlas Application

To get started with JavaScript in Atlas, fire up Visual Studio .NET, and create a new blank Atlas web site by selecting File ➤ New Website and then selecting ASP.NET 'Atlas' Web Site from the New Web Site dialog box (see Figure 3-1).

When you click OK, Visual Studio .NET will create a new workspace for you that contains everything you need to get started with Atlas. You can see the structure it sets up in Figure 3-2.

The template copies the Microsoft.Web.Atlas.dll assembly dependency into your \Bin directory so that your dependencies when running the application will be straight. You'll have to deploy this file with your application if you are moving it to a production server.

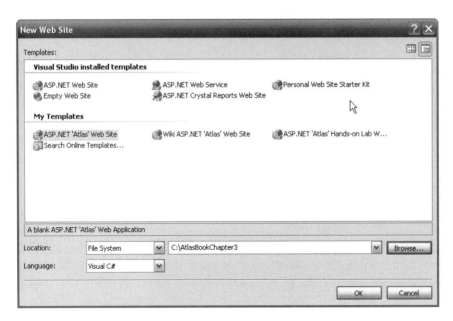

Figure 3-1. *Creating a new Atlas web site*

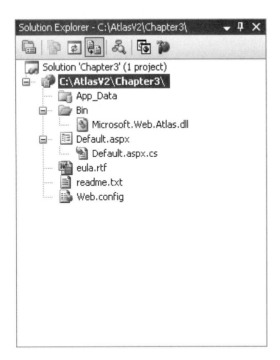

Figure 3-2. *Default Atlas solution structure*

At runtime, this DLL generates the script libraries and downloads them to the browser. The libraries are broken down into the following:

- The core libraries (Atlas.js and AtlasRuntime.js) provide the lowest-level runtime support for the other libraries as well as base functionality for your JavaScript (such as the Type.registerNamespace and Type.registerClass functions in this example).

- The compatibility libraries offer a compatibility layer for a graceful Atlas experience across different browsers. This is an area where Atlas excels—you can code your application without worrying about the differing underlying implementations of XMLHttpRequest. Atlas handles that for you.

- The Atlas UI libraries offer UI services to your applications, allowing functionality such as maps, drag and drop, and UI glitz to make your presentation layers sparkle!

Adding a Custom JavaScript Class

Next, you will create your own .js file that includes the code for a namespace that contains a class definition for a car. As you will see in the next sections, Atlas brings object-oriented programming to JavaScript, providing namespaces, inheritance, interfaces, and other goodies. If you are familiar with using object orientation, the advantages are obvious. If you aren't, then the next sections, which show how namespaces, inheritance, and so on, work with JavaScript, should help you understand how they make your code simpler to write, debug, and understand.

To create this file, right-click the project within Solution Explorer, and select Add New Item (see Figure 3-3).

In the ensuing dialog box, you then select Jscript File and name it. In this case I have called it AtlasBook.js (see Figure 3-4). You can of course call it anything you like, but this is the name I'll use in this book's examples.

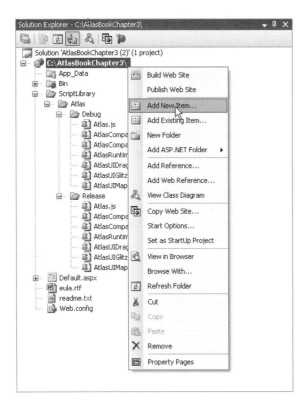

Figure 3-3. *Adding a new script to your application*

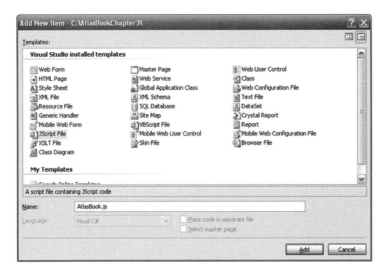

Figure 3-4. *Creating a new Atlas Script library*

You can now add the code that implements the Car class. When you use Visual Studio 2005 to create and edit JavaScript code, you get syntax coloring to make your code easier to understand and maintain. Figure 3-5 shows the Car class code in the editor.

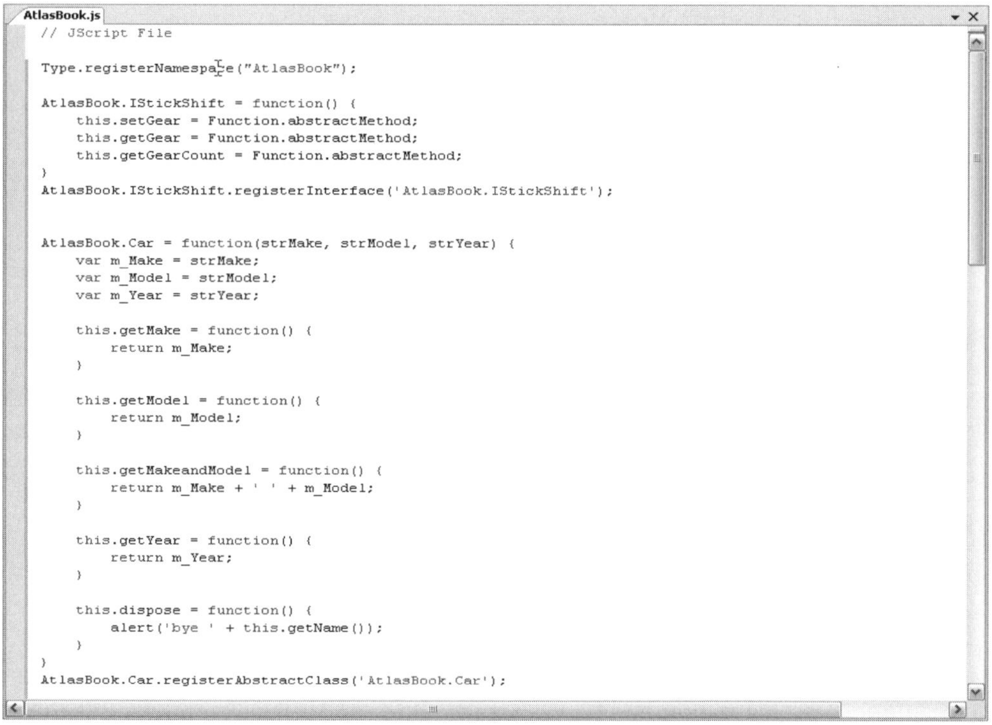

```
AtlasBook.js                                                            ▾ ✕
    // JScript File

    Type.registerNamespace("AtlasBook");

    AtlasBook.IStickShift = function() {
        this.setGear = Function.abstractMethod;
        this.getGear = Function.abstractMethod;
        this.getGearCount = Function.abstractMethod;
    }
    AtlasBook.IStickShift.registerInterface('AtlasBook.IStickShift');


    AtlasBook.Car = function(strMake, strModel, strYear) {
        var m_Make = strMake;
        var m_Model = strModel;
        var m_Year = strYear;

        this.getMake = function() {
            return m_Make;
        }

        this.getModel = function() {
            return m_Model;
        }

        this.getMakeandModel = function() {
            return m_Make + ' ' + m_Model;
        }

        this.getYear = function() {
            return m_Year;
        }

        this.dispose = function() {
            alert('bye ' + this.getName());
        }
    }
    AtlasBook.Car.registerAbstractClass('AtlasBook.Car');
```

Figure 3-5. *Implementing your class in JavaScript*

Using the Atlas Script Manager to Deliver Your Custom Class

To implement a web form that uses this class, use the same procedure as earlier to add a new item, except this time add a new web form, and call it TestAtlasNamespace.aspx (see Figure 3-6).

To this web form, you will add an Atlas ScriptManager. This server-side control manages the downloading of scripts to the client side so that the support files for Atlas code will be automatically installed when the user hits your Atlas-enabled web site. For example, your JavaScript uses the following command:

```
Type.registerNameSpace("AtlasBook");
```

The Type object is implemented in these script libraries, so you'll need them on the client before you can run your test application. The easiest way to do this is with the ScriptManager. You can add this using simple drag-and-drop functionality in the page designer.

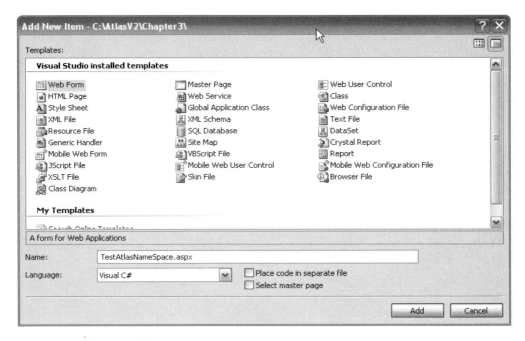

Figure 3-6. *Adding a web form to test your JavaScript*

If this is your first time using Atlas, you will likely not have the controls available to you in your Visual Studio 2005 Toolbox. Adding them is simple. First, make sure your TestAtlasNameSpace.aspx file is open in Design view. Your Toolbox will likely have tabs for Standard, Data, Navigation, and HTML, among others, and will look something like Figure 3-7.

Figure 3-7. *Visual Studio .NET Toolbox*

Right-click anywhere in this window, and select New Tab. A new tab will be created with a text editor in it that you can use to name it. Call it Atlas, and hit Enter. The Atlas tab will now be selected with no controls in it.

Right-click anywhere in this Atlas tab, and select Choose Items. The Choose Toolbox Items dialog box will appear (see Figure 3-8).

Figure 3-8. *Choosing Toolbox items to add to your Atlas project*

Click the Browse button, and look in your application directory for the C:\Program Files\ Microsoft ASP.NET\Atlas directory. In this you will have a version folder (v2.0.50727 for the July CTP), and this contains an 'Atlas' subfolder. Find the file called Microsoft.Web.Atlas.dll, and choose it. Some new items will be added to the .NET Framework Components tab in the Toolbox Items folder. Click the Assembly Name column to sort it in order of namespace, and find the Microsoft.Web.Atlas items (see Figure 3-9). Check each of them, and click OK.

You'll now see the suite of Atlas controls in your Toolbox. I'll discuss these controls throughout this book, but for now, I'll just show how to use the ScriptManager control. Drag and drop this control onto the designer for TestAtlasNameSpace.aspx (or whatever you called the file). Also drag and drop (from the HTML tab) an Input (Button) control to the web form. You can see the result in Figure 3-10.

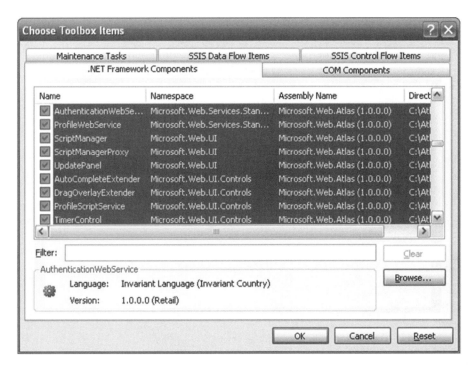

Figure 3-9. *Adding the Atlas web controls*

Figure 3-10. *The Atlas ScriptManager control*

Coding and Running the Application

If you double-click the button in the designer, Visual Studio .NET will create the onclick attribute on the HTML element to point to the Button1_onclick function and implement the stub of the function within the HTML head.

You can then put the following script into this function:

```
function Button1_onclick() {
    var testCar = new AtlasBook.Car('Honda','Pilot','2005');
    alert(testCar.getMakeandModel());
    alert(testCar.getYear());
    return false;
}
```

The last step you have to take is to add a reference containing the class definition for Car to the JavaScript. It is important to place this *after* the reference to the ScriptManager; otherwise, once the browser sees the Type.registerNamespace command, it will get confused and throw an error.

So, look through the HTML code on TestAtlasNameSpace.aspx for the <div> element that contains the <atlas:ScriptManager> declaration. Immediately after this, add the following line:

```
<script language="javascript" src="AtlasBook.js"
        type="text/javascript">
</script>
```

Note how Visual Studio .NET provides autocompletion for you so you can select which JavaScript file to use (see Figure 3-11).

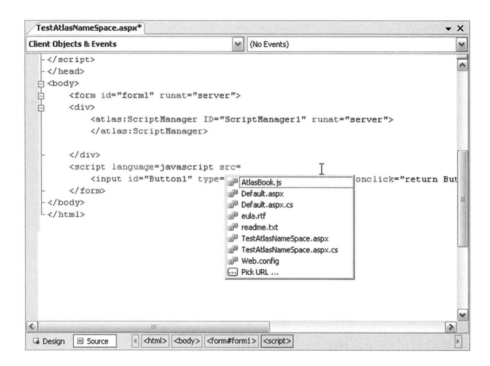

Figure 3-11. *Adding your JavaScript class to your application*

You can now run your application to get a pretty dull web form with a single button that, when clicked, returns the values for the properties of make, model, and year for this instance of a Car object (see Figure 3-12).

Figure 3-12. *Running your first Atlas application using JavaScript objects and namespaces*

Using Namespaces in JavaScript

The Atlas core library (AtlasCore.js) contains the facility to register namespaces and classes using the Type.registerNamespace and Type.registerClass commands. You can use these to build objects in JavaScript and assign them to namespaces for clearer, easier-to-read, and easier-to-debug code. Listing 3-1 shows the definition of the Car class you used earlier. This class is registered to the AtlasBook namespace.

Listing 3-2. *Creating a Car Namespace*

```
Type.registerNamespace("AtlasBook");
AtlasBook.Car = function(strMake, strModel, strYear) {
    var m_Make = strMake;
    var m_Model = strModel;
    var m_Year = strYear;

    this.getMake = function() {
        return m_Make;
    }

    this.getModel = function() {
        return m_Model;
    }

    this.getMakeandModel = function() {
        return m_Make + ' ' + m_Model;
    }
```

```
    this.getModel = function() {
        return m_Model;
    }

    this.getMakeandModel = function() {
        return m_Make + ' ' + m_Model;
    }

    this.getYear = function() {
        return m_Year;
    }

    this.dispose = function() {
        alert('bye ' + this.getName());
    }
}
AtlasBook.Car.registerAbstractClass('AtlasBook.Car');
```

In this code, first the namespace is registered as AtlasBook using the Type.registerNamespace command. Next, the class is implemented using a JavaScript function. Properties of the class are implemented using var declarations, and methods of the class using functions within the master function are assigned to the "this" object.

So to implement a getModel method, you would simply use the following:

```
this.getModel = function() {
// Add Implementation here
}
```

Finally, the class is registered to the namespace using the AtlasBook.Car.registerAbstract-Class command. This takes a single parameter—the fully qualified name of the clas.

Now, any JavaScript that includes this page will be able to create an instance of an AtlasBook.Car object by using the following script:

```
var testCar = new AtlasBook.Car('Honda', 'Pilot', '2005');
```

Your code can then invoke methods on this object in the usual manner:

```
Alert(testCar.getYear());
```

Using Inheritance in JavaScript

As you saw in the previous section, when you register your class, you can specify the base class type from which your class derives. One of the goals of Atlas is to make your JavaScript easier to read and debug, and inheritance is a useful methodology to prevent replication of member variables and methods amongst your classes, helping you achieve this goal.

This is probably best demonstrated by example. Earlier you created a Car class for a generic car. Lots of different types of cars exist; for example, a sports utility vehicle (SUV) is different from a sports car in that it will usually have a four-wheel drive (4WD) and the sports car will not. If you want to implement car classes, where you will query the type of 4WD the car has, it makes sense to have a subclass of Car called SUV that has a 4WD property.

You can try this by adding the following code to the bottom of the .js file you created earlier:

```
AtlasBook.SUV=function(strMake, strModel, strYear, strDriveType)
{
    AtlasBook.SUV.initializeBase(this,[strMake,strModel,strYear]);
    var m_DriveType = strDriveType;
    this.getDriveType = function() {
        return m_DriveType;
    }
}
AtlasBook.SUV.registerClass('AtlasBook.SUV', AtlasBook.Car);
```

The earlier code implemented an AtlasBook.Car class that took a make (strMake), model (strModel), and year (strYear) as constructors. This code now implements the SUV class that takes the same parameters, as well as an additional one (strDriveType) that specifies the type of 4WD the vehicle will use.

The first line passes the make, model, and year up to the base class, so this instance will handle initialization through the base class, and initializors for these properties don't need to be rewritten:

```
AtlasBook.SUV.initializeBase(this,[strMake,strModel,strYear]);
```

It then implements its distinct property (for DriveType) and the method to read that property:

```
var m_DriveType = strDriveType;
    this.getDriveType = function() {
        return m_DriveType;
    }
```

Finally, it registers this class and specifies the base class to be AtlasBook.Car and hence derives from the AtlasBook.Car class:

```
AtlasBook.SUV.initializeBase(this,[strMake,strModel,strYear]);
```

To see it in action, return to the web form you created earlier, and change the Button1_onclick script to this:

```
function Button1_onclick() {
    var testCar = new AtlasBook.Car('Honda','Pilot','2005');
    alert(testCar.getMakeandModel());
    alert(testCar.getYear());

    var testSUV = new AtlasBook.SUV('Honda','Pilot','2005','Active');
    alert(testSUV.getMakeandModel());
    alert(testSUV.getYear());
    alert(testSUV.getDriveType());
```

```
        return false;
}
```

The testSUV stuff is added, and methods for getMakeandModel as well as getYear are called. These methods are implemented on the base (Car) class and inherited by the derived (SUV) class. Run the application, and you'll see them in action (see Figure 3-13).

Figure 3-13. *Calling a method from the base class on the derived class*

Implementing Interfaces in JavaScript

Earlier you saw that when you define a class, you can also define the interfaces it implements. By implementing these interfaces, an object of this class will have those functions available to it. So, as an example, consider the following case. This definition has two types of sports cars: a "real" sports car that implements a manual stick shift that can be set to whatever you like and a "cheap" sports car that doesn't and is just a standard car in a sleek body.

Here is the code that defines the stick shift interface:

```
AtlasBook.IStickShift = function() {
    this.setGear = Function.abstractMethod;
    this.getGear = Function.abstractMethod;
    this.getGearCount = Function.abstractMethod;
}
AtlasBook.IStickShift.registerInterface('AtlasBook.IStickShift');
```

It defines three methods that any class using this interface will support. These are to set the current gear, to get the current gear, and to get the count of available gears to the car.

Now, a good sports car is one that implements this interface and these functions:

```
AtlasBook.SportsCar=
    function(strMake, strModel, strYear, strGears)
{
    AtlasBook.SportsCar.initializeBase(this,
            [strMake, strModel, strYear]);
    var m_Gears = strGears;
    var m_CurrentGear = 0;
```

```
    this.setGear = function(strGearToSet){
        m_CurrentGear = strGearToSet;
        return true;
    }
    this.getGear = function(){
        return m_CurrentGear;
    }
    this.getGearCount = function(){
        return m_Gears;
    }
}
AtlasBook.SportsCar.registerAbstractClass('AtlasBook.SportsCar',
        AtlasBook.Car, AtlasBook.IStickShift);
```

You can see from the registerAbstractClass call that the sports car is being subclassed from a Car class and implements the AtlasBook.IStickShift interface.

Conversely, a cheap sports car is just a normal car, so its definition will look like this:

```
AtlasBook.CheapSportsCar =
    function(strMake, strModel, strYear, strGears)
{
    AtlasCheapSportsCar.initializeBase(this,
            [strMake, strModel, strYear]);
}
AtlasBook.CheapSportsCar.registerClass('AtlasBook.CheapSportsCar',
        AtlasBook.Car);
```

In code, you can check your class to see whether it implements the IStickShift interface so you can derive which type of sports car the car is or to check whether it implements a stick shift before you try to use it.

The following example uses the web form from earlier but changes the code-handling onclick event of the button to this:

```
function Button1_onclick() {
 var testSportsCar = new
    AtlasBook.SportsCar('Porsche','999','2005','6');
 var testCheapSportsCar = new
    AtlasBook.CheapSportsCar('Shorspe','123','2005');
 ProcessCar(testSportsCar);
 ProcessCar(testCheapSportsCar);
 return false;
}
```

This calls a helper function named ProcessCar that looks like this:

```
function ProcessCar(theCar)
{
  if(AtlasBook.IStickShift.isImplementedBy(theCar))
   {
    alert("Current Car: "
              + theCar.getMakeandModel()
              + " This is a good sports car "
              + " -- I can set the gear with a stick shift.");
    theCar.setGear(5);
    alert(theCar.getMakeandModel()
              + " is now cruising in gear number: "
              + theCar.getGear());
   }
   else
   {
    alert("Current Car: "
              + theCar.getMakeandModel()
              + " This is a cheap sports car "
              + " -- it's an automatic with a sleek body.");
   }
}
```

This function looks at the car that is being passed into it. If it is a "real" sports car, it implements the IStickShift interface (AtlasBook.IStickShift.isImplementedBy(theCar) returns true), and you know you can call the setGear and getGear methods on it. Otherwise it doesn't, and if you try to call these methods, you'll get an exception.

You can see it in action in Figure 3-14.

Figure 3-14. *Using the IStickShift interface*

Accessing Server Resources from JavaScript

A typical design pattern in web applications is that your application consumes a web service and presents an interface to this web service to your user. This forms a typical *n*-tier architecture, with the web service and the information resources it consumes being a resource tier for your web application, which is a presentation tier. To consume the web service, you would require a server application because the ASP.NET technology doesn't have a pure client-side implementation of web service proxies. You would build a web application, create a proxy to the web service using Visual Studio .NET or the wsdl.exe tool, and implement this proxy within your application.

With Atlas, you can now have a pure client-side implementation of a web service consumer. When you build your Atlas client, you can use the `<Services>` tag within the ScriptManager and embed an `<atlas:ServiceReference>` element in this to point to your web service. You'll see this in action in a demonstration shortly.

Web services are ideally suited for business logic that has to be shared amongst a number of applications. For example, in this case, I will show how to write a web service that calculates the value of a car based on its make and model and how much it has depreciated in value because of its age. Depreciation is interesting here, because it is date-specific, and hence it is ideal for a hosted business analytic and therefore a web service. This simple algorithm deducts $2,000 in value for each year the car has aged (a real service would have a far more complex formula).

Now you may think you can do the same thing from a client-side application, but the problem with this approach is that everybody has a different clock on their computer, and the time-based calculation of the value should come from a master clock; hence, having a master process to manage the calculation makes sense, and web services are the ideal technology on which to do it, because they are designed for remote accessibility.

So, to see this in action, you should first implement a web service. Add a new web service to your project, and call it CarService.asmx.

To this web service you can add a new WebMethod called getCarValue with the following code:

```
[WebMethod]
public int GetCarValue(string strCarMake,
                       string strCarModel,
                       int strCarYear)
{
    int nReturn = 0;
    if (strCarMake == "Honda")
      nReturn = 30000;
    else
      nReturn = 20000;
    if (strCarModel == "Pilot")
      nReturn += 10000;

    int nDepreciation =
      (System.DateTime.Now.Year - strCarYear) * 2000;
    nReturn -= nDepreciation;
    return Math.Max(0,nReturn);
}
```

This crude calculation establishes the value of a Honda at $30,000, unless it is a Pilot, in which case it is $40,000. Other makes have a base value of $20,000, unless they are Pilots, in which case they are $30,000. Depreciation is counted as $2,000 per year of age.

Next, create a new web form, and call it CalcCarValue.aspx. Drag an Atlas ScriptManager control to the design surface, and add HTML Input (Text) controls and an Input (Button) control to it. Label the three text fields as Make:, Model:, and Year:, and call them txtMake, txtModel, and txtYear, respectively. Give the button the text Get Value.

Your screen should look like Figure 3-15.

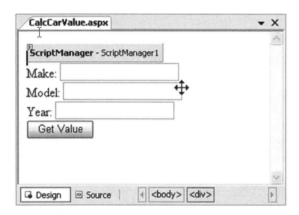

Figure 3-15. *Designing the web services client application*

Next, go to the Source view for this form, and find the `<atlas:ScriptManager>` tag. Enter a new `<Services>` tag inside this one, and create a ServiceReference instance that points to CarService.asmx. The code to do this should look like this:

```
<atlas:ScriptManager ID="ScriptManager1" runat="server">
  <Services>
    <atlas:ServiceReference Path="CarService.asmx" />
  </Services>
</atlas:ScriptManager>
```

Finally, you will create the code that invokes the Service proxy and passes it the parameters derived from the text fields on the form. In Design view, double-click the button to wire up the event handler function for it. You will automatically be returned to the Source view and will be inside the Button1_onclick function.

Add the following code to this function:

```
function Button1_onclick() {
    requestValue = CarService.GetCarValue(
        form1.txtMake.value,
        form1.txtModel.value,
        form1.txtYear.value,
        OnComplete,
        OnTimeOut);

    return false;
}
```

In JavaScript, you refer to an HTML control by prefixing it with the name of the form that it is on. In this case, the form is called form1, and hence you can get the value of the txtMake field using form1.txtMake.value.

Your web service proxy has the same name as the service itself. In this case, the service is called CarService and thus so is the proxy. In many cases you may have a dot-separated hierarchy of names for your web service (that is, MathFunctions.Services.DepreciationService), in which case you would use that as the name of your proxy too. The rule of thumb you can use, if in doubt, is to look up the value of the Class= attribute in the .asmx file and use that.

Now, you may notice that your getCarValue web method took only three parameters, but now you are passing five parameters. The additional ones are the callback functions that you specify upon successful completion of the service call and upon a timeout of the service call. This handles Ajax asynchrony for you completely under the hood!

In this example, you implement the callback functions like this:

```
function OnComplete(result)
{
    alert("Car is worth: $" + result);
}

function OnTimeOut(result)
{
    alert("Timeout: " + result);
}
```

The web method returns a value, and this is passed as "result" to both the successful and the timeout callbacks. In the case of a successful request/response, this will contain the calculated value of the car.

Figure 3-16 shows the application calculating the price of a 2005 Honda Pilot at $38,000, with the client JavaScript invoking the web service and displaying the result.

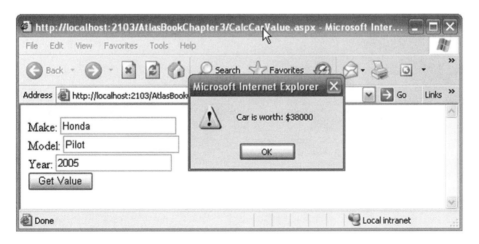

Figure 3-16. *Running the JavaScript web service consumer*

Summary

In this chapter, you began looking at the power of JavaScript in Atlas. You learned about the extensions to JavaScript implemented in the Atlas.js library that allow you to use true object orientation within your JavaScript, enabling such technologies such as inheritance, name-spaces, and interfaces. Through hands-on coding, you saw how these features work and how you can use them to make JavaScript easier to code, debug, and maintain. Additionally, you looked at the JavaScript features that automatically encapsulate asynchronous web service calls from your browser application. You saw how to implement and consume a web service as well as how to wire up the asynchronous call to it. Comparing the complexity of this call to the Ajax code in Chapter 1, you can see it is accomplishing a more complex task (a SOAP call to a web service as opposed to a straight HTTP GET) with less code and in an easier-to-read and easier-to-maintain manner.

From here you can begin to see the value that Atlas brings to Ajax-style applications. In the following chapters, you will start looking into the libraries of controls that Atlas offers, including looking at the client-side controls in Chapters 4 and 5.

CHAPTER 4

■ ■ ■

Introducing Client Controls in Atlas

In the first three chapters, you looked at Ajax and Atlas and how you can use them to build web applications that provide slick, clean, high-performing user interfaces by restricting the need for postbacks to the server and that use the intelligence of the browser on the client side. In this chapter, and the next, you will learn more details about the controls that Atlas gives you to empower your development skills. Although Atlas provides a foundation for building rich client applications using scripting, Atlas implements many common functionalities for you via client-side controls. I will cover these controls in this chapter and cover the server-side controls in Chapter 5.

Specifically, in this chapter you will learn how to use the following:

Atlas client-side controls: You will learn how to use the built-in client-side controls available to JavaScript or the XML-based Atlas Script.

Atlas Script: You will learn how to construct client-side interfaces using XML with the new Atlas Script. You will define how controls appear on the page and hook them up to events, also defined in XML.

In Chapter 5, I'll cover actions, behaviors, and data binding, and I'll cover how to extend existing controls and how to create new controls.

Seeing a Basic Example in Action

When writing web pages that use client-side controls in Atlas, you define the controls within the HTML code as usual and then create references to these controls using Atlas Script or JavaScript. You can then manipulate these references via code to affect the underlying objects; this process is much easier than if you were to manipulate the underlying object directly.

In this example, you will create a page that contains a button and a label, and you'll toggle the visibility of the label by clicking the button:

1. To create this page, first add a blank page (ChangeVisibility.aspx) to your project, and drag an Atlas ScriptManager control onto it.

2. Next, add a `<div>` element (you can drag and drop it from the HTML section in the Toolbox), and give it the ID of **panel**. Add some text to it.

3. Finally, drag and drop an Input (Button) control onto the page. Your screen should look like Figure 4-1.

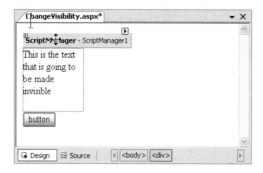

Figure 4-1. *Designing the page*

The code behind this page should look something like this:

```
<%@ Page Language="C#" AutoEventWireup="true"
   CodeFile="ChangeVisibility.aspx.cs" Inherits="ChangeVisibility" %>

<!DOCTYPE html PUBLIC "-//W3C//DTD XHTML 1.0 Transitional//EN"
   "http://www.w3.org/TR/xhtml1/DTD/xhtml1-transitional.dtd">

<html xmlns="http://www.w3.org/1999/xhtml" >
<head runat="server">
    <title>Untitled Page</title>
</head>
<body>
    <form id="form1" runat="server">
    <div>
        <atlas:ScriptManager ID="ScriptManager1" runat="server">
        </atlas:ScriptManager>

    </div>
        <div id="panel" style="width: 100px; height: 100px">
            This is the text that is going to be made invisible</div>
        <input id="Button1" type="button" value="button" />
    </form>
</body>
</html>
```

The next task is to add the Atlas code that allows you to change the visibility of the panel whenever the user clicks the button. You will do this using some JavaScript. Add the following JavaScript to the bottom of the page, beneath the closing </form> element and above the </body> element:

```
<script language="JavaScript">
      var g_panel;
      function pageLoad()
      {
          // Set up the atlas panel and set up the initial css
          g_panel = new Sys.UI.Control($('panel'));
          g_panel.initialize();
          g_panel.set_cssClass('normal');

          var btnVisibility = new Sys.UI.Button($('Button1'));
          btnVisibility.initialize();
          btnVisibility.click.add(onSetVisibilityClick);
      }
      function onSetVisibilityClick() {
          g_panel.set_visible(!g_panel.get_visible());
      }
</script>
```

■Note When you create a new Sys.UI.Control, you pass it the name of the underlying HTML element prefixed with $ like this:

```
g_panel = new Sys.UI.Control($('panel'));
```

Control constructors take an element reference, not the string with the ID. Using the prototype function ($('elementname')) generates the reference so it can be recognized correctly.

This script triggers when the page loads (pageLoad() event in Atlas) and creates a new instance of a Sys.UI.Control, which is constructed using the panel element. This constructor must be an existing control that is on the page. Should you try to call it with something else—for example, panel999—Atlas will throw an error. So, in this case g_panel is a reference to the actual HTML control that is defined in the <div> tag. It makes life much easier to then manipulate this reference to change the underlying object.

Similarly, a reference of type Sys.UI.Button is created to point to the button you created earlier. Interestingly enough, you can add events to controls, and in this case, the click event is given the handler onSetVisibilityClick. Whenever the user clicks the button, the Atlas framework will call this function to handle the click.

The function is then implemented in this script. It simply uses the set_visible and get_visible methods of the Sys.UI.Control class (of which g_panel is an instance) to set the visibility of the object to the logical inverse (using the not, or !, operator) of its current state, thus toggling its visibility.

Running the page gives the results in Figure 4-2.

Figure 4-2. *Now you see me…and now you don't (after clicking the button).*

As you can see, when using client-side GUI objects, the Atlas framework gives you a nice, script-based, object-oriented approach that will make your coding a lot simpler.

Using the Atlas UI Client Controls

The file Atlas.js contains the JavaScript definition for each of the UI control objects. In the following sections, you will look at each of these UI objects and how you can use them to manipulate HTML objects to form true object-oriented client-side controls.

The UI Control

The UI control, from which all the other controls in this chapter derive, provides the foundational functionality shared by all client controls.

It exposes the methods described in Table 4-1.

Table 4-1. *UI Control Methods*

Method Name	Function
addCSSClass(String className)	Attaches the class specified in className to the control. It must be a valid, defined CSS class available to the host page.
focus()	Passes focus to the control.
scrollIntoView()	If the control is off the page, scrolls the page until it is in view.
removeCSSClass(String className)	Unattaches the CSS class specified in className.
toggleCSSClass(String className)	If the CSS className is currently attached, unattaches it; otherwise, attaches it.

The properties described in Table 4-2 are available.

Table 4-2. *UI Control Properties*

Property Name	Function
bindings	Returns an array of strings indicating the data bindings for this control.
dataContext	Gets the data context for the binding associated with the control.
id	Returns the ID for the control.
accessKey	Allows the access key for quick access to this control to be set or read.
associatedElement	Returns an object reference to the associated element.
behaviors	Returns an array of strings indicating the behaviors associated with this control.
cssClass	Gets or sets the cssClass for this control. You can also use the various CSS methods of the control to manipulate its CSS class.
enabled	Gets or sets whether the control is enabled. When true, the control is enabled; when false, the control is grayed out.
style	Returns an object containing the element's style settings.
tabIndex	Gets or sets the value of the control in the tab index.
visible	Gets or sets the visibility of the control. If true, the control is visible; if false, it is invisible.
visibilityMode	Returns a string containing the CSS definition for the object's visibility.

The event described in Table 4-3 is available.

Table 4-3. *UI Control Event*

Event Name	Function
propertyChanged	Fires upon the changing of a property. Supports actions (for more about actions, see Chapter 5).

The Label Control

The Label control is defined in the Sys.UI.Label class. It encapsulates the functionality used to manipulate an HTML `<span>` element as an object within JavaScript.

You define the label in HTML like this:

```
<span id="MyLabel">This is the label</span>
```

You can also define it using a `<label>` tag like this:

```
<label id="MyLabel">This is the label</label>
```

The script to create an instance of an Atlas Label control from this HTML upon the page loading looks like this:

```
<script language=javascript>
    var g_label
    function pageLoad()
        {
            g_label = new Sys.UI.Label($('MyLabel'));
        }
</script>
```

The Label control exposes the methods described in Table 4-4.

Table 4-4. *Label Control Methods*

Method Name	Function
addCSSClass(String className)	Attaches the class specified in className to the `<span>` element. It must be a valid, defined CSS class available to the host page.
focus()	Passes focus to the `<span>` element.
scrollIntoView()	If the `<span>` element is off the page, scrolls the page until it is in view.
removeCSSClass(String className)	Unattaches the CSS class specified in className.
toggleCSSClass(String className)	If the CSS className is currently attached, unattaches it; otherwise, attaches it.

The properties described in Table 4-5 are available.

Table 4-5. *Label Control Properties*

Property Name	Function
bindings	Returns an array of strings indicating the data bindings for this control.
dataContext	Gets the data context for the binding associated with the control.
id	Returns the ID for the control.
accessKey	Allows the access key for quick access to this control to be set or read.
associatedElement	Returns an object reference to the associated element.
behaviors	Returns an array of strings indicating the behaviors associated with this control.
cssClass	Gets or sets the cssClass for this control. You can also use the various CSS methods of the control to manipulate its CSS class.
enabled	Gets or sets whether the control is enabled. When true, the control is enabled; when false, the control is grayed out.
style	Returns an object containing the element's style settings.
tabIndex	Gets or sets the value of the control in the tab index.
visible	Gets or sets the visibility of the control. If true, the control is visible; if false, it is invisible.
visibilityMode	Returns a string containing the CSS definition for the object's visibility.
text	Gets or sets the text within the Label control.

The event described in Table 4-6 is available.

Table 4-6. *Label Control Event*

Event Name	Function
propertyChanged	Fires upon the changing of a property. Supports actions (for more about actions, see Chapter 5).

The Button Control

The Button control is a Sys.UI.Button that corresponds to and controls an HTML button object.
You define it in HTML using the <input> tag, like this:

```
<input id="Button1" type="button" value="button" />
```

or using the <button> tag, like this:

```
<button id="Button1">button</button>
```

You can then set up the script in Atlas like this:

```
var g_button = new Sys.UI.Button($('Button1'));
```

The Button control exposes the methods described in Table 4-7.

Table 4-7. *Button Control Methods*

Method Name	Function
addCSSClass(String className)	Attaches the class specified in className to the Button control. It must be a valid, defined CSS class available to the host page.
focus()	Passes focus to the Button control.
scrollIntoView()	If the Button control is off the page, scrolls the page until it is in view.
removeCSSClass(String className)	Unattaches the CSS class specified in className.
toggleCSSClass(String className)	If the CSS className is currently attached, unattaches it; otherwise, attaches it.

The Button control has the properties described in Table 4-8.

Table 4-8. *Button Control Properties*

Property Name	Function
bindings	Returns an array of strings indicating the data bindings for this control.
dataContext	Gets the data context for the binding associated with the control.
id	Returns the ID for the control.
accessKey	Allows the access key for quick access to this control to be set or read.
associatedElement	Returns an object reference to the associated element.
behaviors	Returns an array of strings indicating the behaviors associated with this control.
cssClass	Gets or sets the cssClass for this control. You can also use the various CSS methods of the control to manipulate its CSS class.
enabled	Gets or sets whether the control is enabled. When true, the control is enabled; when false, the control is grayed out.
style	Returns an object containing the element's style settings.
tabIndex	Gets or sets the value of the control in the tab index.
visible	Gets or sets the visibility of the control. If true, the control is visible; if false, it is invisible.
visibilityMode	Returns a string containing the CSS definition for the object's visibility.
command	Gets or sets the command associated with this button (it can be a regular button, a Submit button, or a Reset button).
argument	The argument associated with the button, such as the URL of the submission processor page for the form.

The Button control can fire the events shown in Table 4-9.

Table 4-9. *Button Control Events*

Event Name	Function
propertyChanged	Fires upon the changing of a property. Supports actions (for more about actions, see Chapter 5).
click	Fires upon the user clicking the button.

The InputControl Control

The Atlas InputControl control is analogous to an HTML input control that can be used for buttons, text boxes, or text fields. You can use it for a text box by defining it in HTML using the following markup:

```
<input id="Text1" type="text" />
```

This then gets associated with an Atlas client InputControl object like this:

```
var g_textbox = new Sys.UI.InputControl($('Text1'));
```

The InputControl control exposes the methods shown in Table 4-10.

Table 4-10. *InputControl Control Methods*

Method Name	Function
addCSSClass(String className)	Attaches the class specified in className to the InputControl control. It must be a valid, defined CSS class available to the host page.
focus()	Passes focus to the InputControl control.
scrollIntoView()	If the control is off the page, scrolls the page until it is in view.
removeCSSClass(String className)	Unattaches the CSS class specified in className.
toggleCSSClass(String className)	If the CSS className is currently attached, unattaches it; otherwise, attaches it.

The InputControl control has the properties described in Table 4-11.

Table 4-11. *InputControl Control Properties*

Property Name	Function
bindings	Returns an array of strings indicating the data bindings for this control.
dataContext	Gets the data context for the binding associated with the control.
id	Returns the ID for the control.
accessKey	Allows the access key for quick access to this control to be set or read.
associatedElement	Returns an object reference to the associated element.
behaviors	Returns an array of strings indicating the behaviors associated with this control.
cssClass	Gets or sets the cssClass for this control. You can also use the various CSS methods of the control to manipulate its CSS class.
enabled	Gets or sets whether the control is enabled. When true, the control is enabled; when false, the control is grayed out.
style	Returns an object containing the element's style settings.
tabIndex	Gets or sets the value of the control in the tab index.
visible	Gets or sets the visibility of the control. If true, the control is visible; if false, it is invisible.
visibilityMode	Returns a string containing the CSS definition for the object's visibility.
validators	InputControls can have validators that automatically validate the data that is being input against programmed criteria such as a number range, a number format, or specific text.

The InputControl can fire the event described in Table 4-12.

Table 4-12. *InputControl Control Event*

Event Name	Function
propertyChanged	Fires upon the changing of a property. Supports actions (for more about actions, see Chapter 5).

The TextBox Control

The Atlas TextBox is analogous to a text box, which uses the underlying HTML
`<input type="text">` tag.

You can define a TextBox control in HTML using the following markup:

```
<input id="Text1" type="text" />
```

This then gets associated with an Atlas client TextBox object like this:

```
var g_textbox = new Sys.UI.TextBox($('Text1'));
```

The TextBox control exposes the methods shown in Table 4-13.

Table 4-13. *TextBox Control Methods*

Method Name	Function
addCSSClass(String className)	Attaches the class specified in className to the text box. It must be a valid, defined CSS class available to the host page.
focus()	Passes focus to the text box.
scrollIntoView()	If the text box is off the page, scrolls the page until it is in view.
removeCSSClass(String className)	Unattaches the CSS class specified in className.
toggleCSSClass(String className)	If the CSS className is currently attached, unattaches it; otherwise, attaches it.

The TextBox has the properties shown in Table 4-14.

Table 4-14. *TextBox Control Properties*

Property Name	Function
bindings	Returns an array of strings indicating the data bindings for this control.
dataContext	Gets the data context for the binding associated with the control.
id	Returns the ID for the control.
accessKey	Allows the access key for quick access to this control to be set or read.
associatedElement	Returns an object reference to the associated element.
behaviors	Returns an array of strings indicating the behaviors associated with this control.
cssClass	Gets or sets the cssClass for this control. You can also use the various CSS methods of the control to manipulate its CSS class.
enabled	Gets or sets whether the control is enabled. When true, the control is enabled; when false, the control is grayed out.
style	Returns an object containing the element's style settings.
tabIndex	Gets or sets the value of the control in the tab index.
visible	Gets or sets the visibility of the control. If true, the control is visible; if false, it is invisible.

Property Name	Function
visibilityMode	Returns a string containing the CSS definition for the object's visibility.
validators	TextBox controls can have validators that automatically validate the data that is being input against programmed criteria such as a number range, a number format, or specific text.
Text	A string containing the text contained in the TextBox.

The TextBox can fire the event described in Table 4-15.

Table 4-15. *TextBox Control Event*

Event Name	Function
propertyChanged	Fires upon the changing of a property. Supports actions (for more about actions, see Chapter 5).

The Image Control

The Atlas Image control corresponds to an HTML image tag, `<img>`, which can be used to place pictures on a web page.

You define an image tag in your page like this:

```
<img src="" id="Image1" />
```

The src attribute indicates the path to the image for the browser to render. It can be a relative path on the web site that the page is hosted on or an absolute path to another server or the physical location of the image on the hard drive of the machine hosting the browser that is viewing the page.

You associate this `<img>` with an Atlas Image control like this:

```
var g_image = new Sys.UI.Image($('Image1'));
```

The Image control exposes the methods described in Table 4-16.

Table 4-16. *Image Control Methods*

Method Name	Function
addCSSClass(String className)	Attaches the class specified in className to the image. It must be a valid, defined CSS class available to the host page.
focus()	Passes focus to the image.
scrollIntoView()	If the image is off the page, scrolls the page until it is in view.
removeCSSClass(String className)	Unattaches the CSS class specified in className.
toggleCSSClass(String className)	If the CSS className is currently attached, unattaches it; otherwise, attaches it.

The Image control has the properties described in Table 4-17.

Table 4-17. *Image Control Properties*

Property Name	Function
bindings	Returns an array of strings indicating the data bindings for this control.
dataContext	Gets the data context for the binding associated with the control.
id	Returns the ID for the control.
accessKey	Allows the access key for quick access to this control to be set or read.
associatedElement	Returns an object reference to the associated element.
behaviors	Returns an array of strings indicating the behaviors associated with this control.
cssClass	Gets or sets the cssClass for this control. You can also use the various CSS methods of the control to manipulate its CSS class.
enabled	Gets or sets whether the control is enabled. When true, the control is enabled; when false, the control is grayed out.
style	Returns an object containing the element's style settings.
tabIndex	Gets or sets the value of the control in the tab index.
visible	Gets or sets the visibility of the control. If true, the control is visible; if false, it is invisible.
visibilityMode	Returns a string containing the CSS definition for the object's visibility.
alternateText	If the browser cannot render the image, this text will appear in its place.
height	The height of the rendered image (in pixels). Every image has an underlying size, but the browser can draw the image in a different size and will stretch or shrink the image accordingly.
imageURL	The source URL for the image. This is analogous to the src attribute on the `<img>` tag.
width	The width of the rendered image (in pixels). Every image has an underlying size, but the browser can draw the image in a different size and will stretch or shrink the image accordingly.

The Image control can fire the event described in Table 4-18.

Table 4-18. *Image Control Event*

Event Name	Function
propertyChanged	Fires upon the changing of a property. Supports actions (for more about actions, see Chapter 5).

The HyperLink Control

The Atlas HyperLink control corresponds to an HTML anchor tag, `<a>`, which can be used to place hyperlinks to external sites or to place internal bookmarks on your page.

You define an image tag in your page like this:

```
<a id="Href1" href="http://www.philotic.com/blog">Hyperlink</a>
```

The href attribute indicates the path to the page or bookmark that the browser will navigate to when the user clicks the hyperlink. It can be a relative path on the web site that the page is hosted on, an absolute path to another server, a reference to a JavaScript function to call, or the location of a bookmark on this specific page.

You associate this <a> with an Atlas HyperLink control like this:

```
var g_href = new Sys.UI.HyperLink($('Href1'));
```

The HyperLink control exposes the methods described in Table 4-19.

Table 4-19. *HyperLink Control Methods*

Method Name	Function
addCSSClass(String className)	Attaches the class specified in className to the anchor. It must be a valid, defined CSS class available to the host page.
focus()	Passes focus to the anchor.
scrollIntoView()	If the anchor is off the page, scrolls the page until it is in view.
removeCSSClass(String className)	Unattaches the CSS class specified in className.
toggleCSSClass(String className)	If the CSS className is currently attached, unattaches it; otherwise, attaches it.

The HyperLink control has the properties described in Table 4-20.

Table 4-20. *HyperLink Control Properties*

Property Name	Function
bindings	Returns an array of strings indicating the data bindings for this control.
dataContext	Gets the data context for the binding associated with the control.
id	Returns the ID for the control.
accessKey	Allows the access key for quick access to this control to be set or read.
associatedElement	Returns an object reference to the associated element.
behaviors	Returns an array of strings indicating the behaviors associated with this control.
cssClass	Gets or sets the cssClass for this control. You can also use the various CSS methods of the control to manipulate its CSS class.
enabled	Gets or sets whether the control is enabled. When true, the control is enabled; when false, the control is grayed out.
style	Returns an object containing the element's style settings.
tabIndex	Gets or sets the value of the control in the tab index.
visible	Gets or sets the visibility of the control. If true, the control is visible; if false, it is invisible.
visibilityMode	Returns a string containing the CSS definition for the object's visibility.
text	The text associated with this anchor. This is the text that will appear on the web page. In the previous example, the text property will be HyperLink.
navigateURL	The location of the destination for this link. This is the text that appears within the href attribute on the HTML tag.

The HyperLink control can fire the events described in Table 4-21.

Table 4-21. *HyperLink Control Events*

Event Name	Function
propertyChanged	Fires upon the changing of a property. Supports actions (for more about actions, see Chapter 5).
click	Fires upon the user clicking the hyperlink. Can be used to preprocess actions before the browser navigates to the destination.

The CheckBox Control

The Atlas CheckBox control corresponds to an HTML input tag, `<input>`, with the CheckBox type set.

You define the HTML in your page like this:

```
<input id="CheckBox1" type="CheckBox" />
```

One of the neat features of Atlas client controls is that they make your code more readable. Instead of dealing with lots of different `<input>` controls of different types, each type is assigned its own control type.

You associate this CheckBox with an Atlas CheckBox control like this:

```
var g_chk = new Sys.UI.CheckBox($('CheckBox1'));
```

The CheckBox control exposes the methods described in Table 4-22.

Table 4-22. *CheckBox Control Methods*

Method Name	Function
addCSSClass(String className)	Attaches the class specified in className to the CheckBox. It must be a valid, defined CSS class available to the host page.
focus()	Passes focus to the CheckBox.
scrollIntoView()	If the CheckBox is off the page, scrolls the page until it is in view.
removeCSSClass(String className)	Unattaches the CSS class specified in className.
toggleCSSClass(String className)	If the CSS className is currently attached, unattaches it; otherwise, attaches it.

The CheckBox control has the properties described in Table 4-23.

Table 4-23. *CheckBox Control Properties*

Property Name	Function
bindings	Returns an array of strings indicating the data bindings for this control.
dataContext	Gets the data context for the binding associated with the control.
id	Returns the ID for the control.
accessKey	Allows the access key for quick access to this control to be set or read.
associatedElement	Returns an object reference to the associated element.
behaviors	Returns an array of strings indicating the behaviors associated with this control.
cssClass	Gets or sets the cssClass for this control. You can also use the various CSS methods of the control to manipulate its CSS class.
enabled	Gets or sets whether the control is enabled. When true, the control is enabled; when false, the control is grayed out.
style	Returns an object containing the element's style settings.
tabIndex	Gets or sets the value of the control in the tab index.
visible	Gets or sets the visibility of the control. If true, the control is visible; if false, it is invisible.
visibilityMode	Returns a string containing the CSS definition for the object's visibility.
checked	Gets or sets the state of the CheckBox. True means the CheckBox is checked; false means it is clear.

The CheckBox control can fire the events described in Table 4-24.

Table 4-24. *CheckBox Control Events*

Event Name	Function
propertyChanged	Fires upon the changing of a property. Supports actions (for more about actions, see Chapter 5).
click	Fires upon the user clicking the CheckBox. Can be used to preprocess actions before the form on which the CheckBox appears is submitted.

The Select Control

The Atlas Select control corresponds to an HTML select tag, `<select>`, which implements various forms of drop-down lists.

You define a select tag in your page like this:

```
<select id="Select1">
    <option selected="selected">Option 1</option>
    <option>Option 2</option>
    <option>Option 3</option>
</select>
```

The select tag specifies the list, and the child option tags specify the elements. The previous snippet defines a selection list with three options, the first option being selected by default.

You associate this CheckBox with an Atlas Select control like this:

```
var g_sel = new Sys.UI.Select($('Select1'));
```

The Select control exposes the methods described in Table 4-25.

Table 4-25. *Select Control Methods*

Method Name	Function
addCSSClass(String className)	Attaches the class specified in className to the select list. It must be a valid, defined CSS class available to the host page.
focus()	Passes focus to the list.
scrollIntoView()	If the list is off the page, scrolls the page until it is in view.
removeCSSClass(String className)	Unattaches the CSS class specified in className.
toggleCSSClass(String className)	If the CSS className is currently attached, unattaches it; otherwise, attaches it.

The Select control has the properties described in Table 4-26.

Table 4-26. *Select Control Properties*

Property Name	Function
bindings	Returns an array of strings indicating the data bindings for this control.
dataContext	Gets the data context for the binding associated with the control.
id	Returns the ID for the control.
accessKey	Allows the access key for quick access to this control to be set or read.
associatedElement	Returns an object reference to the associated element.
behaviors	Returns an array of strings indicating the behaviors associated with this control.
cssClass	Gets or sets the cssClass for this control. You can also use the various CSS methods of the control to manipulate its CSS class.
enabled	Gets or sets whether the control is enabled. When true, the control is enabled; when false, the control is grayed out.
style	Returns an object containing the element's style settings.
tabIndex	Gets or sets the value of the control in the tab index.
visible	Gets or sets the visibility of the control. If true, the control is visible; if false, it is invisible.
visibilityMode	Returns a string containing the CSS definition for the object's visibility.
data	Specifies the Web.Data.DataTable associated with this control. This is used to automatically populate the list. For more about data binding and control population, see Chapter 5.
firstItemText	Gets or sets the text for the first item on the list.
selectedValue	Specifies the value for the currently selected item.
textProperty	Specifies the text for a specific item on the list.
valueProperty	Specifies the value for a specific item on the list.

The Select control can fire the events described in Table 4-27.

Table 4-27. *Select Control Events*

Event Name	Function
propertyChanged	Fires upon the changing of a property. Supports actions (for more about actions, see Chapter 5).
selectionChanged	Fires upon the user changing the current selection. This property supports actions (for more about actions, see Chapter 5).

Using Atlas Script

The typical and familiar method for managing the interaction between controls on your web page and updating their states based on various stimuli is to write Javascript to do so. You saw examples of this in Chapter 3, where you declared a button like this:

```
<input id="Button1" type="button" value="Get Value"
    onclick="return Button1_onclick()" />
```

Within the HTML declaration of the button, the property onclick was set to point to a function, which in this case is called Button1_onclick. Somewhere else on your page you would define a script block that implements the function Button1_onclick, something like this:

```
<script language="javascript" type="text/javascript">
function Button1_onclick() {
    // Do Whatever
    return false;
}
</script>
```

This can be a little difficult to track and debug, so Atlas introduces a new methodology, Atlas Script, for defining the controls on your page and for defining how they can interact with each other using a simple XML-based syntax. It is also intended for future designer applications so that you can use a visual designer to define the page layout and the actions, bindings, and behaviors of the controls in a similar manner to what you may be familiar with when using web forms.

When using Atlas Script, you follow the same process as you did with the JavaScript-based approach in the previous sections; namely, you define the controls in HTML and then create references to them. You then manipulate these references to manipulate the underlying controls. This is best shown by example. All of the code listings in this chapter are available in the download on the Apress web site at http://www.apress.com. You'll be looking at snippets of the full pages, so if you are following along, you may want to download the code first.

These examples use a CSS file called intro.css, shown in Listing 4-1.

Listing 4-1. *intro.css*

```
body           { text-align:left; margin:20,0,0,0;}
table, td      { font-size:10pt;font-family:Verdana; }
td.products td { text-align:center; font-size:8pt;
                 vertical-align:top; height:248 }

td.select      { color:#ffffff; background-color:#000000;
                 font-size:14pt;}
td.select select { width:130 }
td.cart        { height:2500 }
td.cart td     { font-size:9pt; font-weight:700}
td.cart a      { font-size:11pt; font-weight:700}

h3             { font-size:22 }
h2             { font-size:22 }
a:link         { color:blue; }
a:visited      { color:blue; }

div.details {background-color:#ffffcc; padding-top:15;
             padding-bottom:20; }
div.details table { width:280; }
div.details table td { font-family:Verdana; font-size:8pt; }
div.demosample {width:250px;height:75px;
                border: dashed 2px black;}
div.demosample1 {width:50%;height:200px;
                 border: dashed 2px black;
                 text-align:center;
                 vertical-align:bottom;}
div.normal {font-size:14pt;text-align:center;
            vertical-align:middle;background-color:yellow;
            border:dotted 3px black}
div.description {padding-top:15; padding-bottom:20;
                 font-family:Verdana;background-color:white}
div.title {background-color:#ffffcc; padding-top:15;
           padding-bottom:20; font-family:Verdana;}

table.nutr td  { font-family: Verdana; font-size:8pt; }

img.selected { border-color:#DC6035;border-style:solid;}
img.unselected { border-color:#ffffcc;border-style:solid;}

table.details td { font-family: Verdana; font-size:12pt;
                   padding-right:50; width:50%  }

span.blurb { font-size:9pt;}
table.form td { padding-right:15 }
```

```
select.itemselect { font-size:12pt; text-align:left;
                    background-color:lightyellow }
.buttonstyle { font-size:12pt;font-family:Verdana;
               background-color:Gray;color:White}
.buttonstyle2 { margin:4px;padding:4px;text-align:center;
                vertical-align:middle;cursor:hand;
                font-size:12pt;font-family:Verdana;
                background-color:Gray;color:White}


.normal {font-size:14pt;color:black;text-align:center;
         width:100%; height:200px;background-color:yellow;
         border:dotted 3px black}
div.red {font-size:14pt;color:white;width:100%;
         height:200px;text-align:center;
         vertical-align:bottom;background-color:red;
         border:dotted 3px black}
.blue {font-size:14pt;width:100%; height:200px;
       color:white;text-align:center;
       vertical-align:middle;background-color:blue;
       border:dotted 3px black}
.special {cursor: hand;}
.notset {border:dotted 3px black}
.textBox {width:400px;font-size:20pt;text-align:center;
          background-color:yellow}
.result {color:white;background-color:green;
         font-size:20pt;font-weight:bold;}
.input {color:black;background-color:yellow;
        font-size:20pt;font-weight:bold;}
.draghandle{background-color:lightblue;
            font-size:12pt;font-weight:bold;
            color:black;
            cursor:move;border:solid 1px black;
            text-align:center;width:100%}
.floatwindow{background-color:#eeeeee;font-size:14pt;
             border:solid 1px black;padding:4px;}
.popupwindow{border:solid 1px black;background-color:lightyellow;}
.hoverlabel {background-color:lightgreen;cursor:pointer;}
```

The following code defines a <div> element on a page and a number of Button controls that will be used to manipulate the <div> element:

```
<div class="description">
  <h3><u>Example 1:</u></h3>
  <div id="panel">Click the buttons to affect this element</div>
  <br />
```

```
<input type="button" id="hideButton"
       class="buttonstyle" value="Hide" /> 
<input type="button" id="showButton"
       class="buttonstyle" value="Show" />
<br/>
<input type="button" id="disableButton"
       class="buttonstyle" value="Disable" /> 
<input type="button" id="enableButton"
       class="buttonstyle" value="Enable" />
<br/>
<input type="button" id="largeButton"
       class="buttonstyle" value="Large" /> 
<input type="button" id="smallButton"
       class="buttonstyle" value="Small" />
</div>
```

You can see how this appears in Figure 4-3.

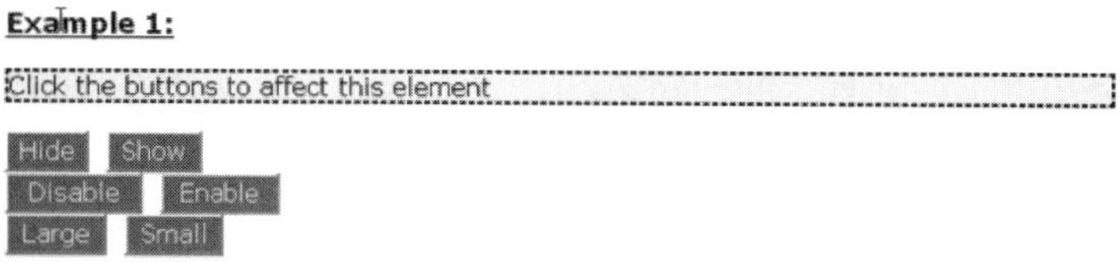

Figure 4-3. *The sample web form*

To affect the `<div>` element when clicking the buttons, you could write a JavaScript function that would be referenced in the onclick attribute of the button, or you could create an Atlas control reference to the button as in the previous section and manage the click event of that reference. The third option is to specify how you want the buttons to behave using Atlas Script.

Please note that you need to add a ScriptManager control to the page to be able to use Atlas Script.

Listing 4-2 shows the full Atlas Script for these buttons; you can find this script at the bottom of the listing before the closing `</body>` tag.

Listing 4-2. *Button Script*

```
<script type="text/xml-script">
<page xmlns:script="http://schemas.microsoft.com/xml-script/2005">
<components>
  <control id="panel" cssClass="start" />
  <button id="hideButton">
    <click>
      <setProperty target="panel" property="visible" value="false" />
    </click>
  </button>
```

```
<button id="showButton">
  <click>
    <setProperty target="panel" property="visible" value="true" />
  </click>
</button>
<button id="disableButton">
  <click>
    <setProperty target="panel" property="enabled" value="false" />
  </click>
</button>
<button id="enableButton">
  <click>
    <setProperty target="panel" property="enabled" value="true" />
  </click>
</button>
<button id="largeButton">
  <click>
    <invokeMethod target="panel" method="removeCssClass">
      <parameters className="small"/>
    </invokeMethod>
    <invokeMethod target="panel" method="addCssClass">
      <parameters className="large"/>
    </invokeMethod>
  </click>
</button>
<button id="smallButton">
  <click>
    <invokeMethod target="panel" method="removeCssClass">
      <parameters className="large"/>
    </invokeMethod>
    <invokeMethod target="panel" method="addCssClass">
      <parameters className="small"/>
    </invokeMethod>
  </click>
</button>
</components>
</page>
</script>
```

To define XML-based Atlas Script, you first define the `<script>` element. You should set this element to be of type text/xml-script so that the browser recognizes it as an XML-based script.

Next, you need to define the page and the namespace that will be used for this page. You do this using the `<page>` element. The current schema for XML Atlas Script is defined at `http://schemas.microsoft.com/xml-script/2005` and as such is associated with the `<page>` element here. This ensures that the browser will be able to correctly parse the XML.

Next, you define the components on the page. If you look at the HTML for the page, you will see that it comprises a <div> element, called panel, and six buttons, called hideButton, showButton, disableButton, enableButton, largeButton, and smallButton.

Atlas Script defines each of these. A base <div> control is defined as an Atlas control named Control. Thus, the tag to define it in Atlas Script is <control>. Thus, to create a reference to the <div> element, you use the following script:

```
<control id="panel" cssClass="start" />
```

This id property specifies the ID of the raw HTML element at which this control is pointing. This is equivalent to the script you saw earlier:

```
var g_ctrl = new Sys.UI.Control($('panel'));
```

Next, you define the buttons, and the neat feature of Atlas Script is that you can define the response to various events directly with the button. So, for example, when defining the Atlas Script for hideButton, you create the <click> child element and specify what happens upon this event:

```
<button id="hideButton">
   <click>
     <setProperty target="panel" property="visible" value="false" />
   </click>
 </button>
```

The <click> element's children specify what should happen upon the button being clicked. In this case, it has the child element <setProperty> that, as you may have guessed, causes properties to be set somewhere. Which properties, and where they should be set, are specified in the attributes of the <setProperty> element. In this case, the target is panel, the property to be set is visible, and the value that should be set on it is false. At runtime, when the button is clicked, Atlas parses this script and follows it, setting the visible property on panel to false, thus rendering the panel invisible. You can see this in Figure 4-4.

Example 1:

Figure 4-4. *The panel has vanished.*

You can see that similar behavior occurs on showButton, disableButton, and enableButton.

One interesting and powerful aspect of this script is that multiple commands may be issued upon an event firing. Take a look at the script for the largeButton control:

```
<button id="largeButton">
    <click>
      <invokeMethod target="panel" method="removeCssClass">
        <parameters className="small"/>
      </invokeMethod>
      <invokeMethod target="panel" method="addCssClass">
        <parameters className="large"/>
      </invokeMethod>
    </click>
  </button>
```

The <click> node has two child elements. They are both <invokeMethod> elements, which, as you may have guessed, call a method on a control. As with setProperty, you define, using attributes, which method on which control uses which parameters.

The base Control class supports methods called removeCssClass and addCssClass. These methods expect a parameter, being the name of the class you want to remove or add, respectively. To call them using the <invokeMethod> element, you can use the following Atlas Script:

```
<invokeMethod target="panel" method="removeCssClass">
  <parameters className="small"/>
</invokeMethod>
```

As you can probably derive, this specifies that the method to be called is removeCssClass; it should be called on the control referenced as panel. The parameter to be passed to the method is className="small".

When clicking largeButton, the user then triggers two actions; the first is that Atlas will invoke the removeCssClass method on the panel, telling it to remove the small Css class. It will then invoke the addCssClass method on the same control and pass it the parameter large. Thus, the effect is to dynamically change the CssClass of the object at runtime. You can see this effect in Figure 4-5.

Example 1:

Click the buttons to affect this element

Figure 4-5. *Dynamically changing CSS at runtime*

Summary

In this chapter, you started looking at client-side controls in Atlas, investigating the common HTML controls that are available as Atlas controls and how you can use and manipulate these using JavaScript or Atlas Script. These controls make the page-level manipulation of objects easier to handle, but they go far beyond just being a scripting methodology for existing functionality. With Atlas you can add new functionality to your client-side controls using behaviors, actions, data binding, and lots of user interface features such as drag and drop. In Chapter 5, you will take what you started with in this chapter and learn in more depth about how to use Atlas Script to associate this functionality with client-side controls.

CHAPTER 5

∎∎∎

Using Client Controls in Atlas

The first three chapters of this book gave you an overview of Ajax and Atlas and discussed how you can use them to build web applications using this technology to restrict unnecessary post-backs and processing on your web pages, thus improving the performance and polish of your web applications. In Chapter 4 you began to look at how Atlas provides controls—such as HTML text areas, anchors, input controls, and more—that help you manage the entities on your web page. The controls framework that Atlas layers on top of HTML standards allows you to write JavaScript code that is easier to maintain than if you were to code directly against the HTML representation of the controls. If you aren't familiar with how this works or don't understand how this helps, it is well worth returning to Chapter 4 before you continue with this chapter.

Additionally, Chapter 4 introduced Atlas Script, which is an XML-based declarative model for programming your web pages. This is a powerful yet easy-to-use construct whereby you specify each of your controls as an XML tag and then, using various child tags such as `<invokeMethod>`, declaratively control the behavior of these controls and how they interact with others. You'll be looking at advanced functionality that uses both forms of manipulation in this chapter, including the following:

Actions: Actions are collections of tasks, bundled into an atomic unit for managing complex tasks in a simple manner.

Behaviors: Behaviors allow you to create specific functionality that can be reused and attached to specific controls and elements on your page.

Data binding: As it sounds, data binding is the built-in facility that allows you to wire controls together to pass data between them.

This chapter will walk you through many examples of web pages that use Atlas to provide sophisticated GUI functionality. You will start with some simple examples and work your way up to more complex ones that use binding, behaviors, and more. I have found this to be the best way to understand the power of Atlas—to work through examples and then to dissect them in order to understand how they work.

Manipulating Controls Using CSS

In this example, you will look at how you can use JavaScript Atlas Script to manipulate the underlying properties of a `<div>` element that contains text and colors on your page. You'll see how Atlas interfaces with CSS styles and how, through the programmatic manipulation of these styles, you can affect how your page looks and performs.

Using JavaScript

First, you need to create your web page, containing the `<div>` tag, and the various controls that will be used to manipulate it.

The page will look like Figure 5-1.

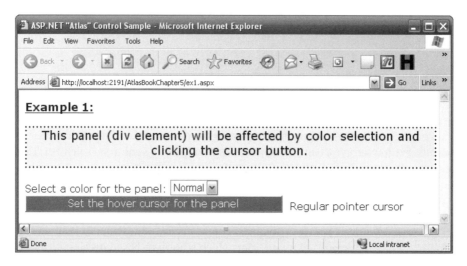

Figure 5-1. *Example screen for changing properties of a* `<div>` *element*

To construct this page, you use the following HTML code:

```
<form id="form1" runat="server">
  <atlas:ScriptManager runat="server" ID="ScriptManager1" />
  <div class="description">
    <h3><u>Example 1:</u></h3>
    <div id="panel">This panel (div element) will be affected
    by color selection and clicking the cursor button.
    </div>
    <br />
    Select a color for the panel: 
    <select id="colorSelect" class="itemselect">
      <option value="normal">Normal</option>
        <option value="red">Red</option>
        <option value="blue">Blue</option>
        <option value="notset">NotSet</option>
    </select>
    <input type="button" id="cursorButton" class="buttonstyle"
           value="Set the hover cursor for the panel" />
    <span id="cursorLabel"></span>
  </div>
</form>
```

This page uses a number of CSS classes. The CSS file is available in the download for this chapter and should be set up in the <head> element of the page using a link tag as follows (the full listing of this CSS file is also available in Chapter 4):

```
<link href="intro.css" type="text/css" rel="Stylesheet" />
```

To edit this page, you can use JavaScript to declare each of the elements as Atlas client controls, and you can then manipulate these controls in code.

First you create holder variables for the <div> element (also called a *panel*), the selection list where you pick the color, and the label where you place the status of the cursor—it will display whether you are using a regular cursor or a hand cursor:

```
var g_panel;
var g_selColor;
var g_label;
```

The pageLoad() function will fire upon the page being loaded and rendered. This is where you initialize the controls. A <div> element is represented by the Sys.UI.Control class, a selection list is represented by the Sys.UI.Select class, a button is represented by the Sys.UI.Button class, and a label is represented by the Sys.UI.Label class (each of these classes is documented in Chapter 4):

```
function pageLoad()
{
  // Set up the Atlas panel, and set up the initial css
  g_panel = new Sys.UI.Control($('panel'));
  g_panel.initialize();
  g_panel.set_cssClass('normal');

  // Set up the select list, and hook up a selection changed event
  g_selColor = new Sys.UI.Select($('colorSelect'));
  g_selColor.initialize();
  g_selColor.selectionChanged.add(onSelectColor);

  // Set up the buttons, and attach the click event
  var btnCursor = new Sys.UI.Button($('cursorButton'));
  btnCursor.initialize();
  btnCursor.click.add(onCursorButtonClick);

  g_label = new Sys.UI.Label($('cursorLabel'));
  g_label.initialize();
  g_label.set_text("Regular pointer cursor");
}
```

To initialize a control, you first assign it to a local variable and then call the initialize() method to set it up. Calling the set_cssClass method on the control will assign the control to the named CSS class. In the previous listing, you can see that g_panel is initialized with the class called normal. If you look at the CSS class file, you can see that this is declared as follows:

```
.normal {font-size:14pt;color:black;text-align:center;width:100%;
        height:60px;background-color:yellow;border:dotted 3px black}
```

Referring to Figure 5-1, you can see that this describes how the box is set up, with a yellow background, a dotted border, and so on.

Next you initialize the selection box. To do this, you assign the variable called g_selColor to a new Sys.UI.Select control. You construct this using the colorSelect parameter, which, if you refer to the HTML, is the ID for the select tag. After initializing, this code is called like this:

```
g_selColor.selectionChanged.add(onSelectColor);
```

This creates an action on g_selColor (and by extension the underlying HTML select control), which adds an event delegate. Whenever the selection changes on the control, the method defined in the parentheses (in this case onSelectColor) will be called. This method is defined like this:

```
function onSelectColor(sender, args) {
  g_panel.set_cssClass(g_selColor.get_selectedValue());
}
```

Therefore, when the user makes a selection, this function is called. What it does is to call the set_cssClass method on the panel, passing it a parameter—the value of the current selectedValue of the selection list. Again, look at the HTML code; the values associated with the various options on the list are normal, red, blue, and notset. These correspond directly with classes defined in the CSS file:

```
.normal {font-size:14pt;color:black;text-align:center;width:100%;
        height:60px;background-color:yellow;border:dotted 3px black}

.red {font-size:14pt;color:white;width:100%; height:60px;text-align:center;
        vertical-align:bottom;background-color:red;border:dotted 3px black}

.blue {font-size:14pt;width:100%; height:60px;color:white;text-align:center;
        vertical-align:middle;background-color:blue;border:dotted 3px black}

.notset {border:dotted 3px black}
```

Thus, for example, if you select the Red option on the list, Atlas will call the onSelectColor function, because it has been added as the event delegate for a selection on the list. The onSelectColor function will receive the value red, because it is the associated value for this selection on the list. The function then will call set_cssClass on the g_panel, passing it the value red, which, as you can see from the previous CSS, sets the background color of the panel to red.

You can see how this appears in Figure 5-2.

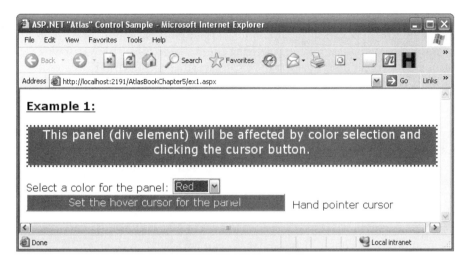

Figure 5-2. *The effect of choosing Red in the selection box*

Another style you can change on the `<div>` element is the cursor that is used when the mouse hovers over it. You can do this in this example with a click of the button to toggle it between the default cursor and a hand cursor. The label indicates the status of the current cursor. You'll now look at how these controls are initialized.

First the button—you set this up by constructing a Sys.UI.Button control with cursorButton, which is the ID of the underlying HTML control:

```
// Set up the buttons, and attach the click event
var btnCursor = new Sys.UI.Button($('cursorButton'));
btnCursor.initialize();
btnCursor.click.add(onCursorButtonClick);
```

Then you assign the onCursorButtonClick function as the delegate event for when the user clicks the button. This function looks like this:

```
function onCursorButtonClick() {
  if (g_panel.containsCssClass('special'))
  {
    g_panel.removeCssClass('special');
    g_label.set_text("Regular cursor");
  }
  else
  {
    g_panel.addCssClass('special');
    g_label.set_text("Hand pointer cursor");
  }
}
```

This function toggles the hover cursor for the panel. To do this, it inspects the panel using the containsCssClass method of the g_panel control. This is a great example of how useful client-side controls are. With Atlas, all the underlying plumbing is handled for you, so you can just call methods like this one to inspect the CSS classes that are attached to a control. If the panel contains the class special, that means it currently has this CSS attached to it:

```
.special {cursor: hand;}
```

And as you can see, this sets the cursor to be a hand. So, if it currently contains this CSS class, the way to toggle it is simply to remove this class from the panel, therefore reverting the panel to its default. You also set the text of the label to Regular Cursor. Otherwise, if it isn't present, you add it and update the label accordingly. Very simple, right?

You can see the effect of clicking this button in Figure 5-3. The button has been clicked to set the cursor to be a hand (first image). Note the state of the label and the cursor as it hovers over the <div> element. In the second image, the button has been clicked again, the special class has been removed, and both the label and the cursor have been updated.

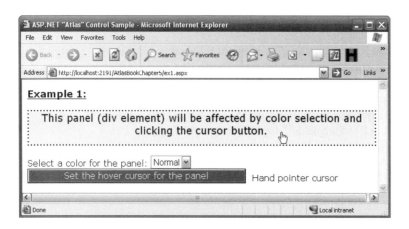

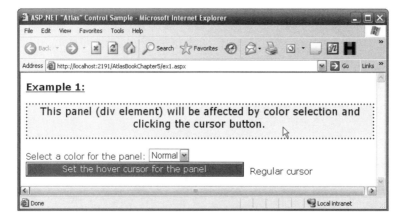

Figure 5-3. *The effect of clicking the button*

This example was a simple one, showing how you can manipulate CSS classes on the underlying controls by using the various methods available to Atlas client-side controls. In addition, you saw how event delegates can be added to controls to allow for complex functionality to be performed upon an event. As you work through this chapter, I will expand on this example to show you how to achieve more sophisticated functionality.

Using Atlas Script

You can achieve the same functionality using Atlas Script instead of JavaScript. In this case, the same HTML is used, but the following XML-based Atlas Script is used instead of the JavaScript code you saw earlier:

```
<script type="text/xml-script">
<page xmlns:script="http://schemas.microsoft.com/xml-script/2005">
<components>

 <control targetElement="panel" cssClass="normal">
  <bindings>
   <binding id="setCss" dataContext="colorSelect"
           dataPath="selectedValue" property="cssClass" />
  </bindings>
 </control>

 <select targetElement="colorSelect">
  <selectionChanged>
    <invokeMethod target="setCss" method="evaluateIn" />
  </selectionChanged>
 </select>


 <button targetElement="cursorButton">
   <click>
     <invokeMethod target="panel" method="toggleCssClass">
       <parameters className="special" />
     </invokeMethod>
     <setProperty target="cursorLabel"
                 property="text" value="Cursor set" />
     <setProperty target="cursorButton"
                 property="enabled" value="true" />
   </click>
 </button>

 <label targetElement="cursorLabel" text="Regular cursor" />

</components>
</page>
</script>
```

This script declaratively achieves the same functionality you saw in the previous expression that used explicit programming. Let's go through it piece by piece so you can understand completely what is happening.

First, you set up the outside tags that define the page:

```
<script type="text/xml-script">
<page xmlns:script="http://schemas.microsoft.com/xml-script/2005">
```

The script tag informs the browser that the processor for the type text/xml-script should be used for the following sections. The Atlas runtime handles this script for you.

Next, the tag appears that defines to Atlas that what is following is Atlas Script defining the page and the controls that are on the page. It uses the xml-script/2005 schema for validation, again informing Atlas to validate the page according to this schema.

Within the page is a `<components>` tag, within which each of the components resides.

Using Data Binding to Map the Select Box to the Panel

The first component to be initialized within the XML is the panel. You set it up like this:

```
<control targetElement="panel" cssClass="normal">
  <bindings>
   <binding id="setCss" dataContext="colorSelect"
           dataPath="selectedValue" property="cssClass" />
  </bindings>
 </control>
```

The `<control>` tag defines a client-side control. It contains a targetElement property that is analogous to the constructor parameter of the JavaScript version. In other words, you should set up this attribute to point to the physical HTML control that this script should reference. In this case, the `<div>` element you will be manipulating is called panel (see its ID property in the HTML), and therefore this `<control>` tag will reference that. Its cssClass will be initialized to normal, which sets it up with a yellow background and dotted border. This class resides in the CSS file associated with this page. If you read the previous section, about how to manipulate this page using JavaScript, you have seen this CSS class.

A child of the `<control>` tag is the `<bindings>` tag. Note the plural—any control may have multiple bindings, each of which is specified using a `<binding>` child tag of the bindings. This example has only a single binding, but you'll see examples of multiple bindings shortly, when the text box is initialized.

It is important to understand how to set up the binding. First, you give the binding an identity so it can be referenced from elsewhere. In this case, you give the binding the ID of setCss. Remember this, because you will be referring to it later. You also give the binding a dataContext. This is a reference to the source control to which this binding is bound. Next, you set up the dataPath—this is the property on the target control to which you are binding. Finally, you declare the property on this control to which you are binding the other control's data path, and this is cssClass. So, in this case, you want to bind the local property cssClass to the selectedValue property of the colorSelect control. You are giving this binding the identity setCss.

To see the other side of this binding, take a look at how the colorSelect control is handled in Atlas Script:

```
<select targetElement="colorSelect">
  <selectionChanged>
    <invokeMethod target="setCss" method="evaluateIn" />
  </selectionChanged>
</select>
```

Here the `<select>` tag specifies that this control is a selection list (analogous to Sys.UI.Select), with its target element being set to colorSelect, which is the ID for the selection control specified in the HTML.

You will notice that this element has a child element called selectionChanged. This is the name of an event that the control supports. For a list of the available properties, methods, and events on this control, see Chapter 4.

Here you are declaring what should happen on a selectionChanged event. What it does is invoke a method on a target. The target in this case is the setCSS binding, which is declared as a binding on the panel. The method itself is evaluateIn (exposed by the binding element), which returns the default value of this control, which, in the case of a select control, is the value (not the text) of the current selection. So, this code, upon the selection change, calls the data binding that was specified on the `<panel>` control, passing it the value of the current selection. Looking back at the definition for the panel control, you will see that the binding is set up to take this value and assign it to the cssClass property of the panel. If you look at the values of the selection options in the HTML (normal, red, blue, and notset), you will see these are the class names in the CSS:

```
.normal {font-size:14pt;color:black;text-align:center;width:100%; height:60px;
         background-color:yellow;border:dotted 3px black}

.red {font-size:14pt;color:white;width:100%; height:60px;text-align:center;
      vertical-align:bottom;background-color:red;border:dotted 3px black}

.blue {font-size:14pt;width:100%; height:60px;color:white;text-align:center;
       vertical-align:middle;background-color:blue;border:dotted 3px black}

.notset {border:dotted 3px black}
```

Thus, the binding sets the CSS class of the panel element to one of these, directly bound to the select control, and updates the appearance of the panel.

Using Method Invocation to Map the Button Box to the Cursor Type

In the JavaScript-based example in the previous section, you saw that clicking the button on the page toggled the cursor for the panel between using a hand and using a normal cursor. You can also achieve this using declarative XML markup.

Let's look at the markup:

```
<button targetElement="cursorButton">
    <click>
      <invokeMethod target="panel" method="toggleCssClass">
        <parameters className="special" />
      </invokeMethod>
      <setProperty target="cursorLabel"
                   property="text" value="Cursor set" />

    </click>
  </button>

  <label targetElement="cursorLabel" text="Regular cursor" />
```

This markup resides within the <components> tag, which itself resides within the <page> tag, so Atlas will assign these to the identified controls within the HTML. This script has two component-level tags: <button> and <label>. These map to the target elements of cursorButton and cursorLabel, respectively. If you inspect the HTML, you will see these are the IDs that have been assigned to the button and the label.

Let's first look at the <button> element. It has one child: <click>. This defines the action for the click event. This action does two things; first it toggles the state of the CSS class called special, turning it on or off, and second, it sets the property of the label to indicate that the property has been set.

It achieves this using the <invokeMethod> tag to invoke the toggleCssClass method on the panel. For more details on the methods, properties, and events of the Panel control, see Chapter 4. This method will turn the specified CSS class on or off when called. In this case, the class called special contains a hand cursor.

The CSS code for the special class looks like this:

```
.special {cursor: hand;}
```

Turning it on will give a hand cursor for the panel; turning it off will revert to the default arrow.

Also, it uses the <setProperty> tag to set the text of the label. You specify the control you are using with the targetElement attribute, and the property attribute should contain the name of the property you want to set. Finally, the value attribute contains the information you want to place in the specified property. Therefore, to set the text property of the cursor label to the text Cursor Set, you use the following markup:

```
<setProperty target="cursorLabel"
             property="text" value="Cursor set" />
```

And because this markup is a child of the <click> node for the button, this action will take place upon the button being clicked.

Manipulating Controls Directly

In this example, you will learn how to manipulate controls directly.

Using JavaScript to Manipulate Controls Directly

In the previous sections, you saw how to use CSS and Atlas client controls to manipulate how a <div> element on your page behaves. When you use Atlas client-side controls, you can also manipulate the controls directly using JavaScript, as you saw in the previous chapter. See Chapter 4 for all the properties, methods, and events on each control.

To manipulate controls, you can call these properties, methods, and events directly. This example is a simple one, showing how you can change the visibility and enabled state of a text box by using Atlas client-side controls and setting their respective properties.

The page will look like Figure 5-4.

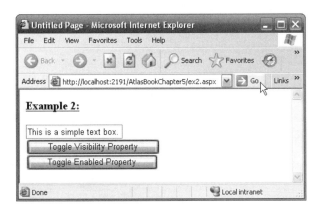

Figure 5-4. *Simple example for manipulating controls directly*

The HTML to set up this page is as follows:

```
<form id="form1" runat="server">
 <atlas:ScriptManager runat="server" ID="ScriptManager1" />
 <div>
  <h3><u>Example 2:</u></h3>
   <input id="textBox" type="text"/>
   <br />
   <input type="button" id="visibilityButton"  class="buttonstyle"
          value="Toggle Visibility Property" />
   <br />
   <input type="button" id="enabledButton" class="buttonstyle"
          value="Toggle Enabled Property" />
 </div>
</form>
```

Take note of the ID tags, because you will use them to construct the client-side controls in JavaScript using Atlas.

When the page loads, it calls the following script:

```
function pageLoad()
{
  // Set up the textBox, and set some properties on it
  g_tbx = new Sys.UI.TextBox($('textBox'));
  g_tbx.initialize();
  g_tbx.set_text("This is a simple text box.");


  var btnVisibility = new Sys.UI.Button($('visibilityButton'));
  btnVisibility.initialize();
  btnVisibility.click.add(onSetVisibilityClick);

  var btnEnabled = new Sys.UI.Button($('enabledButton'));
  btnEnabled.initialize();
  btnEnabled.click.add(onSetEnabledClick);
}
```

This sets up each of the controls. First, a Sys.UI.TextBox is constructed from the control called textbox, which as you may guess is the text box. Next, the two buttons are initialized based on the <input> controls on the page. Note that the two <input> controls were called visibilityButton and enabledButton; these IDs are passed to the Sys.UI.Button controls as constructors, thus setting them up. Each button is then initialized, and event delegates are set up for the click events on each, mapped to the onSetVisibilityClick and onSetEnabledClick functions, respectively.

Let's take a look at onSetVisibilityClick:

```
function onSetVisibilityClick() {
  g_tbx.set_visible(!g_tbx.get_visible());
}
```

This function calls the set_visible method of the TextBox control. The current instance of the TextBox control is called g_tbx, which was set up in the pageLoad event as you saw earlier. To toggle visibility, you call the current visibility state, using the get_visible() method, and set it to the opposite by using the not operator (!) to invert the value.

In a similar manner, you can enable the TextBox control in script like so:

```
function onSetEnabledClick() {
  g_tbx.set_enabled(!g_tbx.get_enabled());
}
```

Viewing the page now allows you to manipulate the visibility and of the text box and whether its enabled by clicking the buttons. This demonstrates simple interaction with a control by calling its methods and events directly.

Using Atlas Script to Manipulate Controls Directly

In the previous section, you looked at using JavaScript and Atlas controls to manipulate the underlying HTML controls directly—showing that you aren't limited to manipulating them through CSS. Now you will learn how to perform the same actions without programming—simply by defining the controls and associated bindings and actions using Atlas Script XML markup.

Figure 5-4 showed the page. The markup that generates this page is as follows:

```
<form id="form1" runat="server">
 <atlas:ScriptManager runat="server" ID="ScriptManager1" />
 <div>
  <h3><u>Example 2:</u></h3>
   <input id="textBox" type="text"/>
   <br />
   <input type="button" id="visibilityButton"  class="buttonstyle"
        value="Toggle Visibility Property" />
   <br />
   <input type="button" id="enabledButton" class="buttonstyle"
        value="Toggle Enabled Property" />
 </div>
</form>
```

The three controls are all HTML `<input>` controls, which can get a little confusing if you aren't familiar with HTML. Buttons are considered `<input>` controls, but the distinguishing factor that makes them buttons is that the type attribute is set to button. Atlas Script clarifies this by defining them as buttons and by defining the text box as a text box. This makes it a lot easier to understand and read your code.

Let's look at the script that sets these up. First, this is the text box:

```
<textBox targetElement="textBox"
        text="This is a simple text box "
        cssClass="textBox">
  <bindings>
    <binding id="setEnabled" dataContext="textBox"
            dataPath="enabled" property="enabled"
            transform="Invert" automatic="false" />
    <binding id="setVisibility" dataContext="textBox"
            dataPath="visible" property="visible"
            transform="Invert" automatic="false" />
  </bindings>
</textBox>
```

The top-level tag here is the `<textBox>` tag, and its target element is the control with the ID textBox, which means the `<textBox>` control becomes associated with the underlying `<input>` control called textBox. Take a look at the previous HTML code, and you will see this. The other attributes on the `<textBox>` tag initialize the control, setting its default text and cssClass.

Next comes the `<bindings>` tag, which contains a couple of `<binding>` tags. These tags demonstrate how you can specify compound bindings on a single object. The desired functionality is that clicking the Enable/Disable button should enable or disable the textbox and that clicking the Show/Hide button should show or hide the TextBox.

If you think of this in terms of properties and data binding, what you want to happen is that the click event of the button should be bound to the appropriate property of the text box. Automatic data validation and transformation of the property at the binding level can handle the toggling behavior.

This is probably a little confusing at first, because you are used to binding controls to data sources, but with Atlas you can actually bind the value of a control to an event. In doing this, what you are saying is that when an event fires, it should do something to the bound control. Because the functionality you want to invoke is a change of visibility or enabled state, no inherent value change takes place—just the toggling of existing Boolean value states. And then you can bind the property to an event. It's enormously useful, but it takes a little while to get used to it.

So, as you look at the `<binding>` element, you will see that each has a number of properties set:

id: This specifies the identity of the binding. When you want to attach something to this binding, you use this ID.

dataContext: This specifies the context to which the binding will occur. In this case, it is mapped to itself.

dataPath: This is the name of the property on the control specified by the dataContext to which the binding will occur. If you were binding to a different control, the dataContext and the dataPath would point to that control and its property, respectively.

property: This is the name of the property on this control to which the binding will occur.

transform: This is the name of the transform that will take place when the binding occurs. The invert transform has the effect of toggling the property specified in the property tag.

automatic: When true, the binding occurs automatically on this control. It defaults to true. Because in this case the control is binding to itself, it is best to make this false, or unexpected results will occur, namely, that it will continue binding to itself!

As you can see, this is a special case. When you want to invert the property of the control based on an external stimulus, you bind the control to itself, you bind the dataContext property of the control to the intended property (thus binding the enabled or visible property to itself), and you turn off automatic binding.

This probably seems a little odd, but currently it is the only way to change a property between known values such as true or false instead of setting it to free-form values such as 1, 2, Hello, or Goodbye. But how do you trigger this?

You can see this by inspecting the button markup. First, here is the button that sets visibility:

```
<button targetElement="visibilityButton">
  <click>
    <invokeMethod target="setVisibility" method="evaluateIn" />
  </click>
</button>
```

WHAT YOU'VE LEARNED FROM THESE EXAMPLES

You may have noticed that there is nothing Ajax about these examples. Atlas is much more than just a methodology for implementing applications that have asynchronous updates. It provides not one but two frameworks on which client-side applications can be coded more easily than ever before. Thus far you've begun to look at these frameworks and how they work.

In the JavaScript-based client controls framework, you learned how to instantiate controls and map them to their corresponding, underlying HTML. You saw how to set properties and call methods on these and, more powerfully, how to assign event delegates to these controls, define these events, and call them.

Alternatively, the Atlas Script–based client controls framework was able to provide the same functionality, but entirely declaratively. Each control has a tag associated with it in the XML script, and these tags have child tags that specify *actions* and *bindings*. You looked at the action of what to do when handling a click of a button; the *binding* that specifies the relationships between, such as a selection list; and the control that the selection would occupy, or the action to take upon pushing a button to trigger an internal binding on a different control to toggle one of its properties.

Although the JavaScript approach is certainly more traditional and you can hit the ground running straightaway with your existing JavaScript skills, I strongly recommend you look at Atlas Script and start getting used to it. The world is heading in the direction of declarative development, allowing for the separation of design and implementation through various forms of XML markup, perhaps the most popular of which will be XML Application Markup Language (XAML), available with the WinFX framework. This separation allows for more fluid design and implementation of applications, as well as easier maintenance, updating, internationalization, and a whole host of other work streams that typically require redevelopment, recompilation, and redeployment.

Additionally, though no tools are available at this time, some will appear that allow applications to be visually designed and wired up to each other, generating Atlas Script. As such, it will be a powerful and prevalent way of designing ASP.NET applications in the future.

As this chapter progresses, you will see more sophisticated examples, continue to dissect them, and then stop to see exactly what you've been seeing.

In the previous examples, you did some basic data binding—binding actions to properties and performing internal binding within a control. In the next two examples, you will look at data binding in a little more detail and start exploring transforms, declarative and programmatic data binding, and directions of data binding. You'll also look into how Atlas Script and JavaScript can work together to help you build the best, easiest-to-maintain application.

The `<click>` tag specifies the action to follow when the button is clicked. In this case, a method needs to be invoked. The method is defined by the binding specified in the target attribute. In this case, the binding is the setVisibility one. So, when the button is clicked, the binding causes a message to be sent to the text box; this message is captured by the binding, which is defined as binding the visibility property to itself. The transform property inverts it, so the Boolean property gets toggled.

Next, the enabled button does the same thing, except it targets the binding called setEnabled:

```
<button targetElement="enabledButton">
  <click>
    <invokeMethod target="setEnabled" method="evaluateIn" />
  </click>
</button>
```

Data Binding with a Transform

In this example, you will look at converting the data from one format to another, as well as at a two-way binding, where the binding maps in both directions. It isn't a case of changing one control to update another, as you saw earlier with the selection box updating the panel, but of either bound control updating the other.

The page looks like Figure 5-5.

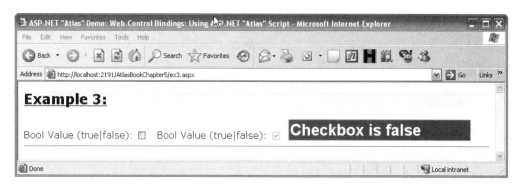

Figure 5-5. *Two-way binding with transforms*

By selecting the checkbox on the left, the checkbox on the right will change its value, and it will be the opposite value of the left one. In addition, the text box on the right will change its text to reflect the value of the left checkbox. Coolest of all, you can type in the text box, and if you change false to true, or vice versa, the checkboxes will update accordingly. So, if you type true, the left checkbox will be selected, and the right one will be cleared.

How does this work? Well, let's first look at the Atlas Script that implements it.

Using Atlas Script

The following is the complete Atlas Script for this page (you can see the whole page, including the HTML markup, in the download for this chapter):

```
<script type="text/xml-script">
<page xmlns:script="http://schemas.microsoft.com/xml-script/2005">
<components>
  <textBox targetElement="textBox">
```

```
    <bindings>
      <binding dataContext="checkBoxBoolean" dataPath="checked"
              property="text" transform="ToString"
              direction="InOut"
              transformerArgument="Checkbox is {0}" />
    </bindings>
  </textBox>
  <checkBox targetElement="checkBoxBoolean" />
  <checkBox targetElement="checkBoxDisabled">
    <bindings>
      <binding dataContext="checkBoxBoolean" dataPath="checked"
              property="checked" transform="Invert" />
    </bindings>
  </checkBox>
</components>
</page>
</script>
```

First, the `<textBox>` tag gets associated with the `<input>` control called textBox in the HTML markup. This has a binding set up with it. This binding has some new attributes set up that you haven't seen before, so let's go through the full set of attributes:

dataContext: This specifies the control to which this binding will happen. In this case, it is set to checkBoxBoolean, which is the checkbox on the left.

dataPath: The property on the dataContext control to which the binding will occur. In this case, the property is checked, so you will be binding to its value.

property: The property on this control that is bound to the control specified in the data-Context. In this case, it is the text property of the text box.

transform: The transform to apply to the data. Because you are binding a text box to a checkbox, you want to transform the raw value of the checkbox from true or false to its string representation of true or false.

direction: The direction can be In, Out, or InOut. In this case, you are using InOut, which creates a two-way binding. This means that not only do changes in the control pointed to by the dataContext change this control, but changes to this control will also change the other one. This is how the functionality whereby editing the checkbox will change the status of how the checkbox works.

transformerArgument: Using a transformer argument is a little like using a printf statement in C. You can embed the arguments {0}, {1}, and so on, in this string and have the relevant properties assigned at runtime. In this case, you have bound to the value of the checkbox, and this value is transformed into a string. This then gets inserted into the string at the position of the argument. So, the string "Checkbox is {0}" will become "Checkbox is True" or "Checkbox is False." The underlying Boolean value of the checkbox is transformed into the string True or False.

Next you set up a <checkBox> control and map it to the checkbox on the left, which has the ID checkBoxBoolean in the HTML markup. It requires no further scripting. Because it is bound to the text box by the markup in the text box (see the earlier explanation), it handles all of the desired functionality.

Finally, you need to configure the other checkbox. Remember, this checkbox is intended to always show the opposite value of the other checkbox, and the best way to achieve this is to bind it to the other checkbox and apply an inversion transform.

You achieve this using the following binding:

```
<binding dataContext="checkBoxBoolean" dataPath="checked"
        property="checked" transform="Invert" />
```

The dataContext is set up to be the other checkbox (called checkBoxBoolean). The property on this control that you want to bind to is configured in the dataPath attribute—so this is set to checked, which is the property that stores the state of the checkbox. Next, the property on this control that you are binding the data to needs to be configured. And because this is also a checkbox, the property you want to bind is the checked property. Finally, you have to apply a transform to make this control have the opposite value of the other one. The Invert transform will perform this, so you configure it using the transform attribute.

Thus, simply by configuring the data bindings for the text box and the check box, all of the functionality to handle the two-way data binding, the updating of the text box, and the inversion of property between the two checkboxes takes place without writing or maintaining any code.

Using JavaScript

You can also implement this functionality in JavaScript by using the client-side control libraries in Atlas.

You do this by creating Atlas controls that reference the underlying HTML controls, as well as using some new controls that you haven't seen before—those that represent the bindings themselves. The best way to understand this is to examine the script itself in detail.

First you need to create the controls that represent the checkboxes and the text box:

```
var textBox = new Sys.UI.TextBox($('textBox'));
var checkBoxBoolean =
    new Sys.UI.CheckBox($('checkBoxBoolean'));
var checkBoxDisabled =
    new Sys.UI.CheckBox($('checkBoxDisabled'));
```

Next you create the binding. This is a control in the Web namespace. You create it using the following code:

```
var binding_1 = new Web.Binding();
```

Next you need to set up the properties for the binding, setting up the dataContext, data-Path, local property, transformer argument, direction, and transform type:

```
binding_1.set_dataContext(checkBoxBoolean);
binding_1.set_dataPath('checked');
binding_1.set_property('text');
binding_1.set_transformerArgument("Checkbox is {0}.");
binding_1.set_direction(Web.BindingDirection.InOut);
binding_1.transform.add(Web.Binding.Transformers.ToString);
```

This is the same as how you set it up in the Atlas Script earlier, pointing the binding at the checkBoxBoolean control's checked property. This is then bound to the text property of this control. Note that the binding hasn't yet been associated with the text box, but this will happen shortly. The transformer argument is set up to create the text that will show in the text box after the binding occurs, as well as the direction type for the binding. The values for the binding direction are available in the Web.BindingDirection enumeration. Additionally, the transform Web.Binding.Transformers.ToString is applied. Other values for the transform are available in the Web.Binding.Transformers enumeration.

To associate this binding with the text box, you need to call the get_bindings() method to get the collection of bindings associated with this control and call its add method, passing it this binding. You do that like this:

```
textBox.get_bindings().add(binding_1);
```

Another binding connects the checkboxes to each other. Again, this is a Web.Binding control, which supports methods that allow you to set the data context, data path, transform, and property to which to bind. You set it up like this:

```
var binding_2 = new Web.Binding();
binding_2.set_dataContext(checkBoxBoolean);
binding_2.set_dataPath('checked');
binding_2.set_property('checked');
binding_2.transform.add(Web.Binding.Transformers.Invert);
checkBoxDisabled.get_bindings().add(binding_2);
```

It is vitally important to then call the initialize() method on the controls after all the binding is set up to make sure it works correctly. Sometimes by habit you may initialize them directly after construction, but in this case you should wait until all of the bindings have been configured first:

```
g_checkBoxBoolean.initialize();
g_checkBoxDisabled.initialize();
g_textBox.initialize();
```

Data Binding with a Custom Transform

In this example, you will continue looking at binding information between controls but will look a little further into the data transformation by using a custom transformation. In this page there is a text box, a selection list, and a label. When you type something into the text box and tab out of it, the label will display the text you typed using the color specified in the selection list. You can achieve this, as you would expect, through a binding between the label and the text box. Additionally, if you change the selection on the list, the label will get updated again, with the new color as well as with a text indicator showing that the update came from the selection list. To do this, you will write a custom transform (using JavaScript) and map it to the binding.

You can see the page in Figure 5-6.

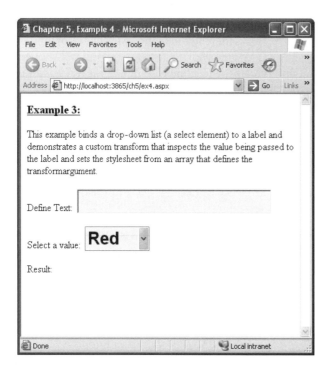

Figure 5-6. *Page containing the custom transform*

The complete script for this page is as follows:

```
<script type="text/xml-script">
<page xmlns:script="http://schemas.microsoft.com/xml-script/2005">
<components>
  <textBox targetElement="textBoxText" />
  <select targetElement="selectStyle">
    <selectionChanged>
      <invokeMethod target="setCss" method="evaluateIn" />
    </selectionChanged>
  </select>
  <label targetElement="labelText">
    <bindings>
      <binding dataContext="textBoxText"
               dataPath="text"
               property="text" />
```

```
    <binding id="setCss"
            dataContext="selectStyle"
            dataPath="selectedValue"
            property="cssClass"
            transform="DoAdditionalHandling" />
    </bindings>
  </label>
</components>
</page>
</script>
```

In this script you can see the initialization of the three components—the text box, the select, and the label.

The initialization of the text box is straightforward—you don't need to do anything special, just point the Atlas control at the underlying HTML tag, which is called textBoxText. You don't specify an ID for the Atlas control, so Atlas gives it the default ID, which is the same as the underlying HTML ID: textBoxText.

To initialize the selection list, you use the `<select>` tag. This is pointed at the underlying HTML `<select>` list, which is called selectStyle, using the targetElement attribute to specify it. On this you specify an action that occurs upon the selection change. You do this using the `<selectionChanged>` child tag. This in turn will call a method using the `<invokeMethod>` tag. The target for this method is setCSS, which, as you will see in a moment, is the name of a binding on the label element. The method attribute is set to evaluateIn, which means the data to be used in this method call is the value of the select box. You will evaluate this input to the selection box and pass that to the setCSS binding.

The workhorse of this application is the label element. You can achieve the functionality I have been discussing—the update of the label via binding with the text and via binding with the selection list—by creating a couple of bindings on the label. The first of these bindings is associated with the element called textBoxText, which is the Atlas identifier for the text box control (see its declaration). The dataPath attribute specifies the property on that control to bind to, which in this case is its text property. The label has a text property too, and you want to update this with whatever is in the text property of the text box. Therefore, you specify the property attribute to be text. With this in place, you have now bound the label to the text box.

The second binding on the label is worth another look:

```
<binding id="setCss"
        dataContext="selectStyle"
        dataPath="selectedValue"
        property="cssClass"
        transform="DoAdditionalHandling" />
```

This binding has a specific ID, called setCss. You will notice that the other binding wasn't given a specific ID, because it is never being explicitly called from elsewhere. This binding, however, is called from the `<invokeMethod>` on the selection list. For Atlas to be able to identify it, it needs this identifier.

The dataContext attribute points to the control to which you are binding. In this case you want to bind to the selection control, and it is called selectStyle.

The dataPath attribute points to the property on the bound control that provides the data to which you are interested in binding. In this case, the property is selectedValue, which contains the value for the item that is currently selected.

The property on the label you want to pass the bound data into is cssClass. If you look at the HTML for the select list, the reason for this will become apparent. Here's the HTML:

```
<select id="selectStyle" class="input">
 <option value="redLocal">Red</option>
 <option value="greenLocal">Green</option>
 <option value="blueLocal">Blue</option>
</select>
```

So, if the user selects Red, the property selectedValue will contain redLocal. This will then be bound to the label, so its cssClass property will become redLocal. On the page you specify the following CSS:

```
<style>
  .redLocal{background-color:red;color:white;font-size:24pt;}
  .greenLocal{background-color:green;color:white;font-size:24pt;}
  .blueLocal{background-color:blue;color:white;font-size:24pt;}
</style>
```

Therefore, the binding will set the label to use the redLocal class in the CSS and thus have a red background.

You can see this in Figure 5-7.

Figure 5-7. *Binding the Label control to the text box and the select list*

Perhaps the most interesting attribute in this example is transform. You may remember earlier that you were able to do some basic transforms such as invert, but now you have a transform called DoAdditionalHandling. This is a *custom* transform where the transform is a JavaScript function on the page, and you specify the name of that function in this attribute.

Let's look at the DoAdditionalHandling function. You'll find this on the same page as the rest of the code:

```
<script type="text/javascript">
function DoAdditionalHandling(sender, eventArgs)
{
  var tbxElem = $('textBoxText').control;
  if (tbxElem.get_text().length > 0)
  {
    // The value is that from the select, so let's ensure it's set
    // The property here is the cssClass
    eventArgs.set_value(eventArgs.get_value());

    // Add text to the output:
    var textElem = $('labelText').control;
    textElem.set_text(tbxElem.get_text() +
          " (You used the style selector)");
  }
}
</script>
```

This script first creates a reference to the text box. It then queries the length of the text in this text box to see whether anything has been typed into it. If it has (the length is less than 0), then you want to update the label with the value of this text plus the custom data, which in this case means you simply add the text that indicates the style selector was used.

You can see the effect of this in Figure 5-8.

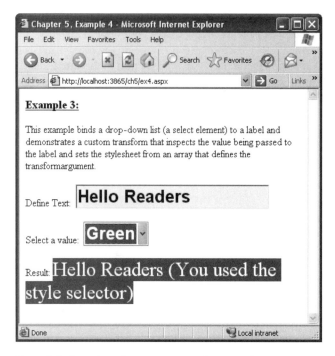

Figure 5-8. *Running the custom transform on the page*

Performing JavaScript Custom Binding

In this example, you will perform a similar binding to that in the previous example but use JavaScript throughout instead of Atlas Script. This custom binding will update the contents of the label with the inverse of the text that is typed into the text box.

You can see it in action in Figure 5-9.

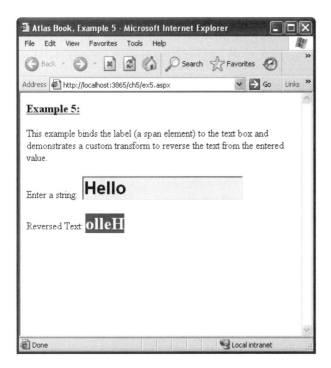

Figure 5-9. *Custom transform to invert text in JavaScript*

The script that implements this functionality is as follows:

```
<script type="text/javascript">
function pageLoad()
{
  var textBoxString = new Sys.UI.TextBox($('textBoxString'));
  var spanLabel2 = new Sys.UI.Label($('spanLabel2'));
  textBoxString.set_text("Hello, World!");

  // Create the binding
  var binding_1 = new Web.Binding();
  binding_1.set_dataContext(textBoxString);
  binding_1.set_dataPath('text');
  binding_1.set_property('text');
  binding_1.transform.add(customTransform);

  // Add the binding
  spanLabel2.get_bindings().add(binding_1);

  // Initialize the controls
  textBoxString.initialize();
  spanLabel2.initialize();
}
```

As you've seen before, the first step you need to take is to create Atlas control objects based on the underlying HTML. This is what the first two lines of the code do, and they create an object based on the underlying HTML input called textBoxString and the underlying HTML span (for a label) called spanLabel2.

Next you need to set up the binding.

First, create a new instance of a binding control:

```
var binding_1 = new Web.Binding();
```

Next, you need to initialize the binding with dataContext, dataPath, and property, which specify the control you are binding to, the property on that control that you are binding to, and the property on this control you are binding to it, respectively.

So, this binding has its context as the text box, and you are binding its text property to the text property of the control that the binding will be associated with. (You will be associating this binding with the label—and will see this in a moment.)

```
binding_1.set_dataContext(textBoxString);
binding_1.set_dataPath('text');
binding_1.set_property('text');
```

Next, you specify the transform. You could use a fixed transform here, such as invert or toString. However, you want a custom binding that reverses the string. No such binding is built into Atlas, but you can write our own and specify it here. On the page is a script called customTransform, so you specify it as the desired transform for this binding like this:

```
binding_1.transform.add(customTransform);
```

Finally, you want to associate this binding with the label. You do this by getting the collection of bindings for the label using the get_bindings() method and adding to this collection with its add() method:

```
spanLabel2.get_bindings().add(binding_1);
```

The custom transform is simple JavaScript that takes the string (passed in as the eventArgs) and uses the Web.StringBuilder Atlas class to build a new string that is the inverse of the original:

```
function customTransform(sender, eventArgs)
{
  var value = eventArgs.get_value();

  var reverseStr = new Web.StringBuilder();
  for (var i=value.length-1; i>=0; i--)
    reverseStr.append(value.charAt(i));

  eventArgs.set_value(reverseStr.toString());
}
</script>
```

Because this function is called from the binding, it will automatically be called whenever the text box loses focus (the trigger for the binding), so if you type into the text box and tab out of it, you will see the label updated with the inverse of what you had typed in the text box.

WHAT YOU'VE LEARNED FROM THESE EXAMPLES

The first examples you saw in this chapter introduced you to the concepts of bindings and actions. You were able to take these to the next level using these examples. First, you were introduced to the concepts of directional binding. Traditionally you would see a binding as a control being associated with data from a data source, so if the data in the source changes, the control would be updated. This is considered an In binding. With Atlas you can also have Out binding, where the destination control updates the source control, and InOut binding, where the data binding is bidirectional. You saw this in the first example where by checking a checkbox, you could update a text field with text indicating its state and by typing into the text box you could also change the state of the checkbox.

   This in turn introduced the concepts of transforming during binding. A checkbox has the Boolean value true or false associated with it. When binding to a text box, this doesn't have the desired semantic meaning, so the ToString transform was used to convert this to a literal string containing true or false. Atlas is smart enough when using an InOut function to reverse this when the text box is updated, so if you type the string "true" or "false" into the text box, the two-way binding will translate this into a Boolean true or false and update the checkbox accordingly.

   Additionally, these examples introduced the concept of custom transformation. In this case, if the transformation is set up with the name of a JavaScript function, Atlas will use this function to perform the transformation. You saw a couple of examples of this, where the custom transformation in one case added new content to the string and in another case reversed the string.

   The next suite of examples will expand further on this, showing how you can perform validation and specify it on controls when using Atlas and how you can associate automatic behaviors with controls, providing functionality such as drag and drop or creating pop-up menus.

Performing Basic Text Validation—Required Fields

A common function of a client web application is data entry through forms. The typical workflow for forms is that the user will enter information, and a special type of input tag called a submit button triggers an HTTP post of the information to a server. The server then processes the submitted information and returns a response. If the data is invalid, the server will return a message indicating this, and the page developer will write a script that emphasizes this to the user. This transaction involves at least one round-trip to the server. You can also perform basic validation in JavaScript prior to form submission; this can be very effective and certainly faster for the user.

   However, performing validation using JavaScript can be a complex task, and thus it's a problem that Atlas components lend themselves naturally to for a fix.

   In this example, you will perform the most basic validation there is—checking whether the user has entered any information into a text box. You can see it in action in Figure 5-10.

   This form will validate the text box and give feedback to the user by putting a red asterisk on the screen beside the text box once the user tabs out of it. It also provides a tooltip on this asterisk, so that if you hover over the asterisk with your mouse, a tooltip will tell you the problem.

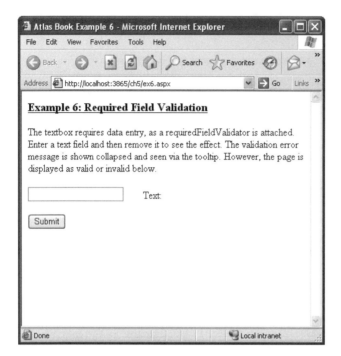

Figure 5-10. *Basic text validation*

Let's look at how to implement this functionality.
First, here is the HTML that defines the controls:

```
<input type="text" id="value1TextBox" class="input" />
<span id="validator1" style="color: red">*</span>
Text: <span id="value1Label" class="result"></span>
```

The HTML is composed of an Input control, which gives you the text box and a couple of <span> tags. The first span contains the asterisk that will appear when the validation rules trip. The second contains nothing currently, but it will be updated with the valid text for the text box once it has been entered.

Now let's look at the Atlas Script that implements this functionality:

```
<script type="text/xml-script">
<page xmlns:script="http://schemas.microsoft.com/xml-script/2005">
 <components>
  <textBox targetElement="value1TextBox">
   <validators>
    <requiredFieldValidator errorMessage="You must enter some text." />
   </validators>
  </textBox>
```

```
<validationErrorLabel targetElement="validator1"
                      associatedControl="value1TextBox" />
<label targetElement="value1Label">
 <bindings>
  <binding dataContext="value1TextBox"
          dataPath="text"
          property="text" />
 </bindings>
 </label>
</components>
</page>
</script>
```

Most of this will look familiar, but you haven't seen a couple of new elements in here. First, a `<textBox>` control points to value1TextBox, which as you will see from the HTML is the `<input>` control. A new child element called `<validators>` is attached to this element. The `<validators>` tag can contain a number of validators that can be rangeValidator, requiredFieldValidator, typeValidator, rangeValidator, or regexValidator, among others.

In this case, you are using a requiredFieldValidator, which fires an error if the field on which the validator is configured is empty. You specify the error message using the errorMessage attribute.

A validation error needs to have a source on the page that it uses to represent the error to the user, or it will not be seen. In this example, you have a `<span>` that contains an asterisk that appears when an error occurs. To achieve this, you use the `<validationErrorLabel>` tag and associate it with this span. The span is called validator1, so the validationErrorLabel is given this as its targetElement. Finally, this validationErrorLabel needs to be tied to the control that it is the error message destination for, and you achieve this with the associatedControl attribute.

Figure 5-11 shows this page after a validation error has been hit. You can see the red asterisk and the tooltip that appears when the user hovers over it.

Note that you didn't have to write any code to make this asterisk appear or disappear, and you don't have to write explicit code for the tooltip. The Atlas framework handles all of this for you!

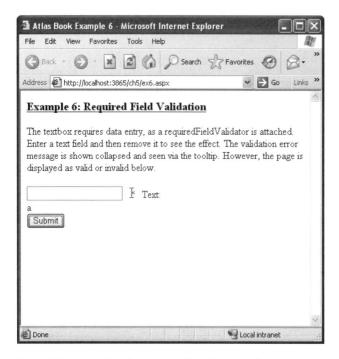

Figure 5-11. *Running the basic validation sample*

Performing Basic Text Validation— Checking for Types and Ranges

In the previous example, you checked to see whether a field was present in your validation rules. This is useful, but for more serious applications, more sophisticated validation is necessary. In this example, you will see what is involved in applying multiple validation rules to a control to not only validate whether you have entered something into it but also to check the data type to ensure you have put in a numeric value and to check that the numeric value falls within a specific range.

You can see the page in Figure 5-12.

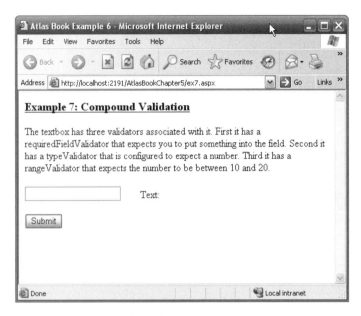

Figure 5-12. *Compound validation*

To understand how this compound validation works, let's inspect the code. The HTML is identical to that used in the previous example, so you'll skip straight to the Atlas Script that manages the compound validation:

```
<script type="text/xml-script">
<page xmlns:script="http://schemas.microsoft.com/xml-script/2005">
<components>
  <textBox targetElement="value1TextBox">
    <validators>
      <requiredFieldValidator
          errorMessage="You must enter a number." />
      <typeValidator type="Number"
          errorMessage="You must enter a valid number." />
      <rangeValidator lowerBound="10" upperBound="20"
          errorMessage="You must enter a number between 10 and 20." />
    </validators>
  </textBox>
  <validationErrorLabel targetElement="validator1"
          associatedControl="value1TextBox" />

  <label targetElement="value1Label">
    <bindings>
      <binding dataContext="value1TextBox"
              dataPath="text" property="text" />
```

```
      </bindings>
    </label>
  </components>
  </page>
</script>
```

The interesting stuff here is in the `<validators>` tag for the `<textBox>` tag, which has three child tags.

The first, `<requiredFieldValidator>`, is similar to what you saw earlier. Should the text box be empty, this validator will fire, and the red asterisk will appear, as shown in Figure 5-13.

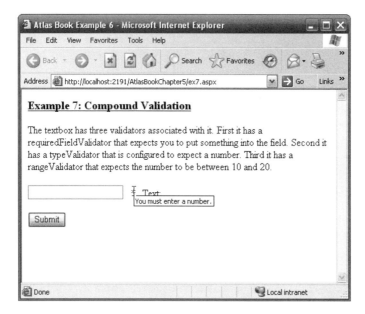

Figure 5-13. *Tripping the required field validator*

The second, `<typeValidator>`, is configured to recognize a Number (which can also be String or Boolean). Should you type something that isn't recognized as a numeric into the text box and tab out, this validator will fire, the red asterisk will appear, and the error tag will appear as "You must enter a valid number."

See Figure 5-14.

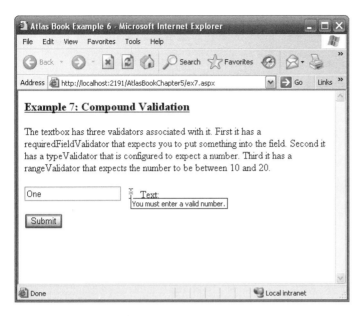

Figure 5-14. *Tripping the type validator*

The third validator is a `<rangeValidator>` that, when used with a number, allows you to specify a maximum and a minimum so that if the value falls outside this range, the validation will trip. You configure these with the lowerBound and upperBound attributes. In this case, these values are set to 10 and 20, respectively. Note that these are inclusive, so 10 and 20 are valid values.

You can see where this validator is tripped in Figure 5-15. In this case, the text box contains something, so the requiredFieldValidator is OK. It contains a valid number, so the typeValidator is also satisfied. However, the number, 8, is outside the range specified by the rangeValidator, so the red asterisk will appear, and the tooltip gives details of why the data is considered invalid.

So, as you can see from this example, you can set up some pretty sophisticated validation rules by stacking validators on top of each other. Where typically you may have programmed rules like this with JavaScript and nested if statements, this declarative approach lends itself nicely for tools to generate these rules.

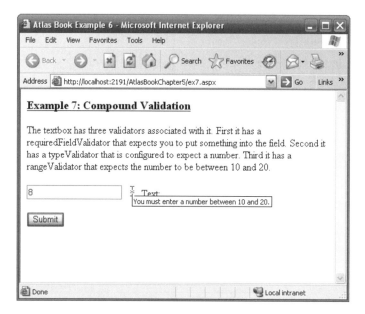

Figure 5-15. *Tripping the range validator*

WHAT YOU'VE LEARNED FROM THESE EXAMPLES

Atlas provides a powerful validation framework for your client-side data. This validation is centered on validation controls, which, when configured with the control, allow for the automatic and declarative validation of the data that is entered into these controls. You looked at validating the presence of the data using the requiredFieldValidator where if the data hasn't been entered, you want to take an action to inform the user.

Additionally, you looked at the typeValidator, which can inspect the data for a specific type. This is particularly useful for filtering input boxes (which are free-format text boxes) for numeric values. Consider the difficulty of this in normal circumstances where you would have to evaluate the contents of the box and use them if they were greater than zero!

Finally, you looked at the range validator, which is used for numeric values and which trips an error if the data falls outside the range. These are also useful for many common tasks and mean you don't need to write any code on either the server or the client.

Another validator that is available is the regExValidator, which validates the input data against a regular expression. Regular expressions are similar to wildcard specifiers but are much more powerful and flexible. They are used to specify search criteria. So, for example, if you want to match a field against a valid U.S. telephone number, you would use this regular expression:

`/\(\d{3}\)( )\d{3}-\d{4}/`

If you are not familiar with regular expressions, this probably looks a little strange. However, regular expressions are incredibly useful for validating data against a fixed structure such as a telephone number or an email address. You can find a great resource on regular expressions at `http://www.regular-expressions.info/`.

Finally, AppleScript also supports custom validators. A custom validator is a function written in JavaScript. This function should accept an eventArgs variable. After performing your custom validation, you should call the set_IsValid function on this with true or false as a parameter. Here's an example:

```
function onValidateValue(sender, eventArgs) {
  var names = [ 'Engineer', 'Manager', 'Performer',
                'Construction Engineer', 'Chef'];
  var valid = names.contains(eventArgs.get_value());

  eventArgs.set_isValid(valid);
}
```

This function contains a list of valid names. The eventArgs sent to the function contains the data that is being validated. This is checked against the string of valid values. If it is found, the validation is successful, and the valid var will be true; otherwise, it will be false. At the end of the function, the eventArgs will have its isValid set with this value, and the custom validation will be complete.

Using the Click Behavior

Many controls support click events that you can use to handle user input. But not everything has a click event that will allow you to specify a handler. If you want to associate an action with a click on an element that doesn't support this, you can use the click behavior. So, for example, you can associate a click behavior with a piece of text on the page by creating a label out of it and applying the click behavior to that.

You can see this example in Figure 5-16.

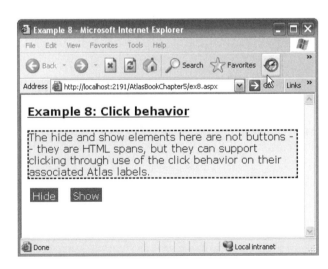

Figure 5-16. *Two HTML* <span> *elements that have click behaviors associated with their Atlas controls*

The HTML for this page is as follows:

```
<div class="description">
<h3><u>Example 8:  Click behavior</u></h3>
<div id="panel">The hide and show elements here are
not buttons -- they are HTML spans, but they can
support clicking through use of the click behavior
on their associated Atlas labels.</div>
  <br />
  <span id="hideLabel" class="buttonstyle2">Hide</span> 
  <span id="showLabel" class="buttonstyle2">Show</span>
</div>
```

You can see that the Hide text and the Show text are implemented as <span> elements and are given the IDs hideLabel and showLabel, respectively. Keep these in mind as you look at the Atlas Script for this page, shown here:

```
<script type="text/xml-script">
<page xmlns:script="http://schemas.microsoft.com/xml-script/2005">
<components>
  <control targetElement="panel" cssClass="start" />
    <label targetElement="hideLabel">
      <behaviors>
        <clickBehavior>
          <click>
            <setProperty target="panel"
                         property="visible"
                         value="false" />
          </click>
        </clickBehavior>
      </behaviors>
    </label>
    <label targetElement="showLabel">
      <behaviors>
        <clickBehavior>
          <click>
            <setProperty target="panel"
                         property="visible"
                         value="true" />
          </click>
        </clickBehavior>
      </behaviors>
    </label>
</components>
</page>
</script>
```

Each of the <span> elements you saw in the underlying HTML has a Label control (<label> tag) associated with it. To configure behaviors for these, you use the <behaviors> tag. Because you are using a <clickBehavior>, you configure this within the <behaviors> tag. Finally, upon a click, you want to set a property on a panel, so you use a <click> action and define it with <setProperty>, which points to the panel. Upon clicking the hideLabel <span> element, the behavior will call a <setProperty> action that will set the visible property of the panel to false. As you'd expect, you use a similar setup to configure the click behavior on the other label to set the visible property of the panel to true.

Thus, using behaviors, you can add click handlers to controls that normally wouldn't support them. You can see the result of clicking the Hide text in Figure 5-17.

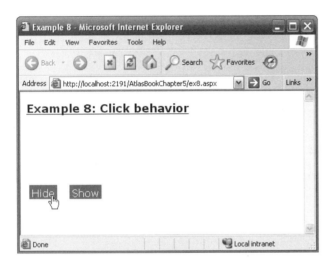

Figure 5-17. *Using the click behavior on a* <span> *element*

Using the Mouse Hover Behavior

You can associate the mouse hover behavior with any element, which allows you to specify an action that should take place when the mouse hovers over an element. A typical use for this would be to implement a custom tooltip, a context menu, a smart tag, or similar. When using Atlas client-side controls, this is straightforward. You can see the mouse hover example in Figure 5-18.

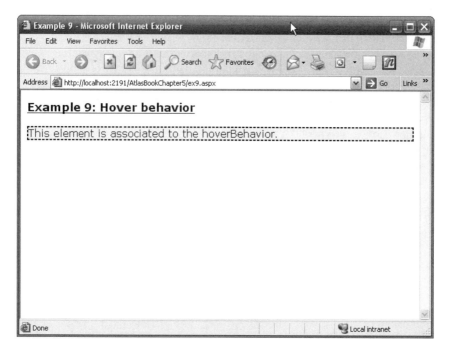

Figure 5-18. *Example page for the hover behavior*

The HTML for this page is here:

```
<div class="description">
  <h3><u>Example 9: Hover behavior</u></h3>
  <div id="panel2">This element is associated
    to the hoverBehavior.</div>
</div>
```

As you can see, it is straightforward. You simply create a <div> element on the page and enter the text into it. In this example, you will change the style of this element when you hover over it for 500 milliseconds. To achieve this, you can use Atlas Script to define the client-side controls and their associated behaviors:

```
<script type="text/xml-script">
<page xmlns:script="http://schemas.microsoft.com/xml-script/2005">
<components>
  <control targetElement="panel2" cssClass="start">
    <behaviors>
      <hoverBehavior unhoverDelay="500">
```

```
      <hover>
        <setProperty target="panel2"
                     property="cssClass"
                     value="hover"/>
      </hover>
      <unhover>
        <setProperty target="panel2"
                     property="cssClass"
                     value="start"/>
      </unhover>
    </hoverBehavior>
  </behaviors>
  </control>
</components>
</page>
</script>
```

When configuring hover behaviors, you should also configure the unhover event, which will typically return control to its default state if you change it (as in this case) or make any pop-up menus disappear.

To configure the hover behavior, you use the <hoverBehavior> tag and set its unHoverDelay attribute to the number of milliseconds you want to wait before the action will take place. The action in this case involves changing the CSS class of the target element when you hover over it, changing its CSS class to hover when you hover over it, and changing its CSS class to start once you leave it:

You can see the styles here:

```
<style>
 .start{background-color:yellow;border:dashed 2px black;}
 .hover{font-size:40pt;background-color:yellow;border:dashed 2px black;}
</style>
```

As you can see from the styles, after hovering over the panel, the font size gets set to 40 points. Returning to the start class removes this and sets the panel to its default view.

You can see the effect of the hover behavior in Figure 5-19.

You will see an extension to this, allowing for a custom context menu, in the next section. This will demonstrate how you can use the pop-up behavior to generate a clickable pop-up menu that can be used for a linkable tooltip, context menu, or smart tag.

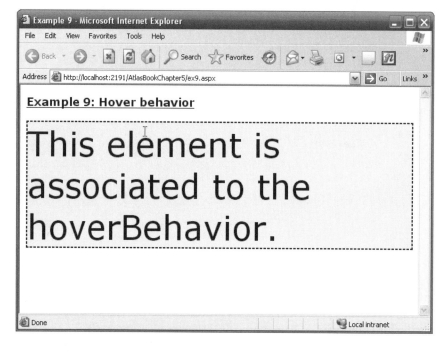

Figure 5-19. *The hover behavior in action*

Using the Pop-up Behavior When You Hover Over an Element

In this example, you will use the hover behavior to trigger the appearance of a context menu that pops up when you hover over a specific word. The context menu will be a list of three hyperlinks. This can be a useful navigational structure where the links are hidden until you need them, instead of them taking up valuable screen real estate when they are not needed. You can see this in action in Figure 5-20.

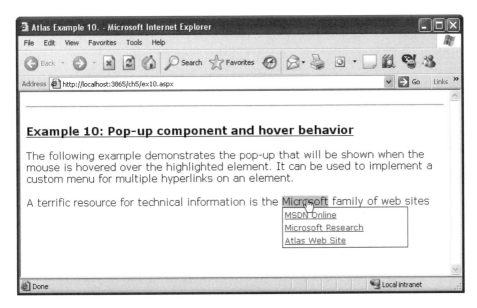

Figure 5-20. *Using the pop-up behavior to implement a link menu*

To better understand how this is implemented, let's take a look at the source code. This is the HTML for the page:

```
<form id="form1" runat="server">
<atlas:ScriptManager runat="server" ID="ScriptManager1">
<Scripts>
  <atlas:ScriptReference ScriptName="AtlasUIDragDrop" />
</Scripts>
</atlas:ScriptManager>
<div class="description">
<hr />
<h3><u>Example 10:  Pop-up component and hover behavior</u></h3>
```

The following example demonstrates the pop-up menu that will appear when the mouse hovers over the highlighted element. You can use it to implement a custom menu for multiple hyperlinks on an element:

```
<p></p>
A terrific resource for technical information is the
<a id="hoverLink" class="hoverlabel">Microsoft</a>
family of web sites
<div id="popup"
style="visibility:hidden;display:none;border:solid 1px black;
        background-color:lightyellow;filter:alpha(opacity=80);">
```

```
<table width="200px">
<tr><td>
<a href="http://msdn.microsoft.com" target="_blank">MSDN Online</a>
<br />
</td></tr>
<tr><td>
<a href="http://research.microsoft.com" target="_blank">
Microsoft Research</a><br />
</td></tr>
<tr><td>
<a href="http://atlas.asp.net" target="_blank">Atlas Web Site</a>
<br />
</td></tr>
</table>
</div>
</div>
</form>
```

What is noteworthy here is that an explicit reference is necessary to the AtlasUIDragDrop library. This is because the ScriptManager doesn't include this in your page by default. The `<floatingBehavior>` that you will see in a moment is implemented in this library, so it is necessary to make this reference, or Atlas will throw an error.

Next you will see that the menu is implemented in a `<div>` element with the ID of popup but is hidden at first because its CSS style implements this (see the visibility:hidden in the style definition). Within this `<div>` element is a table containing the three links.

Now let's look at the Atlas Script and how it uses the behavior to implement this as a pop-up menu:

```
<script type="text/xml-script">
<page xmlns:script="http://schemas.microsoft.com/xml-script/2005">
<references>
  <add src="AtlasUIDragDrop.js" />
</references>
<components>
  <control targetElement="popup">
    <behaviors>
      <popupBehavior id="popupBehavior"
                  parentElement="hoverLink"
                  positioningMode="BottomLeft"/>
      <floatingBehavior handle="popup" />
    </behaviors>
  </control>

  <hyperLink targetElement="hoverLink">
    <behaviors>
      <hoverBehavior unhoverDelay="1000" hoverElement="popup">
```

```
      <hover>
        <invokeMethod target="popupBehavior" method="show"/>
      </hover>
      <unhover>
        <invokeMethod target="popupBehavior" method="hide"/>
      </unhover>
      </hoverBehavior>
    </behaviors>
  </hyperLink>
</components>
</page>
</script>
```

First you use a `<control>` tag to create an Atlas client control that is targeted at the element called popup. This is the `<div>` element that contains the menu you looked at earlier. It has a `<popupBehavior>` associated with it, and this is given the ID popupBehavior. The other attributes on this behavior are parentElement, which specifies the element on the page to which to attach the pop-up menu. If you refer to the HTML, you will see that the anchor for the word *Microsoft* over which the menu will appear has the same ID. Also, later in the script you will see where an Atlas control gets associated with this element. Finally, there is the positioningMode attribute, which determines how the pop-up menu will appear relative to the anchor. Setting this to BottomLeft means the tag will appear over the bottom-left corner of the element to which the menu is attached. You can also use other values in this field: Absolute, Center, TopLeft, BottomRight, and TopRight.

Finally, a floating behavior gets associated with the pop-up menu, allowing it to float on the page. To assign this behavior to this element, you tag it with its handle.

The next part that is necessary is to connect this menu to the anchor tag. You achieve this using the `<hyperlink>` tag, which is associated with the element called hoverLink. As you can see in the HTML, this is the word *Microsoft*; if you hover over the word, you will get the menu. Now that you have a control associated with this element, it is straightforward to implement a pop-up on it. You attach a hoverBehavior element to this control and implement actions for `<hover>` and `<unhover>`.

These actions then simply call the show and hide methods of the `<popupBehavior>` to make it appear and disappear when hovering over and hovering off, respectively.

Implementing Drag-and-Drop Behaviors

In the previous example, you saw the floatingWindowBehavior and how you can use it to implement a pop-up menu. You can also use this behavior to implement true floating windows where you can drag and drop to rearrange information on your screen. You are probably familiar with this if you have used portals such as Live.com or Start.com that allow you to arrange the screen according to your preferences.

In this example, you'll do exactly that. You'll have a page with a number of HTML panes in it that can be rearranged as you desire. This uses the `<floatingBehavior>` control to implement this functionality. This is the power of behaviors. You simply have to identify an element and add the behavior to it.

You can see this example in action in Figure 5-21.

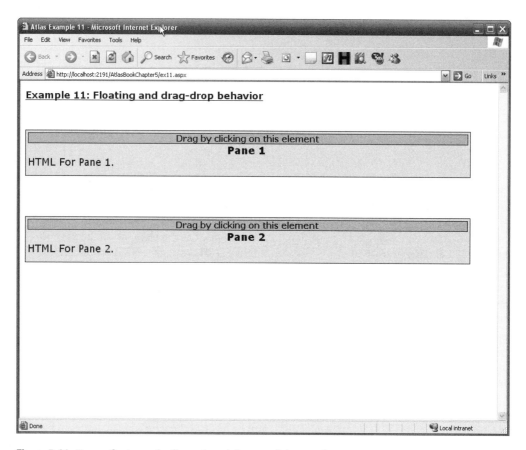

Figure 5-21. *Panes that may be floated and drag and dropped*

Implementing this using behaviors is easy. Before you begin, however, make sure you have the full stylesheet called intro.css that defines the styles used by these panes. You can find it listed in Chapter 4, and it is also available as part of the download with this book. First you need to implement the panes in HTML and assign identities to them. You can see the two panes from the example here:

```
<div id="Description">
 <div id="DragHandle">
 Drag by clicking on this element
 </div>
 <div style="text-align:center;font-weight:bold;">
 Pane 1
 </div>
```

```
 HTML For Pane 1.
</div>
<div id="Description2">
 <div id="DragHandle2">
 Drag by clicking on this element
 </div>
 <div style="text-align:center;font-weight:bold;">
 Pane 2
 </div>
 HTML For Pane 2.
</div>
```

This simply sets up the HTML and associates the IDs Description and Desription2 with the panes and DragHandle and DragHandle2 with the draggable title area in each pane.

You then configure the Atlas Script for these panes, attaching the behavior and implementing the draggable functionality like this:

```
<control targetElement="DragHandle" cssClass="draghandle" />
<control targetElement="Description" cssClass="floatwindow">
 <behaviors>
  <floatingBehavior handle="DragHandle">
  </floatingBehavior>
 </behaviors>
</control>

<control targetElement="DragHandle2" cssClass="draghandle" />
<control targetElement="Description2" cssClass="floatwindow">
 <behaviors>
  <floatingBehavior handle="DragHandle2">
  </floatingBehavior>
 </behaviors>
</control>
```

First you want to create a control that maps to the element containing the title of each pane. These elements are called DragHandle and DragHandle2, respectively. You associate these with the cssClass dragHandle, which gives them their appearance.

Next, you need to associate floatingBehavior with the content of the panes, which are called Description and Description2. To implement a draggable functionality, you simply use this and tag a handle to it. This specifies the name of the element that is used to handle the drag.

And that's all you have to do. As long as you drop the element over a part of the page that currently has markup, it will drop in place; otherwise, it will snap back to where you started from. As you drag the pane over the page, you will see its contents (see Figure 5-22).

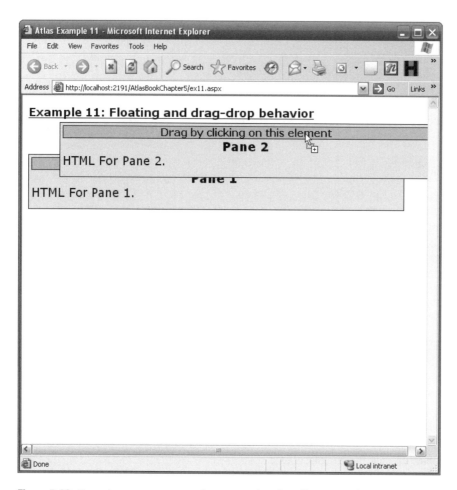

Figure 5-22. *Dragging a pane across the page using the* <floatingBehavior> *element*

WHAT YOU'VE LEARNED FROM THESE EXAMPLES

Behaviors are enormously powerful and immensely useful aspects of the Atlas framework that you can use to give your applications more sophisticated GUIs but keep them easy to develop and maintain.

You looked at how to use the click behavior to add click event handling to elements that may not normally have this, enable more complex functionality to be implemented on simple elements such as `<div>` tags, and make them clickable without needing to use buttons or custom JavaScript hyperlink workarounds.

Next, you looked at the behaviors that allow for mouse hovering and hot tracking. This allows you to update your UI or implement features such as tooltips that improve the user experience upon hovering over various elements of the page. You saw how you can use these behaviors to trigger style updates or implement custom actions. You used this to implement a pop-up menu that contained a list of hyperlinks. You could use such functionality to implement custom smart tags on your pages, context menus, or more.

Finally, you extended on the floatingWindow behavior that was used for the pop-up menu to learn how easy it is to implement panes that can be dragged and dropped across your page.

Ultimately, behaviors give you the facility to implement complex GUI functionality without explicitly coding it. As you progress through this book, you will see where the behaviors are used extensively to empower the GUI.

Summary

This chapter intended to take you through many simple examples of using Atlas client-side controls and demonstrate how to implement and manipulate them using Atlas Script and JavaScript. It was intended to be very hands-on; in other words, you learned by doing. You went through 11 examples of different functionalities, using data binding, actions, behaviors, and more, to implement some complex GUI functionality.

You'll get into more client controls and client functionality later in the book, particularly as you work through the full example in Chapter 12. However, now is a good time to put these new tools that you've learned into your pencil box and move onto the other side—the server side. In the next few chapters, you will start looking at implementing Atlas applications using the ASP.NET Atlas server-side controls.

CHAPTER 6

Introducing Server Controls in Atlas

The first three chapters of this book gave you an overview of Ajax and Atlas and how you can use them to build web applications using this technology to restrict unnecessary postbacks and processing on your web pages, thus improving the performance and polish of your web applications. Chapters 4 and 5 introduced you to the client-side controls presented by Atlas and stepped you through many examples of how to use these controls in JavaScript and in a new XML-based script called Atlas Script.

You looked at some advanced aspects of the scripting framework, including *actions*, which are compound commands associated with an event or stimulus on a control; *behaviors*, which are automatic units of functionality that can be associated with a control, enabling things such as drag and drop; and *data binding*, which allows for controls to be wired up to each other or to themselves in order to pass data between them.

In this chapter, you will go to the other side of the action—the server—and begin exploring the various server-side controls available to you when building your Atlas applications. You have seen one of these controls, the ScriptManager control, already. In this chapter you will look at ScriptManager in more detail. In Chapter 7, you will start learning about how these controls work by navigating through some examples.

Adding the Atlas Server Controls to Visual Studio 2005

Visual Studio 2005 and ASP.NET offer some great design tools that allow you to visually construct pages. This fits in neatly with the concepts that Atlas introduces; developers can place controls on a page, and these controls generate the JavaScript that is necessary to implement the Ajax functionality. In the following sections, you'll look at how to use these controls within the integrated development environment (IDE).

Creating an Atlas Web Site

If you haven't done so already, now is a good time to take a look at Atlas projects in Visual Studio 2005. You can create a new web site by selecting File ➤ New Web Site in the Visual Studio 2005 IDE. This opens the dialog box shown in Figure 6-1. To create an Atlas-based web site, select the ASP.NET 'Atlas' Web Site template.

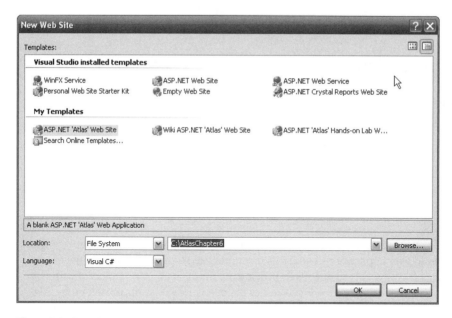

Figure 6-1. *Creating a new ASP.NET Atlas web site*

This creates a solution containing everything you need for an Atlas web site including the Atlas binaries and required support files, including the settings to web.config that allow for Atlas Web services. For more on this, see Chapter 3.

Adding the Server Controls to the Toolbox

On the Toolbox, if you right-click, you will find an option called Add Tab (see Figure 6-2).

Selecting this adds a new tab to the Toolbox. This tab has a text box where you can type in a new title. Call the tab Atlas, and you will see a new, empty tab with no controls in it (see Figure 6-3).

To populate this tab with the suite of Atlas server controls, right-click it, and select Choose Items, which opens the dialog box shown in Figure 6-4. It may take a few moments if it is the first time you've done this, because the dialog box will be evaluating all the references and type libraries for the .NET and COM controls. Make sure the .NET Framework Components tab is selected.

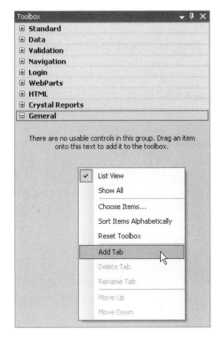

Figure 6-2. *Using the Toolbox Add Tab functionality*

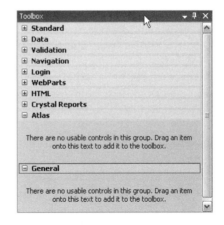

Figure 6-3. *Your new, empty tab*

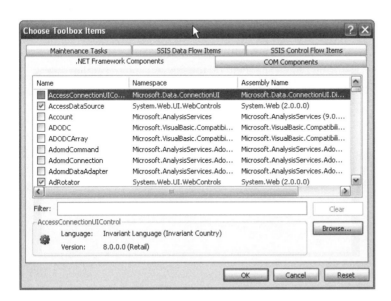

Figure 6-4. *Choosing Toolbox items*

By default, this dialog box lists the controls in alphabetical order of name. Click the Namespace column header to sort by namespace.

The Atlas controls appear in the Microsoft.Web.UI and Microsoft.Web.UI.Controls namespaces. If these namespaces are missing, click the Browse button, and find the Microsoft.Web.Atlas.DLL file in the \Bin directory of your web site.

You can see the Atlas controls from this assembly in Figure 6-5.

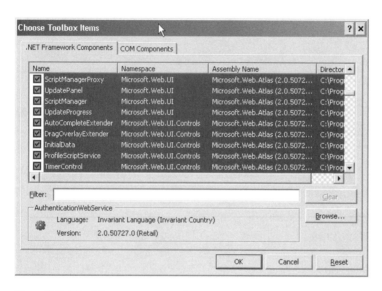

Figure 6-5. *The Atlas server controls*

Once you've added these controls, you'll see them on the tab you created earlier (see Figure 6-6).

Figure 6-6. *Your Toolbox tab containing Atlas server controls*

Now that you have the controls in your Toolbox, you can drag and drop them onto your web forms. For the rest of this chapter, I'll discuss these controls and their object models, and in Chapter 7 you will start using these controls in hands-on examples.

Introducing the ScriptManager Control

The ScriptManager control is at the heart of Atlas. This control, as its name suggests, manages the deployment of the various JavaScript libraries that implement the client-side runtime functionality of Atlas.

Using the ScriptManager Designer Interface

You've used the ScriptManager control already to create references on the client side to the Atlas script libraries. Using the control is simple. When you drag and drop the control onto a page, you get a design-time user interface that allows you to set up some of the common elements of the ScriptManager control (see Figure 6-7).

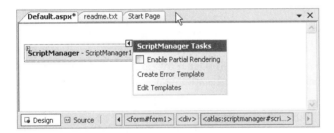

Figure 6-7. *ScriptManager design-time user interface*

This designer allows you to visually set up partial rendering, which is a tag that enables partial-page updates and is specified in UpdatePanel controls; this designer also allows you to create error templates and manage other ScriptManager templates. You'll be seeing more about these features throughout this chapter.

Now, if you take a look at the code behind this .aspx page, you will see that placing the ScriptManager control has led to the following script being added to the page:

```
<atlas:ScriptManager ID="ScriptManager1" runat="server">
</atlas:ScriptManager>
```

When you run the page, you'll see the following source code when you select the View ➤ Source command in the browser:

```
<script src="ScriptLibrary/Atlas/Debug/Atlas.js" type="text/javascript"></script>
<div>
</div>
<script type="text/xml-script">
```

```
<page xmlns:script="http://schemas.microsoft.com/xml-script/2005">
  <components />
</page></script>
<script type="text/javascript">
</script>
```

In this case, at runtime, ASP.NET renders the server-side control as a number of statements. The first is a reference to the script library Atlas.js, which will get downloaded automatically. Next is a `<script>` tag containing any client-side Atlas Script for the page components. Finally, another script tag appears for any JavaScript you may want to use on the page, such as custom actions or transforms.

Programming with the Script Manager

The ScriptManager control is in many ways the core of an Atlas-enabled ASP.NET page. In addition to managing the download of the scripts to the client, it also orchestrates how the page updates and refreshes.

Performing Partial Rendering

The EnablePartialRendering property of this control sets how your page will behave insofar as updates are concerned. If this is false (the default), full-page refreshes will occur on round-trips to the server. If this is true, then postbacks and full-page refreshes are suppressed and replaced with targeted and partial updates. Instead of the application performing a full post-back, the application will simulate full postbacks using the XMLHttpRequest object when this is set to true (as you would expect from an Ajax application).

On the server side, the page will be processed in the normal way, responding to any controls that call _doPostBack(). Existing server-side postback events will continue to fire, and event handlers will continue to work as they always have. It is intended, by design, that Atlas-enabled applications change existing ASP.NET applications as little as possible.

The power of the ScriptManager control, when partial rendering is enabled, comes at render time. It determines, with the aid of the UpdatePanel control, which portions of the page have changed. The UpdatePanel, which you will see more of later in this chapter, defines regions in the page that get updated as a chunk. If, for example, you have a page containing a number of chat rooms and you want to update only a single chat room, you would surround that area of the page with an UpdatePanel control.

The ScriptManager control will override the rendering of the page and instead will send HTML down to the XMLHttpRequest object for each of the UpdatePanel controls on the page.

Enabling Script Components

When you browse to an Atlas-enabled application, two script libraries get downloaded to the client; these are Atlas.js for Internet Explorer and AtlasCompat.js for other browsers. These script libraries effectively bootstrap Atlas functionality on the client side. The ScriptManager control handles the rendering of these references on the page (as `<script>` tags), so you don't need to manually add them to your page.

If you add a ScriptManager control to a blank page and then execute the application, you'll see the following tag embedded in your page (in this case, it is running in debug mode) when running Internet Explorer:

```
<script src="ScriptLibrary/Atlas/Debug/Atlas.js"
        type="text/javascript">
</script>
```

And you'll see this one when running it in Firefox:

```
<script src="ScriptLibrary/Atlas/Debug/AtlasCompat.js"
        type="text/javascript">
</script>
<script src="ScriptLibrary/Atlas/Debug/Atlas.js"
        type="text/javascript">
</script>
```

Specifying Additional Script Components

The ScriptManager control has a `<Scripts>` child tag that can specify additional scripts to download to the browser. This should contain one or more `<atlas:ScriptReference>` tags that specify the path to the script and the browser the script targets.

This tag has three parameters:

Browser: This attribute allows you to target the script at a specific browser. Here's an example that instructs the ScriptManager control to download the script at the path myff.js to Firefox-based callers:

```
<atlas:ScriptReference Browser="FireFox" Path="myff.js" />
```

Path: This specifies the path where the ScriptManager control can find the script file to download. In the previous example, myff.js was in the same directory as the page containing the `<ScriptManager>` tag.

ScriptName: If you want to target one of the built-in Atlas scripts, instead of a custom one, you can reference them by name here. This means you don't have to specify the directory of the script, so you can have consistent `<atlas:ScriptReference>` tags on your pages regardless of their location within the directory structure on the page. Here's an example that instructs the ScriptManager control to download the script AtlasUIGlitz.js to Firefox-based browsers:

```
<atlas:ScriptReference Browser="FireFox" ScriptName="AtlasUIGlitz" />
```

So when using the optional script components on a page, your ScriptManager control will look something like this:

```
<atlas:ScriptManager ID="ScriptManager1" runat="server">
<Scripts>
  <atlas:ScriptReference Browser="Firefox"
      Path="hello.js" ScriptName="Custom" />
```

```
    <atlas:ScriptReference Browser="Firefox"
        ScriptName="AtlasUIGlitz" />
</Scripts>
</atlas:ScriptManager>
```

When you run the page containing this script on Internet Explorer, you will see this:

```
<script src="ScriptLibrary/Atlas/Debug/Atlas.js"
        type="text/javascript">
</script>
```

When you run the page containing this script on Firefox, you will see this:

```
<script src="ScriptLibrary/Atlas/Debug/AtlasCompat.js"
        type="text/javascript">
</script>
<script src="ScriptLibrary/Atlas/Debug/Atlas.js"
        type="text/javascript"></script>
<div> </div>

<script type="text/xml-script">
<page xmlns:script="http://schemas.microsoft.com/xml-script/2005">
  <references>
    <add src="hello.js" />
    <add src="ScriptLibrary/Atlas/Debug/AtlasUIGlitz.js" />
  </references>
  <components />
</page></script>
```

Specifying Services

In Chapter 2 you saw how a service can be directly consumed in a client application through a script-based proxy to it. You can use the ScriptManager control to reference this using the <Services> child tag. This tag should contain one or more <atlas:ServiceReference> tags that specify the service you want to reference.

This tag has two attributes:

Path: This specifies the path to the service. You saw in Chapter 2 that JavaScript proxies to web services on Atlas web sites can be automatically generated by postfixing "/js" at the end of its URI. So, for example, the web service at test.asmx would return a JavaScript proxy that could be used to call it at test.asmx/js. When using the <atlas:ServiceReference> tag to specify the service, this would automatically be generated for you on the client side when the ScriptManager control is rendered. Here's an example:

```
<atlas:ServiceReference Path="wstest.asmx"/>
```

GenerateProxy: This is a Boolean value (true or false) that specifies whether the service reference should generate a proxy class or not. The default is true.

When running a page that contains this within a ScriptManager control, you will get the following code on the client:

```
<script type="text/xml-script">
<page xmlns:script="http://schemas.microsoft.com/xml-script/2005">
  <references>
    <add src="wstest.asmx/js" />
  </references>
  <components />
</page>
</script>
```

As you can see, a `<reference>` tag has been added to the Atlas Script, and this references the JavaScript proxy for the wstest.asmx web service. You'll see some examples on how to use web services and their proxies in Chapter 7.

Using Error Templates

The ScriptManager control provides an error handling mechanism whereby you can specify the HTML to render when an error condition is met. This is particularly useful for the client experience because you can then help your users gracefully handle errors. Within the Script-Manager control, you can use the `<ErrorTemplate>` tag to define your error message in HTML. So, for example, the following script will produce a user-friendly response to an error:

```
<atlas:ScriptManager ID="ScriptManager1" runat="server">
<ErrorTemplate>
    There was an error processing your action.<br />
    <span id="errorMessageLabel"></span>
    <hr />
    <button type="button" id="okButton">OK</button>
</ErrorTemplate>
</atlas:ScriptManager>
```

The HTML defined within the `<ErrorTemplate>` element will render in a simulation of a modal dialog box. This is achieved by the rest of the page being partially obscured using a semitransparent overlay. The HTML within the `<ErrorTemplate>` element is enabled and active. This allows you to design a pretty rich error display according to your preferences.

■Note The `<ErrorTemplate>` element is meaningful only when used in conjunction with an UpdatePanel control because it triggers the asynchronous communication used by the UpdatePanel control. So, although the `<ErrorTemplate>` is defined on the ScriptManager control, it will do nothing until an error is received during an asynchronous update.

It's important to remember the ID values used in this example. You must always use these values (errorMessageLabel and okButton). The ScriptManager control generates XML script that uses these controls to bind controls to the error message property and to clear error methods on the PageRequestManager control.

You can also design this HTML using the Visual Studio 2005 IDE. When you mouse over the ScriptManager control in the page designer, you'll see a small right-pointing arrow on its top-right corner (see Figure 6-8).

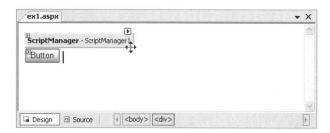

Figure 6-8. *The ScriptManager control*

If you click this arrow, the ScriptManager Tasks Assistant will appear. From this assistant, you can configure or remove the error template and enable partial rendering (see Figure 6-9).

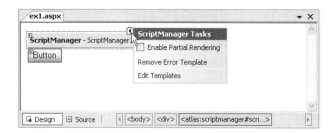

Figure 6-9. *The ScriptManager Tasks Assistant when an* <ErrorTemplate> *element is already configured*

As in this case, the ScriptManager control already has a template associated with it, and the option Remove Error Template is present. Figure 6-10 shows how the ScriptManager Tasks Assistant will appear when no template is present.

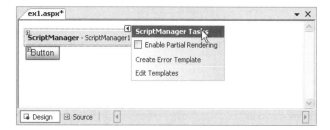

Figure 6-10. *The ScriptManager Tasks Assistant when there is no* <ErrorTemplate> *element present*

To create an error template, click the Create Error Template link. This will not only create a new Error Template for you, but it will also populate it with the standard error message HTML you saw earlier.

If you select Edit Templates, the ScriptManager control surface will open a basic HTML editor that you can use to customize your error template (see Figure 6-11).

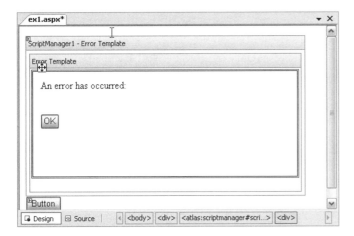

Figure 6-11. *Editing the HTML for your* `<ErrorLayout>` *tag on your ScriptManager control*

As mentioned earlier, you can use the HTML editor to specify how you want this error box to appear. Figure 6-12 shows a customized version of the error template.

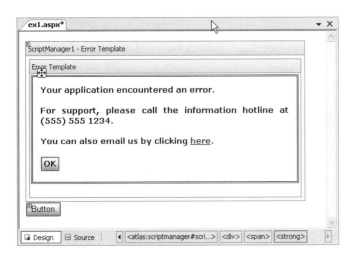

Figure 6-12. *A custom error template*

The designer then generates the `<ErrorTemplate>` code for you. Here is the code associated with the custom error template shown in Figure 6-12:

```
<atlas:ScriptManager ID="ScriptManager1" runat="server">
<ErrorTemplate>
<div style="padding: 12px; width: 400px; height: 140px;
        border: #000000 1px solid;background-color: white; text-align: justify">
<span style="font-size: 10pt; font-family: Verdana">
<strong>
Your application encountered an error.
<br />
<br />
For support, please call the information hotline at (555) 555 1234.
<br />
<span id="errorMessageLabel">
</span>
<br />
You can also email us by clicking
<a href="mailto:support@supporthotline.com">here</a>.
<br />
<br />
</strong>
</span>
<input id="okButton" type="button" value="OK"
style="font-weight: bold; font-size: 10pt; font-family: Verdana" />
<spanstyle="font-size: 10pt; font-family: Verdana">
</span>
</div>
</ErrorTemplate>

</atlas:ScriptManager>
```

To run an application that creates an error, you can add a button to the page. This button, when clicked, will trigger the error.

First add a button:

```
<asp:Button runat="server"
        ID="MyButton"
        Text="Click Me!"
        OnClick="MyButton_Click" />
```

When you click this button, you will call the MyButton_Click event. You define this using a server-side script:

```
<script runat="server">
  private void OnScriptManagerPageError(object sender,
                              PageErrorEventArgs e)
  {
    e.ErrorMessage = "Please do not press that button again.";
  }
```

```
void MyButton_Click(object sender, EventArgs e)
{
    throw new ArgumentException("Please do not press
        that button again.", "MyButton");

}
</script>
```

This script throws an exception when you click the button. The ScriptManager control is also configured to call OnScriptManagerPageError when a page error occurs:

```
<atlas:ScriptManager runat="server"
    ID="scriptManager"
    EnablePartialRendering="true"
    OnPageError="OnScriptManagerPageError">
```

Now when you click the button, the error will fire, and your page will display the HTML defined in the error template (see Figure 6-13).

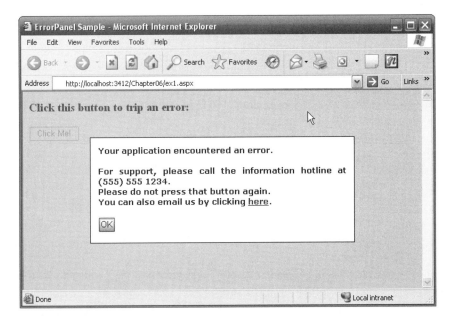

Figure 6-13. *Atlas showing an error*

This concludes the tour of the ScriptManager control. In the rest of this chapter, you will look at the other server-side controls offered by the Atlas framework, and in the next chapter you will go through several examples that use these controls.

Introducing the ScriptManagerProxy Control

The ScriptManagerProxy control is available as an additional script manager for a page. Only one ScriptManager control is allowed, and if you, for example, place a ScriptManager control on a master page but need to add script references to your content page, then you can use the ScriptManagerProxy control.

So, if you have the following master page:

```
<%@ Master Language="C#" AutoEventWireup="true"
      CodeFile="MasterPage.master.cs" Inherits="MasterPage" %>

<!DOCTYPE html PUBLIC "-//W3C//DTD XHTML 1.0 Transitional//EN"
      "http://www.w3.org/TR/xhtml1/DTD/xhtml1-transitional.dtd">

<html xmlns="http://www.w3.org/1999/xhtml" >
<head runat="server">
    <title>Untitled Page</title>
</head>
<body>
    <form id="form1" runat="server">
    <div>
        <atlas:ScriptManager ID="ScriptManager1" runat="server">
        </atlas:ScriptManager>
            This is the Master Page.<br />
            It contains this ScriptManager control:<br />
        <br />
        <asp:contentplaceholder id="ContentPlaceHolder1" runat="server">
            <br />
        </asp:contentplaceholder>
         
    </div>
    </form>
</body>
</html>
```

and you create a new content page based on this master page, your new page will look like this at design time:

```
<%@ Page Language="C#" MasterPageFile="~/MasterPage.master" AutoEventWireup="true"
      CodeFile="Default3.aspx.cs" Inherits="Default3" Title="Untitled Page" %>
<asp:Content ID="Content1" ContentPlaceHolderID="ContentPlaceHolder1"
Runat="Server">
</asp:Content>
```

When you run this page and look at the source code that is generated by ASP.NET from this design-time definition, you will see this:

```
<!DOCTYPE html PUBLIC "-//W3C//DTD XHTML 1.0 Transitional//EN"
        "http://www.w3.org/TR/xhtml1/DTD/xhtml1-transitional.dtd">

<html xmlns="http://www.w3.org/1999/xhtml" >
<head><title>
        Untitled Page
</title></head>
<body>
    <form name="aspnetForm" method="post" action="Default3.aspx" id="aspnetForm">
<div>
<input type="hidden" name="__VIEWSTATE"
        id="__VIEWSTATE"
        value="/wEPDwULLTEwMDUyNjYzMjhkZERQ3hQz51DsahcItBSVyAcTtqP7" />
</div>


<script src="ScriptLibrary/Atlas/Debug/Atlas.js" type="text/javascript"></script>
    <div>

            This is the Master Page.<br />
            It contains this ScriptManager control:<br />
        <br />


         
    </div>

<script type="text/xml-script">
<page xmlns:script="http://schemas.microsoft.com/xml-script/2005">
  <components />
</page></script>
<script type="text/javascript">
</script>
</form>
</body>
</html>
```

You can see here where the `<script>` tag is generated, referencing the Atlas.js core libraries. However, if this page requires using the AtlasUIGlitz library and you don't want to add a reference to that library to the template (because this page is the only one on your site that needs it), then you can use a ScriptManagerProxy control.

So, if you return to the content page that was generated by the master page, you can add a ScriptManagerProxy control to it in the designer (see Figure 6-14).

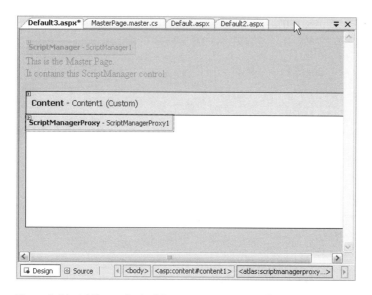

Figure 6-14. *Adding a ScriptManagerProxy control to a content page*

By adding the ScriptManagerProxy control to the content page, you added the following code to the page; you can see this in the Source view:

```
<asp:Content ID="Content1" ContentPlaceHolderID="ContentPlaceHolder1"
        Runat="Server">
    <atlas:ScriptManagerProxy ID="ScriptManagerProxy1" runat="server">
    </atlas:ScriptManagerProxy>
</asp:Content>
```

Now you can simply add the scripts that you want to this page using the <Scripts> child tag in the same manner as you did with the ScriptManager control.

Here's an example:

```
<asp:Content ID="Content1" ContentPlaceHolderID="ContentPlaceHolder1"
        Runat="Server">
    <atlas:ScriptManagerProxy ID="ScriptManagerProxy1" runat="server">
        <Scripts>
            <atlas:ScriptReference ScriptName="AtlasUIDragDrop" />
        </Scripts>
    </atlas:ScriptManagerProxy>
</asp:Content>
```

So now when you run the page, you will see that AtlasUIDragDrop has been included in this page:

```
<!DOCTYPE html PUBLIC "-//W3C//DTD XHTML 1.0 Transitional//EN"
        "http://www.w3.org/TR/xhtml1/DTD/xhtml1-transitional.dtd">
```

```
<html xmlns="http://www.w3.org/1999/xhtml" >
<head><title>
        Untitled Page
</title></head>
<body>
    <form name="aspnetForm" method="post" action="Default3.aspx" id="aspnetForm">
<div>
<input type="hidden" name="__VIEWSTATE"
        id="__VIEWSTATE"
        value="/wEPDwUKLTc4NzcwODI3NmRk9YXV49GLEVNvGzvlq/8dm4TNJOg=" />
</div>
<script src="ScriptLibrary/Atlas/Debug/Atlas.js" type="text/javascript"></script>
    <div>
            This is the Master Page.<br />
            It contains this ScriptManager control:<br />
        <br />
         
    </div>

<script type="text/xml-script">
<page xmlns:script="http://schemas.microsoft.com/xml-script/2005">
  <references>
    <add src="ScriptLibrary/Atlas/Debug/AtlasUIDragDrop.js" />
  </references>
  <components />
</page></script>
<script type="text/javascript">
</script>
</form>
</body>
</html>
```

Introducing the UpdatePanel Control

In typical ASP.NET 2.0 applications, if you do a postback on the web page, the entire page will be rerendered. This causes a "blink" or a "flash" in the client or browser. On the server, the postback is detected, which triggers the page life cycle. This ends up raising the specific postback event handler code for the control that caused the postback, and this calls upon the page's event handler.

When you use UpdatePanel controls along with a ScriptManager control, you eliminate the need for a full-page refresh. The UpdatePanel control is similar to a ContentPanel control in that it marks out a region on the web page that will automatically be updated when the postback occurs (but without the aforementioned postback behavior on the client).

It will instead communicate through the XMLHttpRequest channel—in true Ajax style. The page on the server still handles the postback as expected and executes, raising event handlers, and so on, but the final rendering of the page means that only the regions specified in the UpdatePanel control's regions will be created.

Using the UpdatePanel Designer

Visual Studio 2005 provides a designer for the UpdatePanel control, including a Tasks pane that helps you set up the control. To use an UpdatePanel control, you simply drag and drop it onto the design surface of your web form (see Figure 6-15).

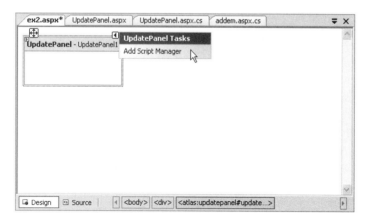

Figure 6-15. *Using the UpdatePanel designer*

As you can see from Figure 6-15, the only task associated with the UpdatePanel control is to add a ScriptManager control. The UpdatePanel control cannot function without a Script-Manager control on the page. Additionally, the ScriptManager control must be located before any UpdatePanel controls on your page. In other words, as you read your source code from top to bottom, the ScriptManager reference should appear before the UpdatePanel ones. Using the Tasks Assistant will ensure that it is placed correctly. If your ScriptManager control is not present or is incorrectly placed, you will get an error (see Figure 6-16).

The UpdatePanel control contains a designer surface where you can place HTML. This code will be the only code updated upon a postback if the ScriptManager control is enabled for partial updates.

Consider Figure 6-17, where several text boxes and a button appear on the screen.

This application has two text boxes, two labels, and a button *outside* the UpdatePanel control, and it has a label *inside* the UpdatePanel designer. The label on the inside is called lblResult. The code behind the button reads as follows:

```
int x = Convert.ToInt16(txt1.Text.ToString());
int y = Convert.ToInt16(txt2.Text.ToString());
int z = x+y;
lblResult.Text = z.ToString();
```

As you can see, the label for the result will get updated to the value of the sum of the values of the text in the text boxes. Because lblResult is in the UpdatePanel control and the ScriptManager control is set to enable partial rendering, clicking the button will update only the text within the UpdatePanel control. You will see and dissect more examples of this in Chapter 7.

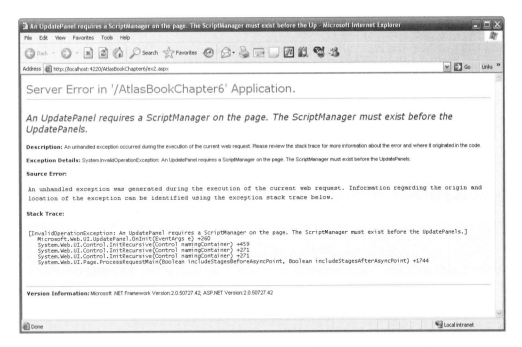

Figure 6-16. *Error page when the UpdatePanel and ScriptManager controls aren't properly configured*

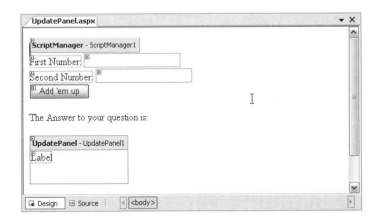

Figure 6-17. *Simple application that uses the UpdatePanel control*

Programming with the UpdatePanel

If you look at the code behind the designer for the UpdatePanel control from the previous example, you'll see the following:

```
<atlas:UpdatePanel ID="UpdatePanel1" runat="server">
<ContentTemplate>
  <asp:Label ID="lblResult" runat="server" Text="Label"></asp:Label>
</ContentTemplate>
</atlas:UpdatePanel>
```

The `<atlas:UpdatePanel>` tag supports two child tags: the `<ContentTemplate>` tag and the `<Triggers>` tag.

Using the ContentTemplate Tag

The `<ContentTemplate>` tag simply defines the HTML or ASP.NET that will get updated by the UpdatePanel control. You can use the designer to generate this HTML. If, for example, you drag and drop a Calendar control onto the UpdatePanel control's content template area (see Figure 6-18), it will be defined within the `<ContentTemplate>` tag area.

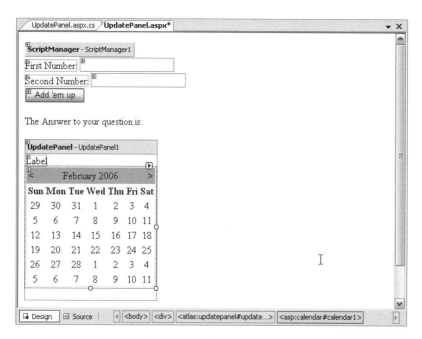

Figure 6-18. *Adding controls to the UpdatePanel control's content template*

You can see the code that is produced by adding the calendar as follows:

```
<atlas:UpdatePanel ID="UpdatePanel1" runat="server">
<ContentTemplate>
  <asp:Label ID="lblResult" runat="server" Text="Label"></asp:Label>
  <asp:Calendar ID="Calendar1" runat="server"></asp:Calendar>
</ContentTemplate>
</atlas:UpdatePanel>
```

Using Triggers

The other child tag for the UpdatePanel control is `<Triggers>`. This allows you to define triggers for the update. The UpdatePanel control has a mode property attribute, and if you set this to Conditional (the other option is Always), then updates to the rendering of the markup will occur only when a trigger is hit. This tag contains the collection of trigger definitions. Two types of trigger exist, defined next.

Using ControlEventTrigger

When using a ControlEventTrigger trigger type, you define a trigger that has an associated control (specified by ControlID) and an event name (specified by the EventName) on that control. If the event is raised on that control, then the trigger fires, and the UpdatePanel control will be rendered.

You specify a ControlEventTrigger with the `<atlas:ControlEventTrigger>` tag. Here's an example:

```
<atlas:UpdatePanel ID="UpdatePanel1" runat="server">
      <ContentTemplate>
        <asp:Label ID="lblResult" runat="server"
                   Text="Label">
        </asp:Label>
        <asp:Calendar ID="Calendar1" runat="server">
        </asp:Calendar>
      </ContentTemplate>
      <Triggers>
        <atlas:ControlEventTrigger ControlID="btnAdd"
                EventName="Click" />
      </Triggers>
</atlas:UpdatePanel>
```

Here the ControlEventTrigger specifies that the source for the trigger is the button called btnAdd, and the event on which to trigger is the Click event. Therefore, when the button is clicked, the ControlEventTrigger will fire, and the partial update will occur.

Using ControlValueTrigger

ControlValueTrigger defines a trigger that fires when the value of a property (specified by PropertyName) for the associated control (specified by ControlID) changes. Upon the change happening, the trigger fires, and the UpdatePanel control will be rendered during the partial rendering of the page on the server. You specify a ControlValueTrigger trigger type with the `<atlas:ControlValueTrigger>` tag.

Here's an example:

```
<atlas:UpdatePanel ID="UpdatePanel1" runat="server">
    <ContentTemplate>
       <asp:Label ID="lblResult" runat="server"
                 Text="Label">
       </asp:Label>
       <asp:Calendar ID="Calendar1" runat="server">
       </asp:Calendar>

    </ContentTemplate>
    <Triggers>
       <atlas:ControlValueTrigger ControlID="txt1"
             PropertyName="Text" />
    </Triggers>
</atlas:UpdatePanel>
```

Here the ControlValueTrigger specifies that the source for the trigger is the txt1 control and that the trigger should fire whenever its text property changes.

Introducing the UpdateProgress Control

Another control that Atlas provides is the UpdateProgress control. This indicates the progress of an asynchronous transaction taking place. Typically the browser's status bar serves as an indicator of activity. With the partial-rendering model, this is no longer applicable, but to make Ajax activity simple and user-friendly, the UpdateProgress control is provided.

Note As with the `<ErrorTemplate>` element you saw earlier, the UpdateProgress control is meaningful only when there is at least one UpdatePanel control on the page. This is because the control is triggered off the asynchronous communication of the underlying XMLHttpRequest object.

To use an UpdateProgress control, you drag and drop it onto your page. This will create an `<atlas:UpdateProgress>` tag on your page.

The HTML to display when the call is taking place is then defined using the `<ProgressTemplate>` tag.

When your application executes calls to the server, the HTML defined in the `<ProgressTemplate>` tag is then displayed.

Here's an example that specifies showing the image of a smiley face while the server is being called:

```
<atlas:UpdateProgress runat="server" ID="updateProgress1">
  <ProgressTemplate>
  <img src="Images/smiling.gif" />
  Contacting Server...
  </ProgressTemplate>
</atlas:UpdateProgress>
```

Introducing Control Extenders

A number of control extenders are available as server-side controls in Atlas. These provide a way to attach rich client-side functionality to the server controls. The available extenders are AutoCompleteExtender and DragOverlayExtender.

Introducing the AutoCompleteExtender

The AutoCompleteExtender control works in conjunction with an AutoCompleteProperties control. It provides for autocomplete functionality on client-side controls, so if you want a text box to provide autocomplete functionality, for example, you would create an AutoCompleteExtender control and an AutoCompleteProperties control. The former would define the extender; the latter would define the target of the autocomplete (in this case the text box) as well as the service and service method that provide the autocomplete values.

This is best demonstrated with a simple example. Here is the HTML for a web form containing a single text box, along with ScriptManager, AutoCompleteExtender, and AutoCompleteProperties controls:

```
<form id="form1" runat="server">
<div>
  <atlas:ScriptManager ID="ScriptManager1"
      runat="server"
      EnablePartialRendering="True">
  </atlas:ScriptManager>
  <asp:TextBox ID="TextBox1" runat="server">
  </asp:TextBox>
  <atlas:AutoCompleteExtender ID="AutoCompleteExtender1"
      runat="server">
    <atlas:AutoCompleteProperties Enabled="True"
      ServiceMethod="GetWordList"
      ServicePath="wordlst.asmx"
      TargetControlID="TextBox1" />
  </atlas:AutoCompleteExtender>
</div>
</form>
```

You can see that the AutoCompleteProperties control points at a web service called wordlst.asmx and a method on this service called GetWordList. You will need to create this service in your project. The code for the GetWordList web method is as follows:

```
[WebMethod]
    public string[] GetWordList()
    {
        String[] theWordList = new String[6];
        theWordList[0] = "Bob";
        theWordList[1] = "Bobby";
        theWordList[2] = "Bobbette";
        theWordList[3] = "Bobbit";
        theWordList[4] = "Bobbles";
        theWordList[5] = "Boba Fett";
        return theWordList;

    }
```

This is pretty straightforward, returning a hard-coded list of words. The autocomplete behavior kicks in once you've typed three characters into the text box. So, at runtime, if you type the letters *bob* into the text box (in memory of Microsoft Bob), you will see the autocomplete list appear (see Figure 6-19).

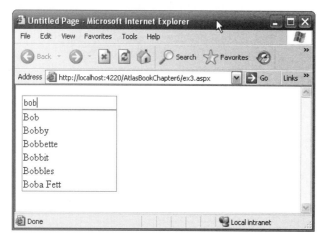

Figure 6-19. *Demonstrating the AutoCompleteExtender control*

Using the DragOverlayExtender

The DragOverlayExtender control allows you to add drag-and-drop functionality to any control in a similar manner to the drag-and-drop behaviors discussed in Chapters 4 and 5. What is nice about this one is that you can declare it on the server side to enhance your existing applications. This demonstrates one of the design tenets of Atlas—it can enhance your existing ASP.NET applications without significantly changing them, so if you have an ASP.NET Label control that you want to add drag and drop to, you can do so, without touching its code. You simply add a DragOverlayExtender control and its associated DragOverlayProperties control and configure them to extend that control.

Consider the following page:

```
<%@ Page Language="C#" AutoEventWireup="true"
        CodeFile="ex4.aspx.cs" Inherits="ex4" %>

<!DOCTYPE html PUBLIC "-//W3C//DTD XHTML 1.0 Transitional//EN"
        "http://www.w3.org/TR/xhtml1/DTD/xhtml1-transitional.dtd">

<html xmlns="http://www.w3.org/1999/xhtml" >
<head runat="server">
<title>Untitled Page</title>
<style type="text/css">
  body{font-family:Verdana;}
  .label{font-weight:bold;}
  .dropArea{height:500px;border:solid 2px Black;background:#ccc;}

</style>
</head>
<body>
  <form id="form1" runat="server">
   <div class="dropArea">

     <asp:Label ID="lbl" runat="server" CssClass="label">
  Drag Me with your mouse!
     </asp:Label>

   </div>
   </form>
</body>
</html>
```

This will provide a simple ASP.NET page containing a gray <div> element with a single label on it (see Figure 6-20).

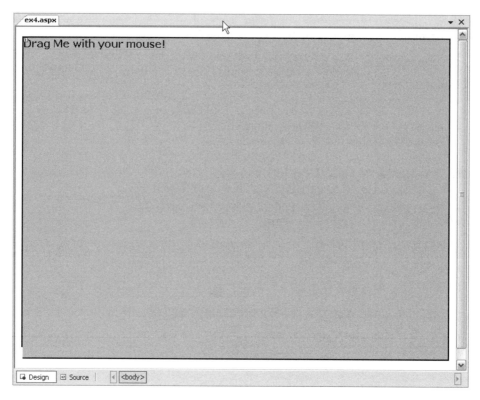

Figure 6-20. *Simple ASP.NET page with a* <div> *element and a* <label> *element*

You can now make the label draggable and droppable using the DragControlExtender control. You achieve this by first adding a ScriptManager control to the page so that the Atlas runtime components will be downloaded to the client.

Once you've done that, you can add a DragOverlayExtender control to the application (see Figure 6-21).

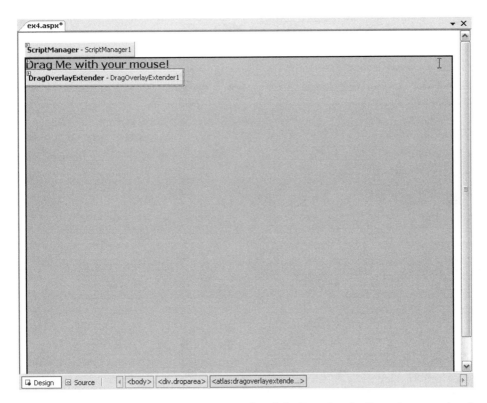

Figure 6-21. *Adding the ScriptManager control and the DragOverlayExtender control to the web form*

This will add the ScriptManager code and the following snippet for the DragOverlayExtender control:

```
<atlas:DragOverlayExtender ID="DragOverlayExtender1" runat="server">
</atlas:DragOverlayExtender>
```

You then use the DragOverlayProperties control to configure this to make the label draggable and droppable. There is no visual designer for this, so you need to add it to the page code like this:

```
<atlas:DragOverlayExtender ID="DragOverlayExtender1" runat="server">
  <atlas:DragOverlayProperties TargetControlID="lbl" Enabled="true" />
</atlas:DragOverlayExtender>
```

Now if you view the page in your browser, you can drag and drop the label anywhere within the gray area (see Figure 6-22).

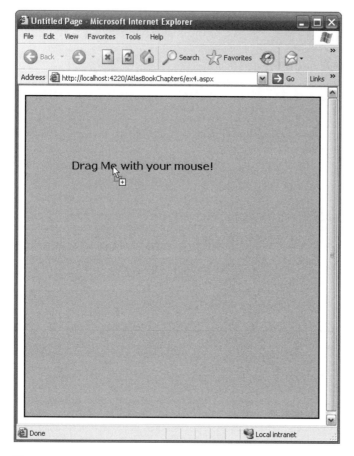

Figure 6-22. *Dragging a label using the DragControlExtender control*

Introducing the ProfileScriptService Control

ASP.NET 2.0 provides a profile application service for persisting custom, per-user data across browser sessions. You add a profile property variable to the Web.config file like this:

```
<profile defaultProvider="AspNetSqlProfileProvider">
  <properties>
    <add name="labelLocation" />
  </properties>
</profile>
```

In this manner, the profile variable will be persisted for you in a SQL Server database. You must have a SQL Server or SQL Server Express Edition already set up to be able to use profiles. For more information on profiles, you can read *Pro ASP.NET 2.0 in C# 2005* (Apress, 2005) or *Pro ASP.NET 2.0 in VB .NET 2005* (Apress, 2006) or refer to Chapter 24 of *Pro ASP.NET 2.0 in VB .NET 2005*.

Once you are using profiles, you can then integrate them with Atlas using the ProfileScriptService control.

To do this, you can drag and drop a ProfileScriptService control onto the design surface for your web form (see Figure 6-23).

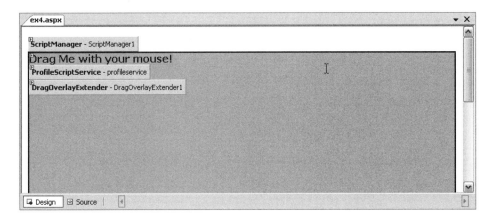

Figure 6-23. *Adding a ProfileScriptService control*

This will add the following tag to your page:

```
<atlas:ProfileScriptService ID="ProfileScriptService1" runat="server">
</atlas:ProfileScriptService>
```

Your page is now able to access profile variables through Atlas.

For an example of this, the DragOverlayProperties control allows you to specify a profile variable that can be used to persist the location of the control that you are dragging and dropping between sessions. So, if you amend the previous drag-and-drop example to specify the profile property that you want to use to persist the location like this:

```
<atlas:DragOverlayExtender ID="DragOverlayExtender1" runat="server">
  <atlas:DragOverlayProperties TargetControlID="lbl"
      Enabled="true" ProfileProperty="labelLocation" />
</atlas:DragOverlayExtender>
```

then you will be able to persist the location of the control between page sessions.

Introducing the Timer Control

Atlas provides a simple-to-use Timer control that can be configured to perform operations repeatedly based on the time elapsed.

You can add a Timer control to a page by dragging and dropping it onto the control surface. To use a Timer control, you will of course need a ScriptManager control on the page. A good use for timers is to update the contents of an UpdatePanel control when the timer ticks.

To see the Timer control in action, you can add an UpdatePanel control to a blank page and use its Tasks pane to add a ScriptManager control to the page. Once you've done this, you can drag and drop a Timer control onto the page. You can see what this looks like in the designer in Figure 6-24.

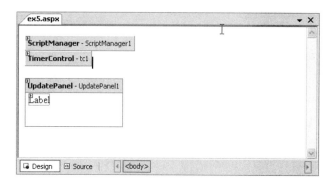

Figure 6-24. *Using a Timer control in the designer*

The code behind your page will now have the <Timer> tag already defined.

Here's an example of a timer that has been customized with a 5,000-millisecond interval (5 seconds in other words), with the name tc1 and the event handler tc1_tick:

```
<atlas:TimerControl ID="tc1" runat="server"
                    Interval="5000" OnTick="tc1_Tick">
</atlas:TimerControl>
```

Now, within the tc1_Tick function, you can write a handler for the timer. Additionally, a useful case for this is to use it to feed a ControlEventTrigger trigger type on an UpdatePanel control. Here's an example:

```
<atlas:UpdatePanel ID="UpdatePanel1" runat="server">
<Triggers>
  <atlas:ControlEventTrigger ControlID="tc1"
         EventName="Tick" />
</Triggers>
<ContentTemplate>
  <asp:Label ID="Label1"
             runat="server"
             Text="Label">
  </asp:Label>
</ContentTemplate>
</atlas:UpdatePanel>
```

And now, whenever the timer ticks, the UpdatePanel control will have an update triggered automatically.

Introducing the Gadget Control

Atlas is designed to work with the new technologies that Microsoft is using to extend public portals at Live.com and Start.com. These sites aggregate panes of information on the screen using a technology called *gadgets*.

Figure 6-25 shows the Live.com site with a number of gadgets, including sports headlines and weather.

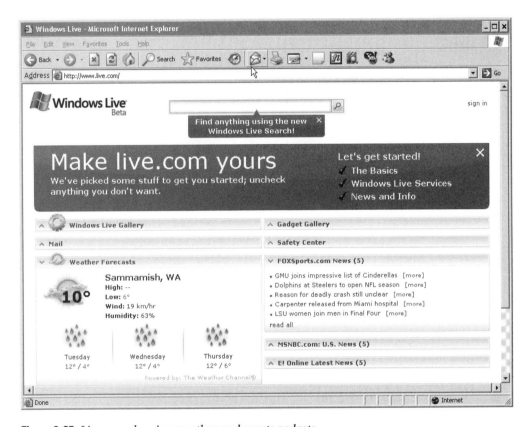

Figure 6-25. *Live.com showing weather and sports gadgets*

You can use the Atlas Gadget server control to implement your own gadgets for Live.com using Atlas.

Doing this is extremely easy. In Visual Studio .NET, you simply drag the Gadget control onto the design surface for an ASP.NET web form. You'll also need to have a ScriptManager control on the web form. You can see this in Figure 6-26.

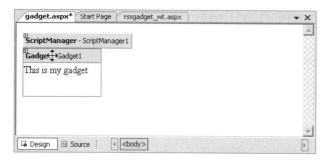

Figure 6-26. *Adding a gadget to an ASP.NET web form*

This generates the following ASP.NET code:

```
<body>
<form id="form1" runat="server">
<div>
 <atlas:ScriptManager ID="ScriptManager1"
                      runat="server"
                      EnablePartialRendering="True">
 </atlas:ScriptManager>
</div>
 <atlas:Gadget ID="Gadget1" runat="server">
  <ContentTemplate>
    This is my gadget<br />
  </ContentTemplate>
  </atlas:Gadget>
</form>
</body>
```

As you can see, as with other controls, a templated area within the control tag specifies what appears at runtime when the control is rendered.

Listing 6-1 shows an example of a full page that hosts a gadget containing an RSS reader. It comes from the Atlas samples download at `http://atlas.asp.net`.

Listing 6-1. *ASP.NET Page Containing RSS Gadget*

```
<%@ Page Language="C#" %>

<!DOCTYPE html PUBLIC "-//W3C//DTD XHTML 1.0 Transitional//EN"
        "http://www.w3.org/TR/xhtml1/DTD/xhtml1-transitional.dtd">

<html xmlns="http://www.w3.org/1999/xhtml" >
<head runat="server">
    <title>Untitled Page</title>
</head>
```

```
<body>
<form id="form1" runat="server">
<div>
 <atlas:ScriptManager runat="server" ID="scriptManager" />

 <atlas:gadget runat="server" ID="AspNetRssFeed"
               Title="ASP.net Forums"
               Description="RSS feeds from ASP.NET forums">
 <ContentTemplate>

    <div style="visibility:hidden;display:none;">
      <div id="RssItemNoDataTemplate">
        <span id="DescriptionLoading">Loading ...</span>
      </div>

      <!-- Layout template for item links -->
      <div id="RssViewLayout">
      <!-- item -->
      <div id="RssItemLayout">
      <div id="RssItemView">
        <span id="RssItemDate"
              style="font-weight:bold;">
        </span>:
        <a target="_blank" href="#"
           id="RssItem" class="ForumLink">
        </a>
      </div>
      </div>
      </div>
    </div>

    <div id="RssViewList" class="Dialog"
         style="position:absolute;width:95%;overflow:auto;">

    <div class="DialogBanner">
      <img src="images/rss.jpg" alt="RSS" /> 
      <div id="ForumTitle"
           style="display:inline;">
        ASP.net "Atlas" Discussion and Suggestions
      </div>
                         
      <a onclick="javascript: return false;"
         href="#" id="RefreshForum">
      <img alt="Get forum feed"
           src="images/refresh.jpg" /></a>
      </div>
```

```
                      <!-- List -->
<div id="RssView"></div>
</div>

<script type="text/xml-script">
<page xmlns:script="http://schemas.microsoft.com/xml-script/2005">
<components>
  <!-- Data -->
  <timer id="sizeTimer" interval="500"
         tick="OnTimerTick" enabled="true" />

  <xmlDataSource id="FeedSource" autoLoad="true"
                 xpath="//item"
                 serviceURL="aspnetforums.asbx?mn=Get">
    <parameters
         feedURL="http://forums.asp.net/rss.aspx?ForumID=1007" />
  </xmlDataSource>

  <!-- Get feed -->
  <button id="RefreshForum">
    <click>
      <invokeMethod target="FeedSource" method="load" />
    </click>
  </button>

  <!-- List of links -->
  <control id="RssViewList" visibilityMode="Collapse" />
  <listView id="RssView"
            itemTemplateParentElementId="rssItemLayout">
  <bindings>
    <binding id="BindListView" property="data"
             dataContext="FeedSource" dataPath="data" />
  </bindings>

  <layoutTemplate>
    <template layoutElement="RssViewLayout" />
  </layoutTemplate>

  <emptyTemplate>
    <template layoutElement="RssItemNoDataTemplate"/>
  </emptyTemplate>
  <itemTemplate>
    <template layoutElement="RssItemView">
    <hyperLink id="RssItem">
     <bindings>
```

```
                <xpathBinding property="text"
                              xpath="./title/text()" />
                <xpathBinding property="navigateURL"
                              xpath="./link/text()" />
              </bindings>
            </hyperLink>
            <label id="RssItemDate">
             <bindings>
              <xpathBinding property="text"
                            xpath="./pubDate/text()"
                            transform="ToDateString" />
             </bindings>
            </label>
           </template>
          </itemTemplate>
         </listView>

         </components>
      </page>
    </script>
</ContentTemplate>

<Scripts>
  <atlas:scriptreference path="rssgadget_wt.js" />
</Scripts>

<Styles>
  <atlas:StyleReference Path="rssgadget.css" />
</Styles>

</atlas:gadget>
</div>
</form>
</body>
</html>
```

Figure 6-27 shows this page in action, reading the RSS string and rendering it using the <ContentTemplate> tag.

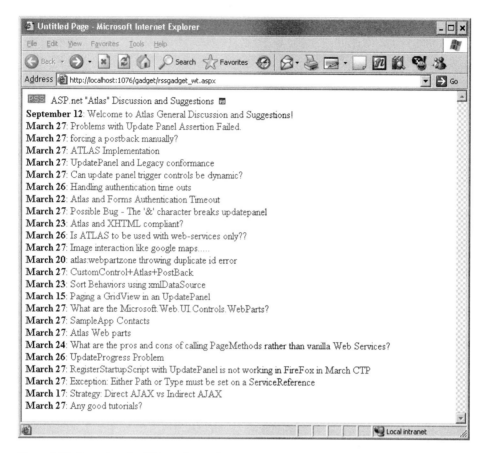

Figure 6-27. *Running the RSS reader gadget*

When you run this and append the text ?gadget=true to the URI, you will receive the output shown in Figure 6-28.

Figure 6-29 shows Live.com when you are signed in. You can sign into this site using Microsoft Passport. To add this gadget to Live.com, you use the Add Stuff link at the top left of the page.

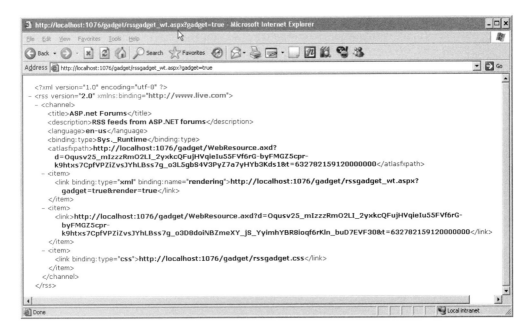

Figure 6-28. *Running the Gadget control with Gadget=True set*

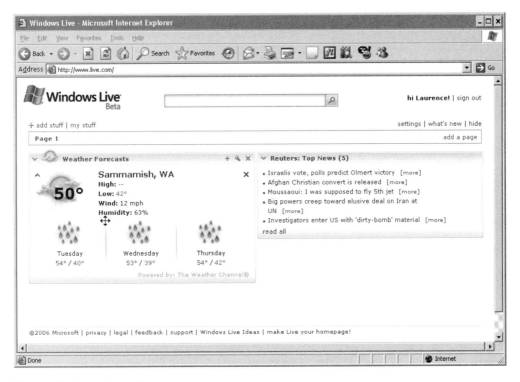

Figure 6-29. *Signed into Live.com*

You can then use the Advanced options to add the URL of your gadget, and you will see it rendered on your Live.com portal. You can see this in Figure 6-30.

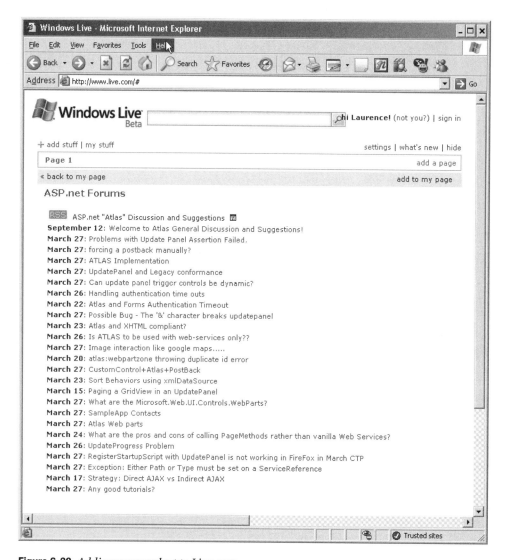

Figure 6-30. *Adding your gadget to Live.com*

One thing to note is permissions and security. If you have trouble viewing the gadget, make sure you have *.live.com and *.start.com in your trusted sites settings within IE.

As you can see, with Atlas creating gadgets is easy. You can integrate these gadgets into Live.com, Start.com, and a number of up-and-coming sites. They'll also be able to be integrated directly into the sidebar of Windows Vista!

Summary

This chapter introduced you to the server controls that are available to Atlas programmers. It walked you through using the ScriptManager control, which is at the heart of Atlas. This control empowers the download of the runtime as well as handles things such as error display messages. Additionally, you looked at the UpdatePanel control, which is at the heart of how Atlas enables Ajax functionality in existing ASP.NET pages using partial-page updates.

Other controls such as the Timer control and the UpdateProgress control are available on the server side to make your UI friendlier. Finally, you looked at some of the control extenders, which provide valuable client-side functionality to existing controls. The extenders are important in that they allow you to easily amend your existing ASP.NET applications unobtrusively. To extend ASP.NET controls for drag and drop, for example, you then simply add an extender to the page and point it at that control.

This chapter gave you a high-level overview of each control and how it works. In the next chapter, you will look at some applications and samples that use this functionality, as well as at the client-side controls you saw in Chapters 4 and 5, dissecting them to understand how you can program similar applications of your own in Atlas.

CHAPTER 7

Using Server Controls in Atlas

This chapter follows on from Chapter 6, which introduced you to the Atlas server controls and showed you how to use them. In this chapter, you will look at several Atlas applications and will dissect them to see how they work. In the process, you will glean lots of new information about how to use the Atlas extensions to ASP.NET to build powerful Ajax-style applications and how to extend your existing applications with asynchrony. At the end of the chapter, you will look into the reference application that was built by Microsoft for Atlas—the Atlas wiki. This application demonstrates how you can put together a powerful and high-performing application using many of the Atlas techniques.

Using the UpdatePanel Control

The first example uses the UpdatePanel control to show a partial refresh of a page. For this example, you will need a web form containing the HTML shown in Listing 7-1.

Listing 7-1. *Partially Refreshing a Page Using the UpdatePanel Control*

```
<%@ Page Language="C#"  %>
<!DOCTYPE html PUBLIC "-//W3C//DTD XHTML 1.1//EN"
        "http://www.w3.org/TR/xhtml11/DTD/xhtml11.dtd">

<script runat="server">
    protected void btnCopy_Click(object sender, EventArgs e)
    {
        lblFirstLineShipping.Text   = lblFirstLineBilling.Text;
        lblSecondLineShipping.Text  = lblSecondLineBilling.Text;
        lblThirdLineShipping.Text   = lblThirdLineBilling.Text;
    }
</script>

<html xmlns="http://www.w3.org/1999/xhtml" >
<head id="Head1" runat="server">
    <style type="text/css">
        .start{background-color:yellow;border:dashed 2px black;}
        .hover{font-size:40pt;background-color:yellow;border:dashed 2px
            black;}
    </style>
```

```
    <link href="intro.css" type="text/css" rel="Stylesheet" />
    <title>ASP.NET &quot;Atlas&quot; Demo: UpdatePanel Control</title>
</head>
<body>
    <form id="form1" runat="server">

        <div id="Div1" class="title">
            <h2>ASP.NET &quot;Atlas&quot; Demo: Server-side
            Controls</h2>
            The following ASP.NET &quot;Atlas&quot; server-side controls
            are shown in this example:
            <ol>
            <li>&lt;atlas:UpdatePanel&gt;</li>
            </ol>

        </div>
        <div class="description">
            <atlas:ScriptManager runat="server"
              ID="ScriptManager1" EnablePartialRendering="true" />
            <hr />
            <h3>Example 1:  Atlas:UpdatePanel</u></h3>
            The UpdatePanel shown in this example updates the 'Shipping
            Address' once the 'Same
            As Billing Address' button is clicked. Notice that the page
            doesn't postback and
            the refresh happens without requiring to reload all the
            current content on the page.<br />
            <br />
            <strong>
            <span style="text-decoration: underline">
            Billing Address
             </span>:<br /></strong>
            <asp:Label ID="lblFirstLineBilling"
                runat="server" Font-Bold="False"
                Text="One Microsoft Way,"></asp:Label><br />
            <asp:Label ID="lblSecondLineBilling"
                runat="server"
                Text="Redmond,"></asp:Label><br />
            <asp:Label ID="lblThirdLineBilling"
                runat="server"
                Text="WA - 98052"></asp:Label><br />
            <br />
            <atlas:UpdatePanel runat="server" ID="UpdatePanel1">
                <ContentTemplate>
                    <strong>
                    <span style="text-decoration: underline">
                    Shipping Address</span>:</strong><br />
```

```
                    <asp:Label ID="lblFirstLineShipping"
                        runat="server"
                        Font-Bold="False"></asp:Label><br />
                    <asp:Label ID="lblSecondLineShipping"
                        runat="server"></asp:Label><br />
                    <asp:Label ID="lblThirdLineShipping"
                        runat="server"></asp:Label><br />
                </ContentTemplate>
            </atlas:UpdatePanel>
            <br />
            <asp:Button ID="btnCopy" runat="server"
                Text="Same As Billing Address"
                OnClick="btnCopy_Click"
                CausesValidation="False" /><br />
        </div>
    </form>
</body>
</html>
```

This page contains an UpdatePanel control whose content template contains three labels: lblFirstLineShipping, lblSecondLineShipping, and lblThirdLineShipping. When the user clicks the button, called btnCopy, the function btnCopy_Click gets called.

As you can see in this function, the values of the labels outside the UpdatePanel control get copied into the labels inside. This triggers a partial refresh on the page, where the server updates only the contents of those three labels.

If you run the page, you'll see a screen like that in Figure 7-1.

Typically in an application like this, if you click the button to change the value of the shipping address labels, the entire page will be posted to and from the server. As the page is rerendered, the entire page will "blink" as the browser deletes the current markup and replaces it with the new one.

With Ajax, you could place the shipping address content within a named <div> element, and then the click of the button could make a call to a JavaScript function that does the copy and builds a new innerHTML property of that <div> element. Or, if the functionality was server side, it would generate a request on XMLHttpRequest and a callback for when the request is complete. The callback would then build HTML code to put on the innerHTML property of the named <div> element.

The latter is exactly how the Atlas UpdatePanel control works under the hood. It uses Web.WebForms.PageRequestManager to set up an asynchronous callback. If you use an HTTP sniffer and run the page in Listing 7-1, you will see the following markup at the bottom of the page:

```
<script type="text/javascript">

Web.WebForms.PageRequestManager._setupAsyncPostBacks(
    document.getElementById('form1'),
    'ScriptManager1', ['UpdatePanel1'], []);

</script>
```

Figure 7-1. *UpdatePanel demonstration*

But all the intricacies of building the HTML and updating the region of the page are handled for you, so you don't have to explicitly code all the asynchronous handling and HTML updating yourself.

Using a Task List Manager

The first reference application publicly available for Atlas was Scott Guthrie's task list manager, ToDo List. This application is a simple yet powerful demonstration of the power of the ASP.NET 2.0 framework and how easy it is to extend it for Ajax-style functionality using Atlas.

Figure 7-2 shows the main screen for this application. It shows a sortable list of tasks that you can add to, edit, or delete. It contains links to another page containing the subitems for a particular item (which you will look at a little later) and a link to an RSS document that is generated from this list.

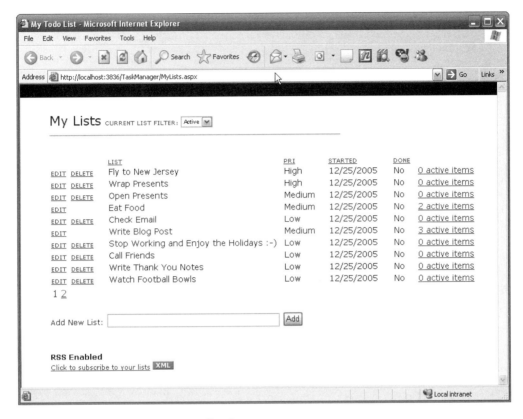

Figure 7-2. *The task list manager application*

Now, let's take a look at this page in the designer. You can see that in Figure 7-3.

The content is stored within a content pane that is hosted by the master page. Master pages in ASP.NET provide template functionality to your pages. If you look at the runtime in Figure 7-2, you will see that the page has a black header and styling that are missing in Figure 7-3. That's because they are implemented on the master page, and the master page defines a content area that changes from implementation page to implementation page. The master page also contains the Atlas ScriptManager control, so in case you noticed you couldn't see it in Figure 7-3, you'll find it on the master page.

This content area is what you see in Figure 7-3 as Content1.

Right at the bottom of the designer you'll see an ObjectDataSource control. An ObjectDataSource control allows you to create a declarative link between your web page controls and data access components that query and update data. It's flexible and can work with many different components, making it suitable for an application such as this one. This ObjectDataSource control ties to a SQL Server Express Edition database that contains the tables for the tasks and items lists.

As far as Atlas controls are concerned, you'll see that there are two UpdatePanel controls on this web form.

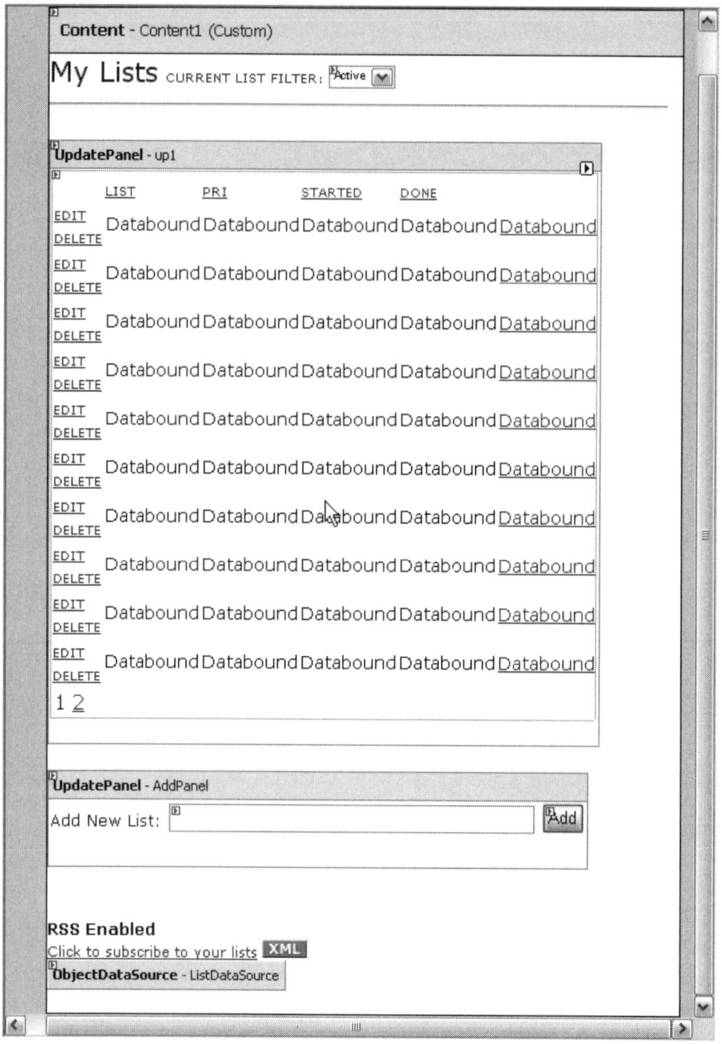

Figure 7-3. *Editing the task list in the ASP.NET designer*

The top UpdatePanel control contains an ASP.NET GridView control. Because it is in an UpdatePanel control and partial rendering is enabled, postbacks caused by actions on this panel should incur only partial refreshes, improving the user experience.

Let's take a look at the code for this UpdatePanel control. First you define the UpdatePanel control and give it the ID of up1:

```
<atlas:UpdatePanel ID="up1" runat="server">
```

Then you use the `<ContentTemplate>` child tag to insert the content you want to partially update. This will be a GridView control, called ListGrid, that will bind to the ObjectDataSource control you saw earlier. This object data source is called ListDataSource and is configured using the `<DataSourceID>` tag:

```
<ContentTemplate>

  <asp:GridView ID="ListGrid" BorderWidth="0px"
                runat="server" AutoGenerateColumns="False"
                DataKeyNames="ListId"
                DataSourceID="ListDataSource"
                AllowPaging="True"
                AllowSorting="True"
                EnableViewState="False"
                GridLines="None">
```

A GridView control defines its content using the <Columns> tag, and each child of this tag defines a column. The <EditItemTemplate> tags define what to present when the grid is in edit mode, and you will see that Update and Cancel link buttons are defined:

```
<Columns>
<asp:TemplateField ShowHeader="False">
<EditItemTemplate>
<asp:LinkButton ID="LinkButton1" runat="server"
    CausesValidation="True" CommandName="Update"
    Text="Update">
</asp:LinkButton>
<asp:LinkButton ID="LinkButton2" runat="server"
    CausesValidation="False" CommandName="Cancel"
    Text="Cancel">
</asp:LinkButton>
</EditItemTemplate>
```

The <ItemTemplate> tag defines what is visible when you are in view mode, showing the grid and the data on it:

```
<ItemTemplate>
<asp:LinkButton ID="LinkButton1" runat="server"
    CausesValidation="False" CommandName="Edit"
    Text="Edit">
</asp:LinkButton>
<asp:LinkButton ID="DeleteBtn"
    Visible='<%# IsDeleteBtnVisible( (int) Eval("ItemCount")) %>'
    runat="server" CausesValidation="False"
    CommandName="Delete" Text="Delete">
</asp:LinkButton>
</ItemTemplate>
<ControlStyle CssClass="buttons" />
<HeaderStyle CssClass="commands" />
</asp:TemplateField>
```

And here is the rest of the grid definition. You can see that it is a standard <asp:GridView> definition and that nothing special for Atlas has been added to it.

```
<asp:BoundField DataField="Name"  HeaderText="List"
                   SortExpression="Name" >
  <ControlStyle CssClass="name_edit" />
  <ItemStyle CssClass="name" />
  <HeaderStyle CssClass="name" />
</asp:BoundField>

<asp:TemplateField HeaderText="Pri"
                   SortExpression="Priority">
  <EditItemTemplate>
  <asp:DropDownList ID="DropDownList1" Width="75"
                   SelectedValue='<%# Bind("Priority") %>'
                   runat="server">
    <asp:ListItem Text="High" Value="3" />
    <asp:ListItem Text="Medium" Value="2" />
    <asp:ListItem Text="Low" Value="1" />
  </asp:DropDownList>
  </EditItemTemplate>
  <ItemTemplate>
  <asp:Label ID="pri"
             Text='<%# FormatPriority((int) Eval("Priority")) %>'
             runat="server" />
  </ItemTemplate>
  <ItemStyle CssClass="priority" />
  <HeaderStyle CssClass="priority" />
</asp:TemplateField>

<asp:BoundField DataField="DateCreated"
    DataFormatString="{0:MM/dd/yyyy}"
    HtmlEncode="False" HeaderText="Started"
    ReadOnly="True" SortExpression="DateCreated" >
  <ItemStyle CssClass="started" />
  <HeaderStyle CssClass="started" />
</asp:BoundField>

  <asp:TemplateField HeaderText="Done"
                   SortExpression="IsComplete">
  <EditItemTemplate>
    <asp:CheckBox ID="CheckBox1" runat="server"
        Checked='<%# Bind("IsComplete") %>' />
  </EditItemTemplate>
  <ItemStyle CssClass="iscomplete" />
  <HeaderStyle CssClass="iscomplete" />
  <ItemTemplate>
    <asp:Label ID="Done"
        Text='<%# FormatDone((bool) Eval("IsComplete")) %>'
        runat="server" />
  </ItemTemplate>
  </asp:TemplateField>
```

```
<asp:HyperLinkField DataTextField="ItemCount"
    DataTextFormatString="{0} active items"
    DataNavigateUrlFields="ListId"
    DataNavigateUrlFormatString="Items.aspx?ListId={0}" >
<ItemStyle CssClass="viewitems" />
</asp:HyperLinkField>

</Columns>
<EmptyDataTemplate>
  <span id="Empty">No lists</span>
</EmptyDataTemplate>

</asp:GridView>

</ContentTemplate>
```

Finally, you close the Atlas UpdatePanel control:

```
</atlas:UpdatePanel>
```

So, from the point of view of Atlas, this is a simple UpdatePanel control. No control event or control value triggers are defined, so postbacks caused by using the controls on the grid for sorting and editing will cause only a partial refresh on this page.

The other UpdatePanel control is a little more interesting. This is where you add a new item to the list and thus affect the grid and the first UpdatePanel that contains it.

Let's inspect the code for it. The first thing you will notice is that on the definition of the panel itself, Mode is set to Conditional. This means it will use triggers for updates. You'll look at the triggers in a moment.

```
<atlas:UpdatePanel ID="AddPanel"
    Mode="Conditional"
    runat="server">
```

The <ContentTemplate> element contains the definition of the HTML to show in the UpdatePanel control. From Figure 7-3 you can see that this is a text box where you can type a new item and an action button that allows you to define it. Here's the code:

```
<ContentTemplate>

  <span>Add New List:</span>
  <asp:TextBox ID="AddItemTxt"
      cssclass="newitem" runat="server">
  </asp:TextBox>
  <asp:Button ID="AddListBtn" runat="server"
      OnClick="AddListBtn_Click" Text="Add" />

</ContentTemplate>
```

Now come the triggers. The idea here is that you want to trigger an update upon the button being clicked. You define that as a ControlEventTrigger control (because the click is an event) using the `<atlas:ControlEventTrigger>` tag. The name of the button, as you saw previously, is AddListBtn, so you define the trigger like this:

```
<Triggers>
  <atlas:ControlEventTrigger ControlID="AddListBtn"
    EventName="Click" />
</Triggers>
```

Finally, you close the tag defining the UpdatePanel control:

```
</atlas:UpdatePanel>
```

Now what you might find interesting about this is that there is nowhere that you explicitly update the first panel. So how does it occur? If you look at the definition of AddListBtn, you'll see that it defines an event to happen when you click it with the OnClick attribute. Atlas is smart enough not to override this with the trigger, so two actions happen when you click the button. The ASP.NET onclick behavior fires and trips the server-side event handler, *and* the Atlas trigger fires to refresh UpdatePanel2.

The code on the server side for that button looks like this:

```
protected void AddListBtn_Click(object sender, EventArgs e) {

  ListsTableAdapters.ListsTableAdapter lists =
    new ListsTableAdapters.ListsTableAdapter();
  lists.Insert(Server.HtmlEncode(AddItemTxt.Text),
    1, false, DateTime.Now);

  AddItemTxt.Text = "";
  ListGrid.DataBind();
}
```

This code inserts a new field into the database, but it's the last two lines that are the most important when looking at this from an Atlas perspective. The first clears out the text box. But because the text box is in an UpdatePanel control, only a partial-page refresh will be triggered. The second binds the ListGrid to the data source; thus, the new item will be rendered. This also is in an UpdatePanel control, so it also will trigger only a partial-page update.

So, if you run the page and play with manipulating the grid by sorting and adding new items, you will see the partial updates in action, based on how they don't "blink" in the way you'd usually expect when adding or manipulating a GridView.

Figure 7-4 shows what happens when you add a new item, called My New Item, to the grid.

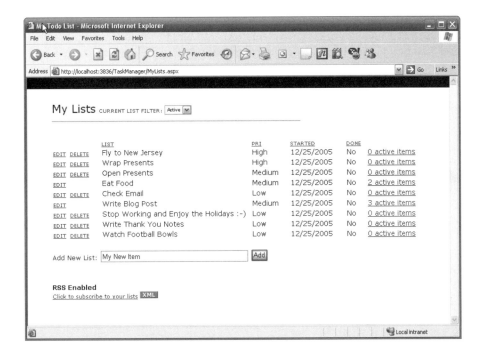

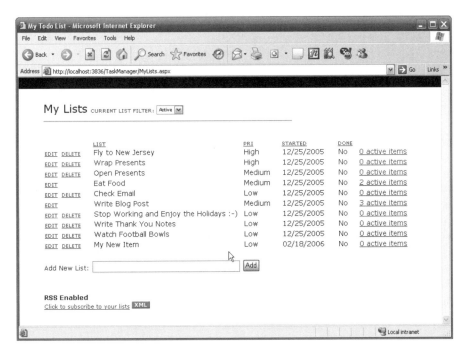

Figure 7-4. *Adding a new item to the list of tasks (first image). The new item now appears on the list (second image).*

The grid had defined an EditItemTemplate that shows how it should behave upon enter-
ing the edit context. This changes the Priority field from a straight text field to a drop-down
list. If you click Edit beside the My New Item field you just added, you will see this in action
(see Figure 7-5).

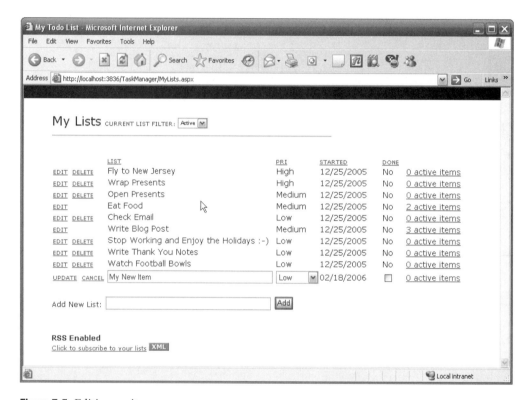

Figure 7-5. *Editing an item*

You can see that you can edit the text, the priority, or the status of the item (done or not).
Each of these actions will result in new data being passed to the database through the data
binding against the ObjectDataSource control and as such will trigger an update on the grid.
Again, because the grid is defined within an UpdatePanel control, this will just be a partial
update and will be cleaner, smoother, and in the style of Ajax.

Another web form in this application is the one that shows your active items under a
particular task. If you look at the Write Blog Post task, you will see that on the right side it has
a hyperlink that says "3 active items." If you click this link, you will be taken to the Items.aspx
page (see Figure 7-6).

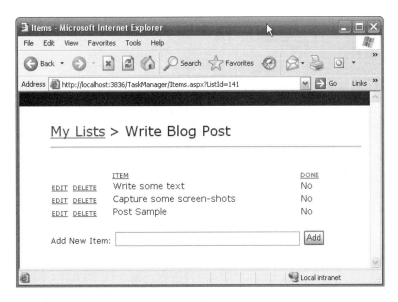

Figure 7-6. *Viewing items for a task*

Let's look at how this page is constructed. Figure 7-7 shows how it appears in the ASP.NET designer.

You will see some similarities between this and the tasks page discussed earlier. It derives from the same master page, so there is no ScriptManager control present. But it does have two UpdatePanel controls: one containing the data grid and one containing the controls that allow you to add a new item to the dataset to which the grid is bound. The data source is represented by an ObjectDataSource control in the same way as the earlier web form.

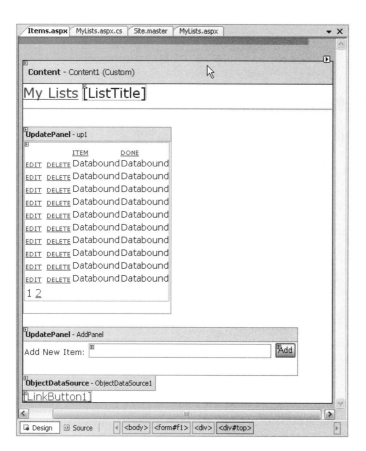

Figure 7-7. *Designing the items page*

The first UpdatePanel control works the same way as the one on the tasks page. Here's the code, with much of the details of the GridView definition omitted for clarity:

```
<atlas:UpdatePanel ID="up1" runat="server">

<ContentTemplate>

  <asp:GridView ID="ItemGrid" BorderWidth="0"
     runat="server" AutoGenerateColumns="False"
     DataKeyNames="ItemId" DataSourceID="ObjectDataSource1"
     AllowPaging="True" AllowSorting="True"
     EnableViewState="False" GridLines="None">

  <Columns>
     // Items Omitted for Clarity of text
  </Columns>
```

```
  <EmptyDataTemplate>
    <span id="Empty">There are no items in this list</span>
  </EmptyDataTemplate>

</asp:GridView>

</ContentTemplate>

</atlas:UpdatePanel>
```

The GridView control is bound to ObjectDataSource1, which in turn is bound to the Items dataset. Columns are set up as before with bindings to fields within the dataset and with an edit item template that provides the controls that allow these fields to be changed.

Because the grid is bound, changes to the underlying dataset will trigger a refresh to the grid and as such an update of the content. The only Atlas amendment you can see is that the whole thing has been embedded within an `<atlas:UpdatePanel>` element. This means that changes to the grid will trigger only a partial-page refresh.

The second UpdatePanel control contains the fields for adding new content to this grid within its `<ContentTemplate>` tag. Also, it is defined as a Conditional UpdatePanel control, meaning that the stimulus to update it will be a trigger.

```
<atlas:UpdatePanel ID="AddPanel"
      Mode="Conditional" runat="server">

  <ContentTemplate>

  <span>Add New Item:</span>
  <asp:TextBox ID="AddBtnTxt" cssclass="newitem"
      MaxLength="50" runat="server">
  </asp:TextBox>
  <asp:Button ID="AddItemBtn" runat="server"
      OnClick="AddItemBtn_Click" Text="Add" />

  </ContentTemplate>
```

The `<Triggers>` tag contains the trigger(s) used to invoke an update to this panel. Because you want to update based on clicking the Add button, you use the ControlEventTrigger type:

```
  <Triggers>
    <atlas:ControlEventTrigger
        ControlID="AddItemBtn" EventName="Click" />
  </Triggers>

</atlas:UpdatePanel>
```

Also, as you saw earlier, *two* things happen when you click the button. The click handler defined in the button's OnClick attribute will fire, as will the trigger defined on the UpdatePanel control. Again, and it is important to emphasize this, using Atlas to provide partial update and asynchronous functionality is extremely unobtrusive. You don't intercept or override the existing click functionality (or any other functionality, for that matter) and just enhance it by providing the additional tags used for the update functionality.

ToDoList is an excellent example of a small ASP.NET application and how it can be enhanced with Ajax functionality using Atlas. The server control set you saw in Chapter 6 has been carefully designed and implemented to allow you to enhance existing applications as easily as possible and in a manner that involves touching your existing code as little as possible. Additionally, for new applications, it involves reusing your existing skills in ASP.NET and lowers the learning curve drastically.

In the next example, you will look at the official reference application for Atlas—the Atlas wiki.

Using the Atlas Wiki Application

The Atlas wiki application is a reference application that demonstrates what a fully featured ASP.NET 2.0 application looks like and how it can be enhanced using Atlas. The Wiki Application was developed and demonstrated on the April CTP of Atlas. It is not presently available for the most recent CTP (July 2006), but may still be downloaded from `http://go.microsoft.com/fwlink/?LinkId=56430`. While it isn't supported on the most recent CTP, it is still worth investigating to learn how a real-world style application may be built using ASP.NET with the Atlas toolkit.

Getting Started with the Wiki Application

If you don't have it already, download the wiki template add-in for Visual Studio .NET from `http://atlas.asp.net`. Once you have installed this, you will be able to create the wiki application.

If you have this template installed, when you issue a File ➤ New command in Visual Studio .NET, you will be presented with the New Web Site dialog box, and it will give you an option to create a Wiki ASP.NET 'Atlas' Web Site, as shown in Figure 7-8.

This will create the entire wiki site for you. Select a location, and click OK.

The example is pretty comprehensive. Figure 7-9 shows the Solution Explorer for this site, and you can see that it contains a lot of good stuff, including master pages, templates, visual themes, back-end databases, controls, and of course web forms. Remember, this is first and foremost an ASP.NET application, built with existing ASP.NET skills and *enhanced* using Ajax/Atlas functionality.

When running the application, you should consider a number of issues.

Sometimes you will find that the browser renders this home page incorrectly when it is loaded for the first time. If this appears to be happening to you, simply click the browser's Refresh button. This should correct the page display. This problem, if it occurs at all, generally is a problem only once: when you load the wiki for the first time in a browser.

The wiki uses SQL Server 2005 Express Edition by default. The initial connection to the wiki's database sometimes times out in SQL Server. You will see a message in the browser about this if it happens. Simply click Refresh in the browser in this case.

If you have other database-related error messages, check that the wiki's App_Data directory permits write access for the anonymous Internet account on the computer. If you are running Windows XP, you will need to add the [server]\ASPNET account to the list of users allowed to write/modify the App_Data folder.

If you are running Windows Server 2003, you should add the [server]\NETWORK SERVICE account. Usually, however, the security settings on this folder are correct by default.

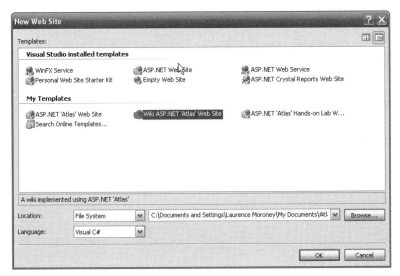

Figure 7-8. *Creating the wiki web site*

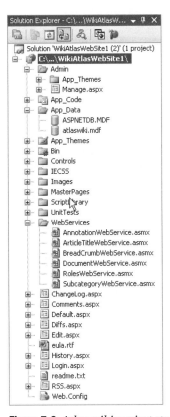

Figure 7-9. *Atlas wiki project structure*

Running the Wiki Application

When you run the wiki application, you will see a screen like in Figure 7-10.

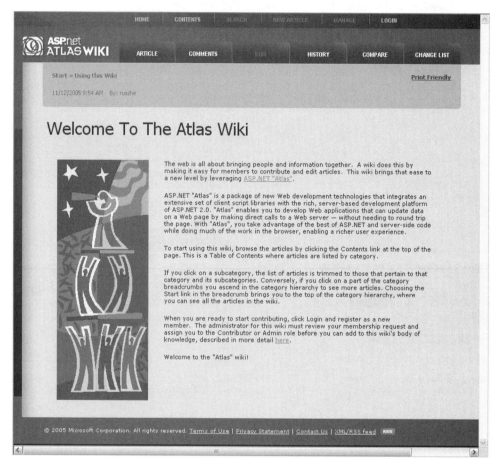

Figure 7-10. *The wiki application*

The first case where you can see some Ajax functionality in action is when you attempt to log in. If you haven't yet used the application or registered any users, try logging in with the username Arnie and any password (see Figure 7-11).

When you attempt to do this and log in, you'll see that the Login pane updates without a complete page refresh (see Figure 7-12).

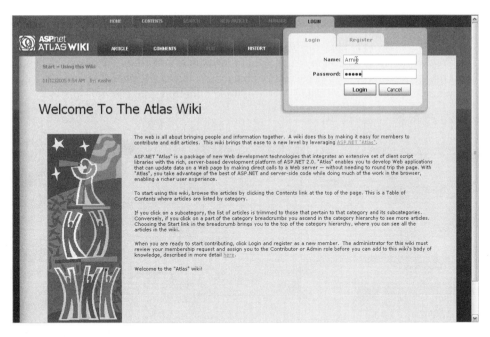

Figure 7-11. *Logging into the wiki application*

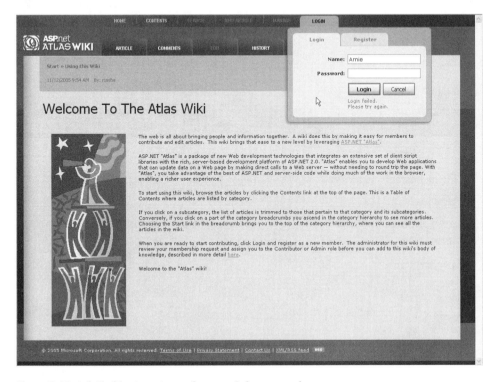

Figure 7-12. *A failed login using only a partial-page update*

Understanding the Login Asynchrony

Let's take a look at how the Login pane realizes this functionality.

The Login pane, along with many of the others, is actually implemented on the master page. This makes sense because you should be able to log in from anywhere. If you view the page Default.master in the ASP.NET designer, you'll see something like Figure 7-13.

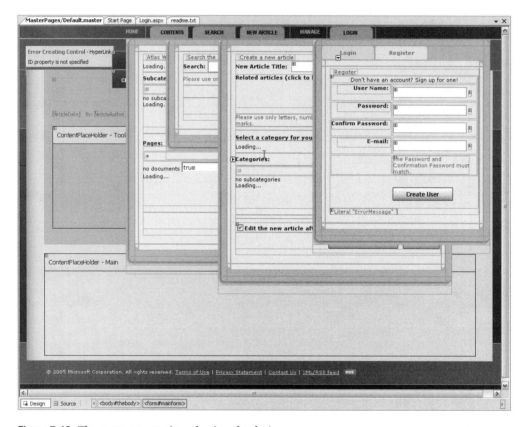

Figure 7-13. *The master page viewed using the designer*

If you look through the code for this page, you'll find the markup for the Login button. It looks like this:

```
<input type="button"
     class="button affirmative"
     id="loginBtn"
     onclick="return OnLogin();"
     value="Login" />
```

You can see that when you click this button, it calls the return Onlogin(); script. Let's take a look at that:

```
function OnLogin() {

  var usernameCtrl = $('username').control;
  var passwordCtrl = $('password').control;
  var loggingInMsgCtrl = $('loggingInMsg').control;
  var loginFailureMsgCtrl = $('loginFailureMsg').control;
  Web.TypeDescriptor.setProperty(loggingInMsgCtrl, 'style',
      'inline', 'display');
  Web.TypeDescriptor.setProperty(loginFailureMsgCtrl, 'style',
      'none', 'display');
  Web.Services.AuthenticationService.login(
      usernameCtrl.get_text(),
      passwordCtrl.get_text(),
      OnLoginComplete);
    return false;
}
```

This script first sets up four vars, each an instance of a control. The first two are the TextBox controls where the username and password are entered. The next two are simple Label controls that are used to mark the progress of the login. When you first click the button, it displays a "Logging in…" message. Later upon a failure, it indicates that you failed (as in Figure 7-12). These labels get referenced using the controls loggingInMsgCtrl and loginFailureMsgCtrl. The script then sets up how they should appear using their style properties.

Most interesting is the call to the web service that processes the login. This is performed in this line:

```
Web.Services.AuthenticationService.login(
      usernameCtrl.get_text(),
      passwordCtrl.get_text(),
      OnLoginComplete);
```

Web.Services.AuthenticationService is a static class contained in the AtlasRuntime.js file that allows you to authenticate using the ASP.NET 2.0 membership application service. You pass it the username and password and the name of the function to call once the logging in is complete. This allows your Atlas applications to use the standard ASP.NET 2.0 authentication system.

As you can see in this call, the script defines OnLoginComplete to handle the callback once the login is complete. Here's the OnLoginComplete script:

```
function OnLoginComplete() {
  var usernameCtrl = $('username').control;
  var passwordCtrl = $('password').control;

  Web.Services.AuthenticationService.validateUser(
      usernameCtrl.get_text(),
      passwordCtrl.get_text(),
      OnLoginValidationComplete);
  return false;
}
```

So, once the login is complete, the next thing it will do is validate the user, establishing not just their identity but also their permissions. You achieve this using the validateUser web method on the authentication service. This method also defines a function to call upon the service completion, again implementing asynchrony.

The function defined as the callback is OnValidationComplete. You can see it here:

```
function OnLoginValidationComplete(result) {
  var loggingInMsgCtrl = $('loggingInMsg').control;
  Web.TypeDescriptor.setProperty(loggingInMsgCtrl,
    'style', 'none', 'display');

  var usernameCtrl = $('username').control;
  var passwordCtrl = $('password').control;
  passwordCtrl.set_text('');
  if (result)
  {
    g_rolesRequest =
      RolesWebService.GetRoles(OnRolesObtained,
                    OnRolesAcquisionTimeout);
  }
  else
  {
    loginFailure();
  }
}
```

This creates a var that references the logging in the message control and sets its style. It then clears the username and password boxes. The function receives a Boolean value from the validation web service that will be true if the user is valid and false otherwise.

Should it be false, as in the case I'm demonstrating, the loginFailure() function will be called:

```
function loginFailure()
{
  var loginFailureMsgCtrl = $('loginFailureMsg').control;
  Web.TypeDescriptor.setProperty(loginFailureMsgCtrl,
      'style', 'inline', 'display');
}
```

This creates a control from the loginFailureMsg region of the page and sets its style to be visible:

```
<span id="loginFailureMsg"
      style="color: Red; display: none;">
      Login failed.<br />
      Please try again.
</span>
```

So, from this flow you can see how Atlas client-side controls, using web services, are providing asynchrony in a simple-to-use, simple-to-follow, and simple-to-understand manner.

Creating a Wiki User

Now that you've investigated the asynchronous login functionality, before you look into the rest of the functionality of Atlas, it's a good idea to create a real user.

You do this by first clicking the Register tab of the Login pane (see Figure 7-14).

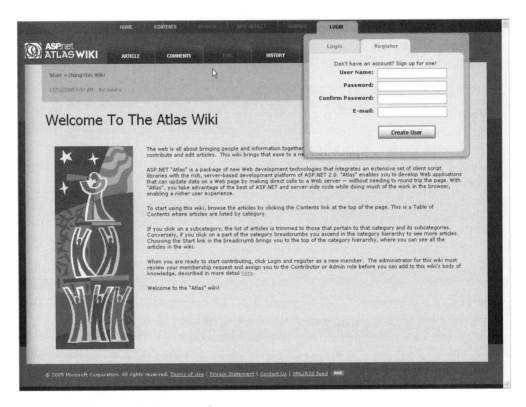

Figure 7-14. *Filling out the Register tab*

Fill these out with details for a wiki user. This will add the user to the database, but it will not give them any permissions. You'll see a dialog box like the one in Figure 7-15 when you create a user.

Figure 7-15. *Status dialog box when creating a new user*

Note that at this point you can log in to the wiki using the username and password you used when registering, but you cannot contribute to the wiki or be an administrator. To get these privileges, you use the ASP.NET 2.0 role management service to configure these users into roles that give them the required functionality.

To do this, select ASP.NET Configuration from the Website menu in Visual Studio .NET. This will take you to the ASP.NET Web Site Administration tool (see Figure 7-16).

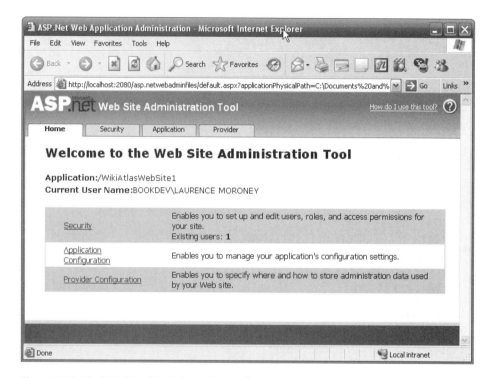

Figure 7-16. *The Web Site Administration tool*

Clicking the Security link on this screen will take you into the user configuration and security tool (see Figure 7-17).

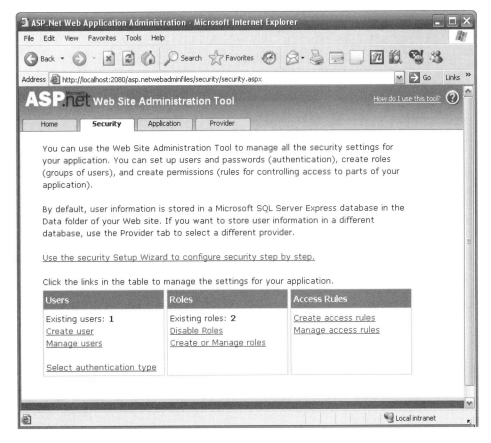

Figure 7-17. *Administering security*

From here, you can select Manage Users to put your new user(s) into their specific roles. This will take you to the user administration settings (see Figure 7-18).

You can see a list of users on this screen. In Figure 7-18, you can see the user Arnie that was created earlier. You can also see that Arnie isn't in any roles yet, so although he can log in and browse the wiki, he cannot be an administrator or contribute content.

If you click Edit User on this screen, you'll be taken to the screen shown in Figure 7-19, which allows you to set his role.

In this case, set the user to be an administrator. You can then sign in with Arnie and take a look at some more features of the wiki and in particular how you can make them Ajax-oriented using Atlas.

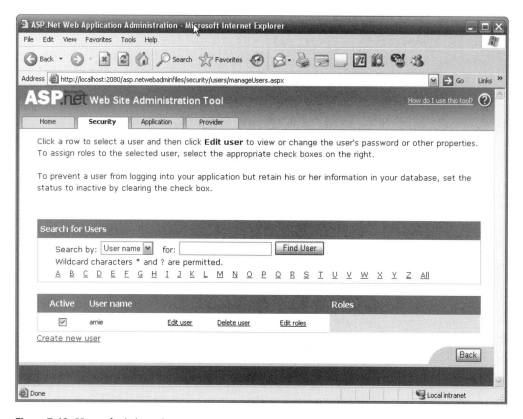

Figure 7-18. *User administration*

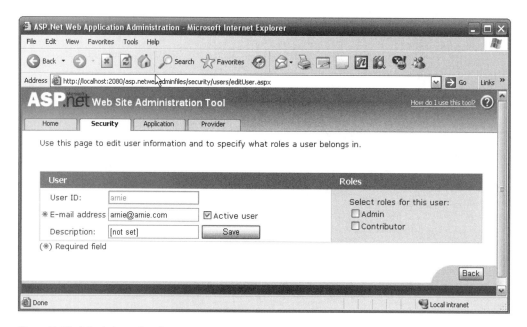

Figure 7-19. *Administration for a user*

Understanding the Create Article Asynchrony

Now that you have a new user who can log in and create articles, you can see a neat piece of asynchronous functionality. Click the New Article tab at the top of the page (see Figure 7-20).

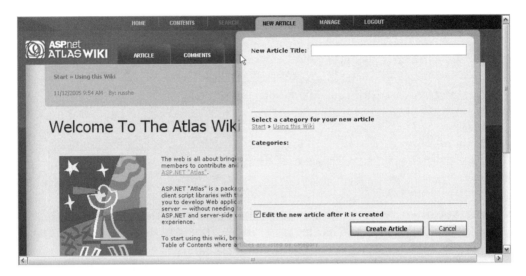

Figure 7-20. *Creating a new article*

When you type letters in the New Article Title text box, autocomplete will kick in and render similar articles in the space beneath. See Figure 7-21 for an example that works if you enter the letters *CRE*.

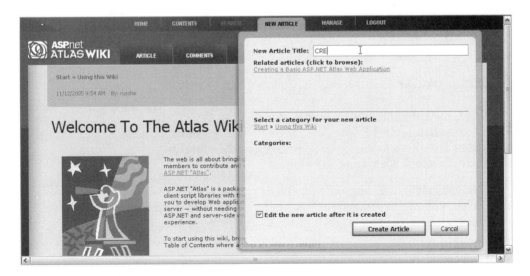

Figure 7-21. *The autocomplete functionality for the New Article Title text box*

Let's take a look at how this has been implemented using Atlas. This functionality, similar to the login functionality you saw earlier, is implemented on the master page. In this case, Atlas Script is used, and you can see the script here:

```
<textBox id="<%= titleTB.ClientID %>">
  <behaviors>
    <wiki:readOnlyAutoComplete
        completionList="newArticleTitleCompletionList"
        serviceURL="<%=ResolveUrl
          ("~/WebServices/ArticleTitleWebService.asmx") %>"
        serviceMethod="GetRelatedDocumentTitlesAsLinks"
        autoHideCompletionListElementParent="true" />
  </behaviors>
<validators>
  <regexValidator regex="/[A-Za-z\d \,\.\?]+/" />
</validators>
</textBox>
```

First it assigns the text box to point at a specific control. It does this using an evaluator that assigns the ID to the bizarre-looking `<%= titleTB.ClientID %>`, which evaluates the ID of the titleTB control and assigns it to the ID of the Atlas TextBox control.

This is good practice when you are using a master page scenario; because the ID is evaluated at runtime, you don't hard-code it at design time.

To get autocomplete functionality with this control, you use a behavior. However, as you'll see from the code, the behavior is a new one you haven't seen yet and is tagged as a `<wiki:readOnlyAutoComplete>` behavior.

The wiki: prefix indicates that it is a control in the wiki namespace, and this namespace is defined in JavaScript libraries as you saw in earlier chapters. In this case, the Editor.js and ReadOnlyAutoComplete.js files in the Controls directory define this namespace. If you look at ReadOnlyAutoComplete.js, you'll see this code:

```
Type.registerNamespace('Wiki');

Wiki.ReadOnlyAutoCompleteBehavior = function(associatedElement) {
    Wiki.ReadOnlyAutoCompleteBehavior.initializeBase(this);
...
Type.registerSealedClass('Wiki.ReadOnlyAutoCompleteBehavior',
        Web.UI.Behavior);
Web.TypeDescriptor.addType('wiki', 'readOnlyAutoComplete',
        Wiki.ReadOnlyAutoCompleteBehavior);
```

This implements the complete behavior. As you can see at the bottom, it is registered as a sealed class that derives from Web.UI.Behavior, making it an overridden behavior.

So, now that you know where this comes from, let's take a look at the behavior declaration again:

```
<wiki:readOnlyAutoComplete
       completionList="newArticleTitleCompletionList"
       serviceURL="<%=ResolveUrl
         ("~/WebServices/ArticleTitleWebService.asmx") %>"
       serviceMethod="GetRelatedDocumentTitlesAsLinks"
       autoHideCompletionListElementParent="true" />
```

The first parameter passed to it is the ID of another control: completionList. This specifies the target control for the results to get loaded into. If you recall from Figure 7-21, there's a big space under the text box where the results get loaded. This is the completion list, and the control loads the results of the autocomplete query into it.

The next parameter is serviceURL. This is the location of the web service that hosts the supporting functionality. Again, an evaluator is used to locate the absolute URI from the relative ~/WebService/ArticleTitleWebService.asmx. The control and behavior could conceivably be used on any page in the directory structure of the web site, so it's a good idea to use an absolute URI to describe the location of the web service.

The next parameter is serviceMethod, which as you can guess is the name of the service method to call. Now, you may remember that typing three letters into the text box triggered this behavior, so these letters should somehow be passed to the web service to determine the correct list of articles to return, but this isn't happening in any of these parameters, so how does the web service get them?

The answer is in the behavior definition itself. If you take a look at the this_onTimerTick definition in the implementation code, you'll see that it pulls the text from the parent control of the behavior. In this case, the parent control for the behavior is the text box, so it gets the text from there and passes it to the service to get the related articles.

Finally, the autoHideCompletionListElementParent attribute is set to True. This is a property on the behavior that overrides the base autocomplete behavior where a drop-down list appears on the parent control. When set to true, the list is hidden, which is logical, because in this case you don't want to show it and instead want to display the friendlier, richer text including the formatting and hyperlinks shown in Figure 7-21.

This example demonstrated the asynchronous updating of an area of the page using Atlas Script, custom behaviors, and back-end web services. You can see how straightforward it was to implement using scripting, with more complex functionality implemented using a custom behavior. It's recommended that you take a look at how the custom behavior was implemented to get a better understanding of how you can implement your own. In this case, the custom behavior was used to replace the base autocomplete behavior, as you've seen in earlier chapters, where the results are rendered in a drop-down list that's attached to the control. If you want to override this type of functionality (or any other behavior) with something different, then the object orientation that Atlas brings to JavaScript is an obvious candidate, and this is a great example. Here, the requirement was to render the results in a separate <div> element, where you can add formatting, hyperlinks, and so on, to the results.

Understanding the Table of Contents Asynchrony

Another place in the application where asynchrony occurs, powered by Atlas-style Ajax, is in rendering the table of contents for the wiki. You can see this screen by selecting the Contents tab at the top of the page (see Figure 7-22).

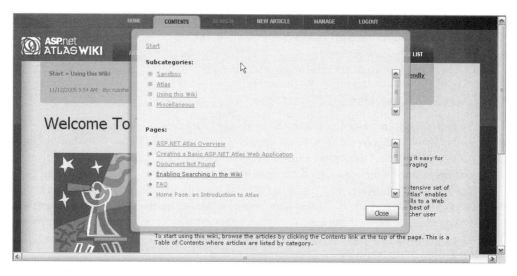

Figure 7-22. *The table of contents page*

As you select the links across the top, the subcategories pane gets populated, and as you select a subcategory, the pages section gets populated. This all happens cleanly and quickly without "blinks" or long refresh cycles due to full-page postbacks.

Let's take a look at how it works. The content pane is divided into three areas. The one at the top (which simply reads Start in Figure 7-22) is the breadcrumb trail showing the category and the path of subcategories used to get to the current position.

The second one, in the middle, is the list of subcategories of the currently selected category.

The third one, at the bottom, is the list of pages within the selected subcategory.

Each of these panes use Atlas-based data binding. (Chapter 8 covers data binding in more detail.)

All three use the same methodology to achieve this result. We'll look at the breadcrumb, because the principles are the same for the others.

The breadcrumb gets rendered in the <div> tag called results5. This tag has a control associated with it in Atlas Script:

```
<listView id="results5"
        itemTemplateParentElementId="resultsTemplateParent5">
  <bindings>
    <binding dataContext="breadCrumbSource5"
            dataPath="data"
            property="data"/>
  </bindings>
  <layoutTemplate >
    <template layoutElement="resultsTemplate5"/>
  </layoutTemplate >
```

```
    <itemTemplate>
      <template layoutElement="resultsItemTemplate5">
      <label id="resultsItemDelimiter5">
        <bindings>
          <binding dataPath="CategoryID"
                   property="text"
                   transform="XFormBreadCrumbDelimeter" />
        </bindings>
      </label>
      <hyperLink id="resultsItemLink5">
        <bindings>
          <binding dataPath="CategoryID"
                   property="navigateURL"
                   transform="XFormSubcategoryLink" />
        </bindings>
      </hyperLink>
      <label id="resultsItemLinkText5">
        <bindings>
          <binding dataPath="Title" property="text"/>
        </bindings>
      </label>
    </template>
    </itemTemplate>
</listView>
```

This control uses a binding called breadCrumbSource5, which is defined here:

```
<dataSource id="breadCrumbSource5"
        serviceURL="<%= ResolveUrl
           ("~/WebServices/BreadCrumbWebService.asmx") %>">
  <bindings>
    <binding dataContext="<%= navCategoryID.ClientID %>"
             dataPath="text"
             property="selectParameters"
             propertyKey="lowestCategoryID"/>
    <binding dataContext="<%= navDefaultDocumentTitle.ClientID %>"
             dataPath="text" property="selectParameters"
             propertyKey="defaultDocumentTitle"/>
  </bindings>
</dataSource>
```

This data source control defines its main data source as a web service at BreadCrumbWebService.asmx. It then binds the navCategoryID control and the navDefaultDocumentTitle control to the lowestCategoryID and defaultDocumentTitle fields returned by the selectParameters method on that web service.

Now, back at the results5 control, you can see that the listView control binds itself to this data source and implements a template that renders a number of hyperlinks. These links get bound to the navigateURL field coming back from the data source. They use a custom transform called XFormSubCategoryLink, which is defined using JavaScript on the master page like this:

```
function XFormSubcategoryLink(sender, eventArgs)
{
  var value = eventArgs.get_value();
  var str =
    'javascript:$("<%= navCategoryID.ClientID %>")
      .control.set_text(' + value + ');
        OnNavCategoryIDChanged(); void(0);';
    eventArgs.set_value(str);
}
```

For more about custom transforms, see Chapters 4 and 5.

Thus, using Atlas data binding, accompanied by custom transforms, the wiki application has been able to provide partial-page updates and refreshes using the data binding methodology. In the next chapter, you'll start looking at this data binding functionality in more detail and how it works in Atlas.

Summary

This chapter took you through some examples of realistic applications that use Atlas controls on the server and on the client. You began by looking at how you can do partial refreshes using the UpdatePanel control, before quickly moving into a couple of real-world use cases for ASP.NET applications, including how they can be enhanced by using Atlas.

In the first case you looked at a simple but powerful task list manager. You looked at how you can use ASP.NET to build this data-driven application and then how you can use Atlas to improve the user experience, making updates cleaner and more straightforward. You saw the important design concept of Atlas—that it can be used to enhance existing ASP.NET applications as unobtrusively as possible. You place new tags in parallel to your existing ones and point them at the existing ones to enable Ajax functionality, or you wrap your existing controls and markup in UpdatePanel controls to give them partial-refresh functionality. You also saw how by assigning triggers to common events such as button clicks, you can enhance the existing behavior on those events *without* rewriting the existing code that handles them.

In addition, you looked at the excellent Atlas wiki reference application that is one of the de facto applications for Atlas. This is a huge application, so the entire code wasn't explored, but three important areas that use three different technologies that empower Ajax functionality were explored: the login functionality, the article creation functionality, and the table of contents area.

It is strongly recommended that you look further into these examples using this chapter as a jumping-off point. Your ASP.NET and Atlas applications will be all the better for it!

CHAPTER 8

■■■

Data Binding in Atlas

Data is at the heart of every application. The key to providing productivity to the developer is making programming your application for data access as easy and as robust as possible. Microsoft tools, from the early days of Visual Basic, have had data binding at the core of the developer experience. The philosophy has been that data should be treated as an appliance. You plug your controls into the data, and they just work. How you achieve this is through defining your data source, pointing your controls at the data points on that data source that you want them to render and/or update, and letting the data binding engine take care of the rest.

Atlas is no different. It empowers your applications to use data to provide asynchronous updates to your pages (amongst other things), including direct connections to web services directly from your client applications. This alone is huge functionality. Previously if you wanted to present data from web services to your applications, you would have to create a server-side application such as a web form and use this to consume a server-side proxy that speaks to the web service on your behalf. Now you can go directly to the web service from your browser by using some of the Atlas client-side libraries or more implicitly by using data source controls that consume the web service on your behalf and to which you bind your controls. This is important because it brings a rich experience to your web application without involving postbacks to a web server application because the data transfer occurs between the browser and the data web service, without requiring a middle tier.

In this chapter, you will look at the client-side classes that are available to Atlas for managing data binding and how you can use them to build applications.

Specifically, you'll look into the following:

- The objects in the Sys.Data and Sys.UI.Data namespaces

- Manually binding the results from a web service to a ListView

- Using the DataSource control to connect to a database

- Using a ListView control to render items from a DataSource control

- Using an ItemView control to present single items from a DataSource control

- Using a DataTable control to render a grid of items

Introducing the Sys.Data Controls

The controls you can use for binding to databases and web service–based datasets are available in the Sys.Data namespace. They include the DataSource control for managing the connection and various controls for looking at columns, rows, tables, and views.

Introducing the DataSource Control

At the heart of all data binding in Atlas is the Sys.Data.DataSource control. This control creates the "connection" between your controls and the back-end datasets. It is an object and is implemented in Atlas in the Atlas.js script library.

The DataSource control exposes the events shown in Table 8-1.

Table 8-1. *DataSource Events*

Event Name	Function
propertyChanged	Fires when a property changes on the control
dataAvailable	Fires when the data source has data available to return

The DataSource control exposes the properties shown in Table 8-2.

Table 8-2. *DataSource Properties*

Property Name	Function
bindings	Returns an array of controls that are bound to this one.
dataContext	Gets or sets the current data context for this control. This is a specific object to which you want to pass the results.
id	Gets or sets the ID for this control.
data	Gets the data for this control.
isDirtyAndReady	Gets the status of the DataSource control. If it is dirty and ready, the control has data to write to the database and is ready to do so.
isReady	Gets the status of the data control and lets you know whether it is in a ready state to read or write data.
rowCount	Returns the number of rows that the source will expose on the next read.
serviceURL	Specifies the URI of the web service that will supply the data.
selectParameters	Gets the parameters that can be used for the select query.
serviceType	Gets or sets the type of service. This can be DataService or Handler. DataService can support reading and writing; Handler supports only reading. So if you have an XML data source that doesn't support updates, you can set serviceType to Handler.

The DataSource control exposes the methods shown in Table 8-3.

Table 8-3. *DataSource Methods*

Method Name	Description
Select()	Explicitly performs the selection of records according to the current criteria
Update()	Explicitly performs the writing and updating of the data source according to the current criteria

Introducing the DataView Control

The Sys.Data.DataView control offers a filtered view of your data. You can bind controls to this as an alternative to the data source should you want to filter the data. You can create filters using the DataFilter and PropertyFilter controls, which you will see in a moment.

This control exposes a single event (as shown in Table 8-4).

Table 8-4. *DataView Event*

Event Name	Description
propertyChanged	Fires when a property changes on the control

The DataView exposes the properties shown in Table 8-5.

Table 8-5. *DataView Properties*

Property Name	Description
bindings	Returns an array of controls that are bound to this one.
dataContext	Gets or sets the current data context for this control. This is a specific object to which you want to pass the results.
id	Gets or sets the ID for this control.
data	Returns a Sys.Data.DataTable control that contains the data for this control.
filteredData	Returns a Sys.Data.DataTable control that contains the filtered data for this control.
Filters	Specifies an array of filters. This uses .NET data filters that are similar in syntax to SQL. For more information, check your ASP.NET documentation for filtering and sorting.
length	Specifies the number of records to return.

You will have noticed that the DataSource and DataView controls return Sys.Data.DataTable objects. Let's look at these next.

Introducing the DataTable Control

This control is returned by the data and filteredData methods of the DataSource and DataView controls.

It exposes the events shown in Table 8-6.

Table 8-6. *DataTable Events*

Event Name	Description
collectionChanged	This event fires whenever the collection of columns has a change. It can be associated with an action to perform when this happens.
propertyChanged	This event fires whenever a property on the control changes. It can be used to trigger a custom action.

The properties shown in Table 8-7 are also available.

Table 8-7. *DataTable Properties*

Property Name	Description
columns	A read-only array of Sys.Data.DataColumn objects that contain the data columns.
keys	An array of strings containing the keys for this table.
length	The number of records in this table.
isDirty	If the table has updates that need to be written to the database, this flag will be true.

The DataTable control supports the methods shown in Table 8-8.

Table 8-8. *DataTable Methods*

Method Name	Description
Add()	Adds a new Sys.Data.DataRow to this table
Clear()	Removes all Sys.Data.DataRow items from this table
Remove(item)	Removes a specific Sys.Data.DataRow item from this table

Introducing the DataColumn Control

This control represents a column in a table. The columns property of the DataTable control will return an array of DataColumn controls.

The DataColumn control supports the properties shown in Table 8-9.

Table 8-9. *DataColumn Properties*

Property Name	Description
columnName	Returns a string containing the column name
dataType	Returns a Sys.Type object containing the data type
defaultValue	Returns the default value for this column

The control doesn't support any methods or events. It is simply used to get a better understanding of a specific column, returning its name, type, and default value.

Introducing the DataRow Control

This control allows you to query the specifics of a particular row. It supports three properties (as shown in Table 8-10).

Table 8-10. *DataRow Properties*

Property Name	Description
_isDirty	Returns true if the row has updated data that hasn't yet been written to the data source
_index	Returns the current index for this row
_rowObject	Returns the object containing the underlying row data

It also supports the event shown in Table 8-11.

Table 8-11. *DataRow Events*

Event Name	Description
propertyChanged	Fires whenever one of the properties of the event changes

Introducing the Sys.UI.Data Controls

Several controls within the Sys.UI.Data namespace provide visual links to your data. You will see examples of using these controls later in the chapter. But before you use them, it's a good idea to understand their interfaces.

Introducing the ItemView Control

You can bind the ItemView control to a `<div>` element in HTML and update it according to the settings within its `<itemTemplate>` child tag. This tag defines a series of controls and their bindings to the data property of the ItemView control. It is designed for viewing a single record at a time and is complemented by the ListView control, which is designed for viewing a range of records at a time.

The control exposes the properties shown in Table 8-12.

Table 8-12. *ItemView Properties*

Property Name	Description
Bindings	Returns an array specifying all the bindings of this control. When used in Atlas Script, this is a child tag that contains `<binding>` tags that define the bindings for this control.
dataContext	Gets or sets the dataContext for the binding.
id	Gets or sets the ID for the ItemView control.
associatedElement	Specifies the underlying `<div>` tag to which this ItemView control will push content.

Continued

Table 8-12. *Continued*

Property Name	Description
behaviors	Returns the behaviors associated with this control. When using Atlas Script, you can specify these behaviors using the `<behaviors>` child tag.
cssClass	Gets or sets the CSS class for this control.
enabled	Gets or sets the enablement of this control.
style	Reads the current CSS style for the control.
tabIndex	Gets or sets the position of this control in the tab index. This is the position that it occupies when the user moves through the UI using the Tab key.
visible	Gets or sets the visibility of the control. If this is false, you will not see the control.
visibilityMode	This can be set to Hide so the control is not seen or to Collapse so the control is minimized to its top label.
canMoveNext	If the current record is the last one in the record set, then you cannot move to the next record, and this will be false; otherwise, it will be true.
canMovePrevious	If the current record is the first one in the record set, then you cannot move to the previous record, and this will be false; otherwise, it will be true.
data	This is a Sys.Data.DataTable that contains the complete set of data that is currently loaded into the ItemView control. This is returned by a select query against the underlying data source.
dataIndex	Specifies the index of the currently selected item in the data source.
dataItem	Specifies the currently selected row on the data source.
length	Specifies the number of rows in the data table within the data property.
itemTemplate	Specifies the template for the items that will be rendered within the ItemView control. It uses the `<itemTemplate>` child tag within Atlas Script, and each `<itemTemplate>` will contain a number of child controls.
emptyTemplate	Specifies what to render within the ItemView control if there are no records within the data.

The ItemView control exposes a single event (as shown in Table 8-13).

Table 8-13. *ItemView Event*

Event Name	Description
propertyChanged	Fires whenever a property of the ItemView control changes

The ItemView control provides several methods (as shown in Table 8-14).

Table 8-14. *ItemView Methods*

Method Name	Description
addCssClass(String className)	Adds the specified CSS class to the ItemView control. Can be used to (for example) change the style of the control based on the current circumstances, such as changing the color to red if the dataset is currently dirty.
focus()	Passes the cursor to this control.
scrollIntoView()	If the control is off the screen, scrolls the browser until it is visible.
removeCssClass(String className)	Removes the specified CSS from the ItemView control. In a similar manner to addCssClass, you can change the visual state of the control based on the current circumstances.
toggleCssClass	Complements the add and remove CSS class methods. If the class is currently active, this will turn it off; otherwise, it will turn it on.
addItem()	Adds a new item to the underlying dataset. This will make the dataset dirty.
deleteCurrentItem()	Removes the current item. This will make the dataset dirty.
moveNext()	Moves to the next record in the dataset and triggers the binding of all controls within the ItemTemplate that are bound to it.
movePrevious()	Moves to the previous record in the dataset and triggers the binding of all controls within the ItemTemplate that are bound to it.

Introducing the ListView Control

The Sys.UI.Data.ListView control complements the ItemView control. This allows you to view a range of records that are selected by the bound DataSource control.

The control exposes the properties shown in Table 8-15.

Table 8-15. *ListView Properties*

Property Name	Description
Bindings	Returns an array specifying all the bindings of this control. When used in Atlas Script, this is a child tag that contains `<binding>` tags that define the bindings for this control.
dataContext	Gets or sets the data context for the binding.
id	Gets or sets the ID for the ListView control.
associatedElement	Specifies the underlying `<div>` tag to which this ListView control will push content.
behaviors	Returns the behaviors associated with this control. When using Atlas Script, you can specify these behaviors using the `<behaviors>` child tag.

Continued

Table 8-15. *Continued*

Property Name	Description
cssClass	Gets or sets the CSS class for this control.
enabled	Gets or sets the enablement of this control.
style	Reads the current CSS style for the control.
tabIndex	Gets or sets the position of this control in the tab index. This is the position that it occupies when the user moves through the UI using the Tab key.
visible	Gets or sets the visibility of the control. If this is false, you will not see the control.
visibilityMode	This can be set to Hide so the control is not seen or to Collapse so the control is minimized to its top label.
canMoveNext	If the current record is the last one in the record set, then you cannot move to the next record, and this will be false; otherwise, it will be true.
canMovePrevious	If the current record is the first one in the record set, then you cannot move to the previous record, and this will be false; otherwise, it will be true.
data	This is a Sys.Data.DataTable that contains the complete set of data that is currently loaded into the ListView control. This is returned by a select query against the underlying data source.
dataIndex	Specifies the index of the currently selected item in the data source.
dataItem	Specifies the currently selected row on the data source.
length	Specifies the number of rows in the data table within the data property.
alternatingItemCssClass	As this control renders a range of items, you can create a different style for alternating rows, giving a "striped" appearance that makes it easier to distinguish the data from different rows. You specify that using a CSS class with this property.
layoutTemplate	This specifies how the range of items will be laid out. It is implemented in Atlas Script using the child tag `<layoutTemplate>` that specifies the HTML for how the bound controls will appear.
itemCssClass	This specifies the CSS for individual items within the range. It is complemented by alternatingItemCssClass.
itemTemplate	Specifies the template for the items that will be rendered within the ItemView control. It uses the `<itemTemplate>` child tag within Atlas Script, and each `<itemTemplate>` will contain a number of child controls.
emptyTemplate	Specifies what to render within the ListView control if there are no records within the data.
selectedItemCssClass	Specifies the CSS class for the selected item. Can be used to highlight the selected item against the range of existing items.
separatorCssClass	This specifies how columns will be visually separated.
separatorTemplate	Defines the HTML code for the column separators. Complements separatorCssClass.

The ListView control exposes a single event (as shown in Table 8-16).

Table 8-16. *ListView Events*

Event Name	Description
propertyChanged	Fires whenever a property of the ListView control changes

The ListView control provides several methods (as shown in Table 8-17).

Table 8-17. *ListView Methods*

Method Name	Description
addCssClass(String className)	Adds the specified CSS class to the ListView control. Can be used to (for example) change the style of the control based on the current circumstances, such as changing the color to red if the dataset is currently dirty.
focus()	Passes the cursor to this control.
scrollIntoView()	If the control is off the screen, scrolls the browser until it is visible.
removeCssClass(String className)	Removes the specified CSS from the ItemView control. In a similar manner to addCssClass, you can change the visual state of the control based on the current circumstances.
toggleCssClass	Complements the add and remove CSS class methods. If the class is currently active, this will turn it off; otherwise, it will turn it on.
addItem()	Adds a new item to the underlying dataset. This will make the dataset dirty.
deleteCurrentItem()	Removes the current item. This will make the dataset dirty.
moveNext()	Moves to the next record in the dataset and triggers the binding of all controls within the ItemTemplate that are bound to it.
movePrevious()	Moves to the previous record in the dataset and triggers the binding of all controls within the ItemTemplate that are bound to it.

Getting Started with Data Binding

This example implements a simple search engine that allows you to query a list of animals. You can search for a particular type of animal, and it will return a list of animals of that type, including data about the animal such as its name and color.

You can see it in action in Figure 8-1.

This example also implements autocomplete functionality, as shown in Figure 8-2.

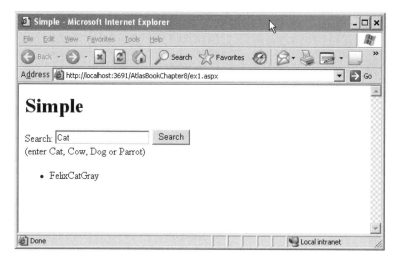

Figure 8-1. *The simple data-bound search engine showing results*

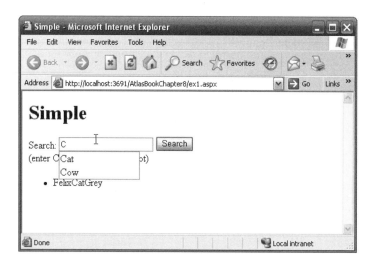

Figure 8-2. *The data-bound application showing autocomplete functionality*

Both of these pieces of functionality are served by a web service to which the controls will bind. Listing 8-1 shows the complete code for the web service.

Listing 8-1. *Data Web Service*

```
using System;
using System.Web;
using System.Collections;
using System.Collections.Generic;
using System.Web.Services;
using System.Web.Services.Protocols;
```

```
namespace Quickstart.Samples.Data
{

  public class Animal
  {
    String _name;
    String _category;
    String _color;

    public Animal()
    {
    }
    public String Name
    {
      get { return _name; }
      set { _name = value; }
    }

    public String Category
    {
      get { return _category; }
      set { _category = value; }
    }

    public String Color
    {
      get { return _color; }
      set { _color = value; }
    }

    public Animal(String name, String category, String color)
    {
      _name = name;
      _category = category;
      _color = color;
    }
  }
}

[WebService(Namespace = "http://tempuri.org/")]
[WebServiceBinding(ConformsTo = WsiProfiles.BasicProfile1_1)]
public class AnimalService : System.Web.Services.WebService
{
[WebMethod]
public string[] GetCompletionList(string prefixText, int count)
{
  prefixText = prefixText.ToLower();
  string[] categories = {
```

```
          "Cat",
          "Dog",
          "Cow",
          "Parrot",
    };

    List<string> suggestions = new List<string>();
    foreach (string category in categories)
    {
      if (category.ToLower().StartsWith(prefixText))
      {
        suggestions.Add(category);
      }
    }
    return suggestions.ToArray();
}

[WebMethod]
public Animal[] GetAnimals(String searchText)
{
  List<Animal> _data = GetAllAnimals();

  if (String.IsNullOrEmpty(searchText))
  {
    return _data.ToArray();
  }

  List<Animal> _dataFiltered = new List<Animal>();
  foreach (Animal animal in _data)
  {
    if (searchText.ToLower().
        CompareTo(animal.Category.ToLower()) == 0)
      _dataFiltered.Add(animal);
  }

   return _dataFiltered.ToArray();
}

  List<Animal> GetAllAnimals()
  {
    List<Animal> _data = new List<Animal>();

    _data.Add(new Animal("Felix", "Cat", "Gray"));
    _data.Add(new Animal("Fido", "Dog", "Brown"));
    _data.Add(new Animal("Rover", "Dog", "Brown"));
    _data.Add(new Animal("Daisy", "Cow", "Black and White"));
    _data.Add(new Animal("Polly", "Parrot", "Green"));
```

```
      return _data;
   }
 }
}
```

You can also find this code in the download for this book or in the QuickStart samples at http://atlas.asp.net.

This web service implements two web methods that will be used in the data binding scenario. The first, GetCompletionList, services the autocomplete functionality of the text box that is used in the application.

The autocomplete functionality is straightforward; you've seen an example of the <autoComplete> behavior:

```
<textBox id="Text1" targetElement="Text1">
  <behaviors>
    <autoComplete serviceURL="AnimalService.asmx"
                  serviceMethod="GetCompletionList"
                  minimumPrefixLength="1"
                  completionList="Text1__autocomplete" />
  </behaviors>
</textBox>
```

As you can see, the <autoComplete> behavior points the serviceURL at the web service that was listed in Listing 8-1. The serviceMethod attribute specifies which web method to call, and in this case it is GetCompletionList, which you can see in Listing 8-1. The minimumPrefixLength attribute specifies the number of characters that the user will enter before the autocompletion behavior kicks in. Finally, the completionList parameter specifies the name of the control that contains the completion list. On this page, it is a <span> element immediately after the text box, as shown in the HTML markup here:

```
<div id="header">
Search:
<input id="Text1" type="text" />
<span id="Text1__autocomplete"></span>
<input id="Button1" type="button"
       value="Search"
       onclick="Button1_onclick();" />
<br />(enter Cat, Cow, Dog or Parrot)
</div>
```

The search results works in a similar way. The HTML markup that specifies how the page will appear is as follows:

```
<!-- Main Content -->
<div id="content">
 <div class="left">
  <div id="searchResults">
  </div>
  <div style="display: none;">
  <div id="searchResults_layoutTemplate">
```

```
    <ul id="searchResults_itemTemplateParent">
      <li id="searchResults_itemTemplate">
        <span id="searchResults_Name"></span>
        <span id="searchResults_Category"></span>
        <span id="searchResults_Color"></span>
      </li>
    </ul>
  </div>
  </div>
 </div>
</div>
```

And here is the Atlas Script that creates the list on the page using this HTML markup:

```
<listView id="searchResults"
          cssClass="listView"
          targetElement="searchResults"
          itemTemplateParentElementId="searchResults_itemTemplateParent"
          alternatingItemCssClass="alternatingItem" itemCssClass="item">
  <layoutTemplate>
    <template layoutElement="searchResults_layoutTemplate" />
  </layoutTemplate>
  <itemTemplate>
    <template layoutElement="searchResults_itemTemplate">
    <label targetElement="searchResults_Name">
      <bindings>
        <binding dataPath="Name" property="text" />
      </bindings>
    </label>
    <label targetElement="searchResults_Category">
      <bindings>
        <binding dataPath="Category" property="text" />
      </bindings>
    </label>
    <label cssClass="bar" targetElement="searchResults_Color">
      <bindings>
        <binding dataPath="Color" property="text" />
      </bindings>
    </label>
    </template>
  </itemTemplate>
</listView>
```

This uses a ListView control that wraps the underlying markup on the page, which is shown here:

```
<div style="display: none;">
  <div id="searchResults_layoutTemplate">
    <ul id="searchResults_itemTemplateParent">
      <li id="searchResults_itemTemplate">
        <span id="searchResults_Name"></span>
        <span id="searchResults_Category"></span>
        <span id="searchResults_Color"></span>
      </li>
    </ul>
  </div>
</div>
```

As you can see, this is an HTML list (`<ul>`) containing a number of list items (`<li>`).

The ListView control contains an item template that fills out this list with three Label controls, with each Label control corresponding to one of the `<span>` elements (such as searchResults_Name) and binding it to a field from the data source.

For example, the name of the animal gets bound to the correct `<span>` element using this definition:

```
<label targetElement="searchResults_Name">
  <bindings>
    <binding dataPath="Name" property="text" />
  </bindings>
</label>
```

Now you might be wondering, how does it get the data? There is no binding to the web service here, so what is going on?

The answer lies in the functionality of the page. This list gets populated upon clicking the button, so let's look at the code behind the button.

It's implemented as a JavaScript function, as shown here:

```
<script language="javascript" type="text/javascript">
  function Button1_onclick()
  {
    Quickstart.Samples.Data.AnimalService.
        GetAnimals(document.getElementById("Text1").value,
        onSearchComplete);
  }

  function onSearchComplete(results)
  {
    var searchResults = document.getElementById("searchResults");
    searchResults.control.set_data(results);
  }
    </script>
```

You can see that when you click the button, the web method GetAnimals is called. The web service is available to script using the following include command (earlier in the page):

```
<atlas:ScriptManager ID="scriptManager" runat="server">
  <Services>
    <atlas:ServiceReference Path="AnimalService.asmx" />
  </Services>
</atlas:ScriptManager>
```

Creating this service reference means that JavaScript functions can now call the web service using its fully qualified name. You can see that the contents of the Text1 text box are passed as the first parameter to the web service, and the second parameter is the name of the callback function.

The callback function, onSearchComplete, then gets the searchResults element and calls the set_data function on it.

The set_data function allows you to explicitly define the data for a control. It uses the same mechanism as data binding but can be used to perform late binding. In other words, you may not have the data at the beginning of the page session, and it arises only as a result of user input. In this case, the data is returned as a parameterized query that involves the user specifying the parameter.

As such, it is ideally suited for this late binding of data, and when the set_data() method is called on the control, it triggers all the bindings as if it were a typical data binding scenario, and the data gets written to the page.

In the next example, you will look at the DataSource control and see how you can use it to consume data that has been exposed.

Using the DataSource Control

In this example, you will create a web service that exposes two special types of web methods (GetData and SaveData) that a data source can use to bind to them. In this case, the web service behaves like a database, so the binding can occur along with Select, Insert, Update, and Remove statements.

The first example will show an HTML list being bound to the data source. This will demonstrate a Select statement being used to show a large range of data. Later you will look at an ItemSelect control that allows you to perform similar functionality to a DataNavigator control, such as moving through a dataset, editing records, and updating records.

Figure 8-3 shows the HTML list, which is bound to the DataSource control.

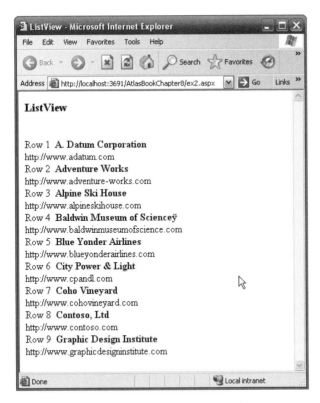

Figure 8-3. *A ListView control bound to the web service DataSource control*

Before seeing the client-side code that provides the binding, you'll look at the data service itself so you can understand how the data gets bound to it.

Listing 8-2 shows the full source code for the service.

Listing 8-2. *Data Service*

```
using System;
using System.Collections;
using System.Collections.Generic;
using System.ComponentModel;
using System.IO;
using System.Web;
using System.Web.Caching;
using System.Web.Services;
using System.Web.Services.Protocols;
using Microsoft.Web.Services;
```

```csharp
[WebService(Namespace = "http://tempuri.org/")]
[WebServiceBinding(ConformsTo = WsiProfiles.BasicProfile1_1)]
public class SampleDataService : DataService
{
  static List<SampleRow> _data;
  static int _nextId;
  static object _dataLock = new object();

  private static List<SampleRow> Data
  {
    get
    {
      if (_data == null)
      {
        lock (_dataLock)
        {
          if (_data == null)
          {
            _data = new List<SampleRow>();
            _data.Add(new SampleRow(0, "A. Datum Corporation",
                      "http://www.adatum.com"));
            _data.Add(new SampleRow(1, "Adventure Works",
                      "http://www.adventure-works.com"));
            _data.Add(new SampleRow(2, "Alpine Ski House",
                      "http://www.alpineskihouse.com"));
            _data.Add(new SampleRow(3,
                      "Baldwin Museum of Science",
                      "http://www.baldwinmuseumofscience.com"));
            _data.Add(new SampleRow(4, "Blue Yonder Airlines",
                      "http://www.blueyonderairlines.com"));
            _data.Add(new SampleRow(5, "City Power & Light",
                      "http://www.cpandl.com"));
            _data.Add(new SampleRow(6, "Coho Vineyard",
                      "http://www.cohovineyard.com"));
            _data.Add(new SampleRow(7, "Contoso, Ltd",
                      "http://www.contoso.com"));
            _data.Add(new SampleRow(8, "Graphic Design Institute",
                      "http://www.graphicdesigninstitute.com"));
            _nextId = 9;
          }
        }
      }
      return _data;
    }
  }
}
```

```
[DataObjectMethod(DataObjectMethodType.Delete)]
public void DeleteRow(int id)
{
  foreach (SampleRow row in _data)
  {
    if (row.Id == id)
    {
      lock (_dataLock)
      {
        _data.Remove(row);
      }
      break;
    }
  }
}

[DataObjectMethod(DataObjectMethodType.Select)]
public SampleRow[] SelectRows()
{
  return SampleDataService.Data.ToArray();
}

[DataObjectMethod(DataObjectMethodType.Insert)]
public SampleRow InsertRow(string organization, string url)
{
  SampleRow newRow;
  lock (_dataLock)
  {
    newRow = new SampleRow(_nextId++, organization, url);
    _data.Add(newRow);
  }
  return newRow;
}

[DataObjectMethod(DataObjectMethodType.Update)]
public void UpdateRow(SampleRow updateRow)
{
  foreach (SampleRow row in _data)
  {
    if (row.Id == updateRow.Id)
    {
      row.Name = updateRow.Name;
      row.Description = updateRow.Description;
      break;
    }
  }
}
```

A helper class, called SampleRow, represents the data:

```
using System;
using System.Collections;
using System.Collections.Generic;
using System.ComponentModel;
public class SampleRow
{
  private string _name;
  private string _description;
  private int _id;

  [DataObjectField(true, true)]
  public int Id
  {
    get { return _id; }
    set { _id = value; }
  }

  [DataObjectField(false)]
  [DefaultValue("New row")]
  public string Name
  {
    get { return _name; }
    set { _name = value; }
  }

  [DataObjectField(false)]
  [DefaultValue("")]
  public string Description
  {
    get { return _description; }
    set { _description = value; }
  }

  public SampleRow()
  {
    _id = -1;
  }

  public SampleRow(int id, string name, string description)
  {
    _id = id;
    _name = name;
    _description = description;
  }
}
```

You'll notice that the web service doesn't expose web methods in a typical manner. In this case, the web service is derived from DataService, and the methods are attributed using [DataObjectMethod]. These are used by the ObjectDataSource control to expose methods that are treated as Select, Insert, Update, or Delete.

For more information about these, take a look at MSDN (in particular at `http://msdn2.microsoft.com/en-us/library/57hkzhy5.aspx`).

Also note that for the sake of simplicity, this example uses an in-memory data source, which is a static array of SampleRow objects. This makes it a stateful web service, which typically isn't good practice!

Now let's look at the data source control and how it is used to bind the HTML list to this data so that you can get results like those you saw in Figure 8-3.

Let's start by looking at the HTML for the page:

```
<div id="dataContents">
</div>

<div style="visibility:hidden;display:none">
  <div id="masterTemplate">
    <div id="masterItemTemplate">
      Row <span id="masterIndex"></span>  
      <b><span id="masterName"></span></b><br />
      <span id="masterDescription"></span><br />
    </div><br/>
  </div>
  <div id="masterNoDataTemplate">No data</div>
</div>
```

This defines two `<div>` elements. The first is dataContents, which will contain the rendered results. The second is masterTemplate, which defines the template for how the data will appear. Both of these elements will have Atlas client controls mapped to them.

Let's look at the Atlas Script code that maps to these elements and binds to the data source:

```
<script type="text/xml-script">
<page xmlns:script="http://schemas.microsoft.com/xml-script/2005">
<components>
  <dataSource id="dataSource"
              serviceURL="SampleDataService.asmx"
              propertyChanged="onChange"/>

  <listView id="masterRepeater"
            targetElement="dataContents"
            itemTemplateParentElementId="masterTemplate"
            propertyChanged="onChange">
    <bindings>
      <binding dataContext="dataSource"
               dataPath="data" property="data"/>
    </bindings>
```

```
      <layoutTemplate>
        <template layoutElement="masterTemplate"/>
      </layoutTemplate>
      <itemTemplate>
        <template layoutElement="masterItemTemplate">
          <label targetElement="masterIndex">
            <bindings>
              <binding dataPath="Id"
                       transform="Add"
                       property="text"/>
            </bindings>
          </label>
          <label targetElement="masterName">
            <bindings>
              <binding dataPath="Name"
                       property="text"/>
            </bindings>
          </label>
          <label targetElement="masterDescription">
            <bindings>
              <binding dataPath="Description"
                       property="text"/>
            </bindings>
          </label>
        </template>
      </itemTemplate>
      <emptyTemplate>
        <template layoutElement="masterNoDataTemplate"/>
      </emptyTemplate>
    </listView>

<application>
  <load>
    <invokeMethod target="dataSource"
                  method="select"/>
  </load>
</application>
</components>
</page>
</script>
```

You can see at the bottom of the script that the action to invoke upon the application loading is the select method on the dataSource control. This will bind the dataSource to the data service and call the select method, which returns all the available rows.

Now, if you remember the HTML, there was this peculiar-looking tag:

```
<div id="dataContents">
</div>
```

It seems pretty odd that there would be a <div> element on the page that contains nothing. All is explained when you look at the Atlas ListView control as defined in the script. It wraps this underlying <div> element, as you can see here:

```
<listView id="masterRepeater"
          targetElement="dataContents"
          itemTemplateParentElementId="masterTemplate"
          propertyChanged="onChange">
```

The target element for the ListView control is specified as dataContents, which means the underlying <div> element, which appears empty, will be treated by Atlas as a ListView control. This list will use an item template to define its contents. The item template is called masterTemplate. Additionally, the bindings for the ListView control are set up, and in this case the control is being bound to the DataSource control. You can see this in the <bindings> tag, as shown here:

```
<bindings>
  <binding dataContext="dataSource"
          dataPath="data" property="data"/>
</bindings>
```

By setting the dataPath to data, you are binding to the data property that is being exposed by the data source. As you saw earlier in this chapter, that property returns the dataset that the dataSource exposes from the underlying data source. It binds it to the data property of the ListView control. As shown in the earlier example, this property was explicitly set in the JavaScript that fires when the page loads.

When the data property is set on a control, as is the case with the ListView control here, template properties can then be bound to the local data property, and the columns on that property can be specified using the dataPath property. So the following item on the template will create a <label> element that is bound to the Name column on the data property of the parent control, which in this case is bound to the Name column on the data source:

```
<label targetElement="masterName">
  <bindings>
    <binding dataPath="Name"
            property="text"/>
  </bindings>
</label>
```

This maps to the text property of the <label> element.

As a result, the template drives the generation of labels within its parent control, and the empty <div> element you saw earlier gets filled up with the data that is served by the underlying data source.

As such, the web service, which is hard-coded to return nine data items, will cause nine sets of labels to be generated within this <div> element, rendering the results of the selection against the data in the manner specified by the template. If you refer to Figure 8-3 again, the code-behind that gets generated at runtime doesn't contain any of the data. The <div> element is still empty.

What happens when the query is made for the binding is that the following data gets posted back to Atlas. This data then gets drawn on the innerHTML of the <div> element at runtime but isn't visible in Source view. If you perform an HTTP sniff of the interaction between the browser and the server, you'll see it, as shown here:

```
new Sys.Data.DataTable(
  [{"Id":0,
    "Name":"A. Datum Corporation",
    "Description":"http://www.adatum.com"},
   {"Id":1,
    "Name":"Adventure Works",
    "Description":"http://www.adventure-works.com"},
   {"Id":2,
    "Name":"Alpine Ski House",
    "Description":"http://www.alpineskihouse.com"},
   {"Id":3,
    "Name":"Baldwin Museum of Science",
    "Description":"http://www.baldwinmuseumofscience.com"},
   {"Id":4,
    "Name":"Blue Yonder Airlines",
    "Description":"http://www.blueyonderairlines.com"},
   {"Id":5,
    "Name":"City Power & Light",
    "Description":"http://www.cpandl.com"},
   {"Id":6,
    "Name":"Coho Vineyard",
    "Description":"http://www.cohovineyard.com"},
   {"Id":7,
    "Name":"Contoso, Ltd",
    "Description":"http://www.contoso.com"},
   {"Id":8,
    "Name":"Graphic Design Institute",
    "Description":"http://www.graphicdesigninstitute.com"}],
[new Sys.Data.DataColumn("Id",Number,null),
 new Sys.Data.DataColumn("Name",String,"New row"),
 new Sys.Data.DataColumn("Description",String,"")],
["Id"])
```

The binding to the data source created a query to the data source that returns a Sys.Data.DataTable that contains a list of constructors for records, which are specified using name/value pairs. It then also specifies the Sys.Data.DataColumn types that represent these and finally the key column.

As you can see, this can be turned into an object at runtime that represents the data. Changing any of these data items on the browser renders the dataset dirty, and when it is considered dirty, you can explicitly write code to update the underlying data source.

In the next example, you'll do exactly that—you'll take a look at an example that not only returns and renders data from the underlying data source but also allows you to create new records, update existing records, and delete unwanted records.

An interesting note is that the web service in this example was explicitly coded for the return of data using the GetData and SaveData web methods. If the underlying service returns a DataTable type, they aren't necessary; therefore, for example, a web service with the following web method would be able to serve a similar data experience and would be interoperable with other technologies. Note that in this case the data is different—it will return employees from the Northwind database:

```
[DataObjectMethod(DataObjectMethodType.Select)]
public DataTable GetDataTable()
{
  SqlConnection connection =
  //Replace server, username, password with
  // your own SQL Server credenials
      new SqlConnection("Server=(local); Database=Northwind;
                          User ID=username; Password=password");

  SqlCommand command =
      new SqlCommand("SELECT FirstName, LastName,
            Title FROM Employees WHERE region = 'WA'
            AND Title LIKE '%pres%'");

  command.Connection = connection;
  connection.Open();

  SqlDataAdapter adapter = new SqlDataAdapter(command);
  DataSet dataSet = new DataSet();

  adapter.Fill(dataSet);
  command.Connection.Close();

  return dataSet.Tables[0];
}
```

Reading and Writing Data from a DataSource Control

This example provides a standard client-side data control that allows you to navigate through a data source. It displays the contents of the fields for the current record and provides read and write binding between them. Therefore, when you navigate to a field, you can edit that field, and your edit will automatically update the underlying dataset.

You can see it in action in Figure 8-4.

The < and > buttons will move you forward and backward through the dataset. If you change an item either within the name field or within the description field, the dirty flag will be set. This enables the Save button so that the changes can be written to the database, as shown in Figure 8-5.

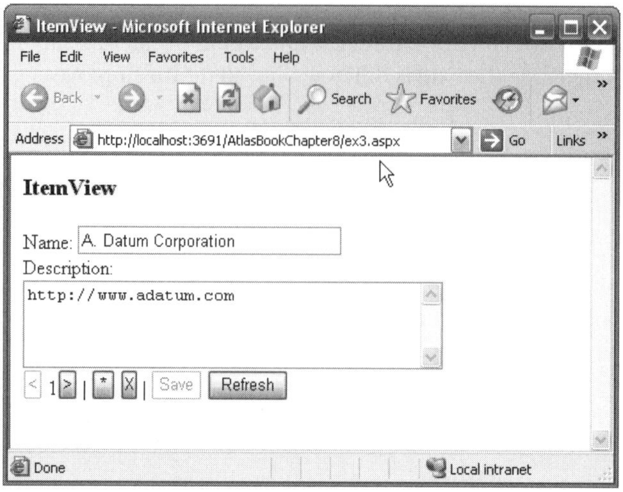

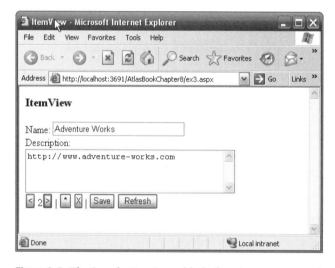

Figure 8-4. *Viewing and editing data items*

Figure 8-5. *The Save button is enabled after changes are made to the data.*

Similarly, the * button, which adds a new row at the end of the dataset, and the X button, which deletes the current row, will enable the dirty flag and thus the Save button to commit the changes. Finally, the Refresh button will reload the data from the underlying dataset, which will lose all unsaved changes.

The back-end data source is the same web service as you used in the previous example, so you'll now look at the client-side code for this to see how it is implemented.

The UI is implemented using the following HTML:

```
<!-- First Section -->
<div id="detailsView"></div>
```

```
<!-- Second Section -->
<input type="button" id="previousButton"
       value="<" title="Go to previous row" />

<span id="rowIndexLabel"></span>

<input id="nextButton" type="button"
       value=">" title="Go to next row" />
    |
<input type="button" id="addButton"
       value="*" title="Create a new row" />

<input type="button" id="delButton"
       value="X" title="Delete the current row" />
    |
<input type="button" id="saveButton"
       value="Save" title="Save all pending changes" />

<input type="button" id="refreshButton"
       value="Refresh"
       title="Discard pending changes and
     get the latest data from the server" />

<br /><br />

<!-- Third Section -->
<div style="visibility:hidden;display:none">
  <div id="detailsTemplate">
      Name:
      <input id="nameField" size="30" /><br />
      Description:<br />
      <textarea id="descriptionField" rows="4" cols="40">
      </textarea>
      <br />
  </div>
</div>
```

This is divided into three sections. The first is an empty `<div>` tag, which will be populated using an Atlas ItemView control, as you will see in a moment.

The second section contains the definitions for all the buttons that are used for navigating, creating new records, deleting records, and saving and refreshing.

The third, and final, section is hidden, but it specifies the UI for the template that will drive the content for the first.

The content for this UI will be driven from the data binding specified in the Atlas Script. Let's take a look at these scripts now. Listing 8-3 shows the entire script for the page. In later pages you will look at this script section by section.

Listing 8-3. *Data Binding Page Script*

```
<script type="text/xml-script">
<page xmlns:script="http://schemas.microsoft.com/xml-script/2005">
<components>
 <dataSource id="dataSource" serviceURL="SampleDataService.asmx"/>

 <itemView targetElement="detailsView">
 <bindings>
  <binding dataContext="dataSource" dataPath="data" property="data"/>
  <binding dataContext="dataSource" dataPath="isReady"
           property="enabled"/>
 </bindings>
 <itemTemplate>
  <template layoutElement="detailsTemplate">
  <textBox targetElement="nameField">
   <bindings>
    <binding dataPath="Name" property="text" direction="InOut"/>
   </bindings>
  </textBox>
  <textBox targetElement="descriptionField">
   <bindings>
    <binding dataPath="Description" property="text" direction="InOut"/>
   </bindings>
  </textBox>
  </template>
 </itemTemplate>
 </itemView>

 <button targetElement="previousButton">
 <bindings>
  <binding dataContext="detailsView" dataPath="canMovePrevious"
           property="enabled"/>
 </bindings>
 <click>
  <invokeMethod target="detailsView" method="movePrevious" />
 </click>
 </button>

 <label targetElement="rowIndexLabel">
 <bindings>
  <binding dataContext="detailsView" dataPath="dataIndex"
           property="text" transform="Add" />
 </bindings>
 </label>
```

```
<button targetElement="nextButton">
 <bindings>
  <binding dataContext="detailsView" dataPath="canMoveNext"
          property="enabled"/>
 </bindings>
 <click>
  <invokeMethod target="detailsView" method="moveNext" />
 </click>
</button>

<button targetElement="addButton">
 <bindings>
  <binding dataContext="dataSource" dataPath="isReady"
          property="enabled"/>
 </bindings>
 <click>
  <invokeMethod target="detailsView" method="addItem" />
 </click>
</button>

<button targetElement="delButton">
 <bindings>
  <binding dataContext="dataSource" dataPath="isReady"
          property="enabled"/>
 </bindings>
 <click>
  <invokeMethod target="detailsView" method="deleteCurrentItem" />
 </click>
</button>

<button targetElement="saveButton">
 <bindings>
  <binding dataContext="dataSource" dataPath="isDirtyAndReady"
          property="enabled"/>
 </bindings>
 <click>
  <invokeMethod target="dataSource" method="update" />
 </click>
</button>

<button targetElement="refreshButton">
 <bindings>
  <binding dataContext="dataSource" dataPath="isReady"
          property="enabled"/>
 </bindings>
```

```
  <click>
    <invokeMethod target="dataSource" method="select" />
  </click>
  </button>

  <application>
    <load>
      <invokeMethod target="dataSource" method="select"/>
    </load>
  </application>
  </components>
  </page>
  </script>
```

First you define the script and start laying out the components. The first component is a data source called dataSource that binds to the web service for its data:

```
<script type="text/xml-script">
<page xmlns:script="http://schemas.microsoft.com/xml-script/2005">
<components>
  <dataSource id-"dataSource"
    serviceURL="SampleDataService.asmx"/>
```

Second you create the `<itemView>` control that will wrap the empty `<div>` element you saw earlier. This control will use two bindings. The first binding is to bind the data returned from the data source to the data property of the ItemView control. This ensures that the ItemView control will receive a full, compatible dataset from the data source through the binding.

The second binding is an interesting and useful one. It ties the enabled property of the ItemView control to the isReady property of the data source. This means that although the data source is not in its ready state—such as when it is in the middle of a read or write cycle— the ItemView control will automatically get disabled, and once the data source is ready, it will be automatically enabled. Thus, functionality that might typically be programmed by hand is managed for you through data binding. This isn't a typical use case for data binding, but as you can see, it's is a handy one!

```
  <itemView targetElement="detailsView">
    <bindings>
      <binding dataContext="dataSource"
               dataPath="data"
               property="data"/>
      <binding dataContext="dataSource"
               dataPath="isReady"
               property="enabled"/>
    </bindings>
```

The `<itemTemplate>` specifies the template for how the bound data will appear on the `<itemView>` control. An Atlas `<textbox>` element is defined that wraps the underlying HTML `<input>` control called nameField. This gets bound to the parent `<itemView>` control's data property (which in turn is bound to the data source specified by the dataSource control).

It binds to the field called Name and connects it to its Text property. The direction attribute is set to InOut, which means changes to the data source will be reflected in the text box *and* changes to the text box will affect the underlying data source. Note that these changes will make the data dirty, meaning that the isDirty flag will be set on the data source, which can trigger the Save button. You'll see this a little later.

```
<itemTemplate>
  <template layoutElement="detailsTemplate">
    <textBox targetElement="nameField">
      <bindings>
        <binding dataPath="Name"
                 property="text"
                 direction="InOut"/>
      </bindings>
    </textBox>
```

You can see that the specification for the description field is similar, except that its target element is an HTML text field instead of an Input control. However, in Atlas parlance the two are both treated as <textBox> controls, which is more logical:

```
<textBox targetElement="descriptionField">
  <bindings>
    <binding dataPath="Description"
             property="text"
             direction="InOut"/>
  </bindings>
</textBox>
```

Now you can define the buttons that allow you to navigate. These show some interesting functionality. Let's first look at the Move Previous button (labeled < in the application):

```
<button targetElement="previousButton">
  <bindings>
    <binding dataContext="detailsView"
             dataPath="canMovePrevious"
             property="enabled"/>
  </bindings>
  <click>
    <invokeMethod target="detailsView" method="movePrevious" />
  </click>
</button>
```

When the <itemView> control has a set of records loaded in it (using its data property), it exposes a number of properties for navigating that data. One of these properties is canMovePrevious, which is false if you are currently looking at the first record in the dataset and true otherwise. Thus, if you bind a button to this property and tie that binding to the button's enabled property, the button will automatically be disabled if you are currently looking at the first record. As such, you can create, declaratively, a set of navigation buttons around a dataset. This is exactly what is being done here. Additionally, you want to implement an action to perform once the button is clicked. Naturally, in this case the action to perform will be to move to the previous record. This is implemented on the <itemView> control as the movePrevious method. As such, you can tie an action on the <click> of this button to this method on the <itemView> and declaratively implement navigational functionality that manages the move to the previous record.

As you can see, the functionality to move to the next record is similar:

```
<button targetElement="nextButton">
  <bindings>
    <binding dataContext="detailsView"
             dataPath="canMoveNext"
             property="enabled"/>
  </bindings>
  <click>
    <invokeMethod target="detailsView"
                  method="moveNext" />
  </click>
</button>
```

You can render the index of the current record by using the dataIndex property of the connected dataset. You can bind this to a label like this:

```
<label targetElement="rowIndexLabel">
  <bindings>
    <binding dataContext="detailsView"
             dataPath="dataIndex"
             property="text"
             transform="Add" />
  </bindings>
</label>
```

When it comes to adding a new record to the dataset, you need to use the addItem method that the itemView exposes. This should be called only when the data source is considered ready for adding data.

You do this by binding the enablement of the control to the isReady property of the *dataSource* (not the itemView), and then upon clicking the button, you invoke the addItem method of the *itemView* to which the data is bound. You do it this way because the readiness of the data to be written to is best established by looking at the dataSource, because it is closer to the data.

```
<button targetElement="addButton">
  <bindings>
    <binding dataContext="dataSource"
             dataPath="isReady"
             property="enabled"/>
  </bindings>
  <click>
    <invokeMethod target="detailsView" method="addItem" />
  </click>
</button>
```

Deleting a record is similar. If the data source is ready, you can invoke the deleteCurrentItem method on the parent ItemView control. You control access to the button (and thus the deletion) by disabling the button when the dataSource isn't ready:

```
<button targetElement="delButton">
  <bindings>
    <binding dataContext="dataSource"
             dataPath="isReady"
             property="enabled"/>
  </bindings>
  <click>
    <invokeMethod target="detailsView"
                  method="deleteCurrentItem" />
  </click>
</button>
```

Saving data is a little more complex. You should save data only when the dataset is considered dirty and the dataSource is considered ready. Remember that the binding is two-way, so when you type something into either of the text boxes, their binding to the itemView will update the dataset within the itemView, and it, in turn, will update the dataset within the dataSource control. Thus, the dataSource will be considered dirty. Once it is also ready, then the isDirtyAndReady flag will be true. You can bind the enablement of the Save button to this flag, and you will then be protected from bad writes. Thus, when the dataSource is dirty and it is ready for writing, the button will be enabled; otherwise, it will be disabled and unavailable for user interaction. When you click the button, the action to update the dataSource should take place.

```
<button targetElement="saveButton">
  <bindings>
    <binding dataContext="dataSource"
             dataPath="isDirtyAndReady"
             property="enabled"/>
  </bindings>
  <click>
    <invokeMethod target="dataSource" method="update" />
  </click>
</button>
```

Refreshing the data involves running another query on the data source to perform another select and get a refreshed dataset. This should happen only when the dataSource is ready to receive the request.

Thus, you bind the enablement of the button to the isReady property of the dataSource, and when you click it, you invoke the select method to get the data. This will trigger all the bindings and refresh the controls on the screen with new data.

All this refreshing and updating of controls of course happens asynchronously using Ajax techniques. Thus, only the <itemView> will update, and the entire page will not blink.

```
<button targetElement="refreshButton">
  <bindings>
```

```
    <binding dataContext="dataSource"
            dataPath="isReady"
            property="enabled"/>
  </bindings>
  <click>
    <invokeMethod target="dataSource" method="select" />
  </click>
</button>
```

Finally, you want to specify what should happen when the page first loads. This application performs a simple action in this circumstance, and that is to do a select against the data source to generate a new dataset and trigger all the bindings, initializing the UI.

```
<application>
  <load>
    <invokeMethod target="dataSource"
                method="select"/>
  </load>
</application>
```

Summary

Data binding is vital to any application, and how a programming language or framework implements data binding is a great gauge of its usefulness. If the data binding APIs handle all the complexities of passing data around controls including reading, writing, and protecting data updates yet give you the flexibility you need to write your applications, then it's a winner.

In this circumstance Atlas is strong; it provides a rich declarative model that gives you powerful but easy-to-use data binding functionality.

In this chapter, you took a tour of the controls that are implemented in the Atlas libraries that give you a data binding API. You started by looking at the nonvisual controls, which implement tables, records, views, filters, and the like. You next moved on to the visual controls of ItemView and ListView and learned how you can use them to render bound data in the browser.

You then put the theory into practice by looking at several examples. First you looked at simple data binding where a DataSource control isn't used and your Atlas controls are simply bound to a back-end web service.

Next you looked at binding a ListView control to a set of data and how you can use it to render a large snapshot of data asynchronously to your page.

Finally, I presented an example of using the ItemView control, and you learned about displaying the data on a web page and providing a user interface that allows for data entry, where you write data back to the service that provided it without going through an intermediary. In addition, you used data protection, controlling access to the write cycles upon the readiness and dirtiness of the local data cache.

After reading this chapter, you should have a good grasp of how to start implementing your own data-aware web applications that use Atlas to provide Ajax-style asynchrony.

In the next chapter, you'll start looking at another client-side library—one that provides additional user interface functionality, or "glitz," to your applications.

■■■

CHAPTER 9

Using the AtlasUIGlitz Library

One of the libraries that comes with Atlas is the AtlasUIGlitz library. This library contains a number of behaviors and controls that you can use to "glitz up" your Atlas applications. This includes setting and changing the opacity of areas of the screen in your application; programmatically setting the layout of areas of the screen, giving you control over the left, top, height, and width of layers on the screen; and running various custom animations on your layers, including property animations, discrete animations, number animations, and more. As you work through this chapter, you'll learn by example, going through each animation and functionality that this library offers you and finding out how to use them in your applications.

Using Opacity

Figure 9-1 shows a page containing two layers that are set to different levels of opacity. You can set these programmatically using JavaScript, or you can use Atlas Script. For example, you could attach behaviors to affect the opacity of a component when the mouse is moving over it.

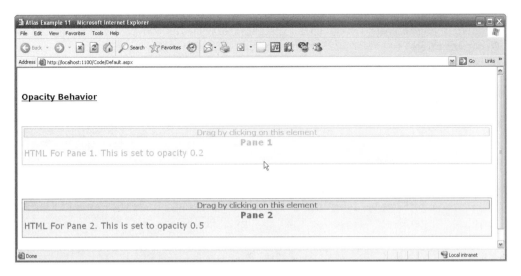

Figure 9-1. *Showing the opacity behavior on two elements*

As you can see in Figure 9-1, these elements have opacities 0.2 and 0.5. So how do you achieve this?

Let's take a look at the code; first, here is the HTML that defines the elements:

```
<div id="Description">
  <div id="DragHandle">Drag by clicking on this element</div>
  <div style="text-align:center;font-weight:bold;">Pane 1</div>
    HTML For Pane 1. This is set to opacity 0.2</div>
<div id="Description2">
  <div id="DragHandle2">Drag by clicking on this element</div>
  <div style="text-align:center;font-weight:bold;">Pane 2</div>
    HTML For Pane 2. This is set to opacity 0.5</div>
```

You need to make sure Atlas loads the AtlasUIGlitz library. You do this using a ScriptReference control. In this case, the code is referencing the AtlasUIGlitz library as well as the drag-and-drop library (called AtlasUIDragDrop), which will be used a little later in this chapter.

```
<atlas:ScriptManager runat="server" ID="ScriptManager1">
  <Scripts>
    <atlas:ScriptReference ScriptName="AtlasUIDragDrop" />
    <atlas:ScriptReference ScriptName="AtlasUIGlitz" />
  </Scripts>
</atlas:ScriptManager>
```

This is the Atlas Script that builds the application from this HTML:

```
<page xmlns:script="http://schemas.microsoft.com/xml-script/2005">
<components>

  <control targetElement="DragHandle" cssClass="draghandle" />
  <control targetElement="Description" cssClass="floatwindow">
    <behaviors>
      <floatingBehavior handle="DragHandle">
      </floatingBehavior>
      <opacity value="0.2">
      </opacity>
    </behaviors>

  </control>

  <control targetElement="DragHandle2" cssClass="draghandle" />
  <control targetElement="Description2" cssClass="floatwindow">
    <behaviors>
      <floatingBehavior handle="DragHandle2">
      </floatingBehavior>
      <opacity value="0.5">
      </opacity>
```

```
    </behaviors>
  </control>
</components>
</page>
```

Each of these elements is assigned a `<control>` element in Atlas. Control elements can have behaviors associated with them. In this case, two behaviors are attached to the elements. The first, floatingBehavior, allows for the layer to be dragged and dropped around the page. (You can see more about this in Chapters 4 and 5.)

The second, opacity, comes from the AtlasUIGlitz library. It takes a parameter, called value, that determines the opacity. This is a number from 0 to 1, with 0 being completely transparent and 1 being completely opaque.

And that's it—it is very straightforward, as you can see!

Using Layout Behaviors

The next behavior that is available from the AtlasUIGlitz library is the layout behavior, which allows you to specify the dimensions and location of an element. As you can see in Figure 9-2, you can declaratively specify how the content will appear using Atlas Script.

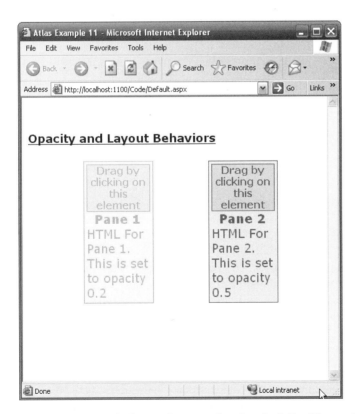

Figure 9-2. *Setting the layout for controls using the "glitzy" layout behavior*

Getting this effect is easy; you simply attach the layout behavior to the control in Atlas Script and then specify the left, top, width, and height properties.

You can see this here:

```
<control targetElement="DragHandle" cssClass="draghandle" />
<control targetElement="Description" cssClass="floatwindow">
  <behaviors>
    <floatingBehavior handle="DragHandle">
    </floatingBehavior>
    <opacity handle="myOp" value="0.2">
    </opacity>
    <layout handle="myLo"
            top="100"
            left="100"
            height="100"
            width="100">
    </layout>
  </behaviors>

</control>

<control targetElement="DragHandle2" cssClass="draghandle" />
<control targetElement="Description2" cssClass="floatwindow">
  <behaviors>
    <floatingBehavior handle="DragHandle2">
    </floatingBehavior>
    <opacity value="0.5">
    </opacity>
    <layout handle="myLo"
            top="100"
            left="300"
            height="100"
            width="100">
    </layout>
  </behaviors>
</control>
```

Thus, if you attach the layout behavior to your control, you can specify the visual appearance of it. Should you not specify a parameter, the HTML layout properties will be used. You can use a partial set of parameters (for example, you can set the left but not the top), and it will still work.

Using Fade Animations

The first animation that you will look at is the fade animation, where the opacity of a layer is changed going either toward value 1 (fade-in) or toward value 0 (fade-out).

Figure 9-3 and Figure 9-4 show the state of a layer at the beginning and at the end of a fade-in animation.

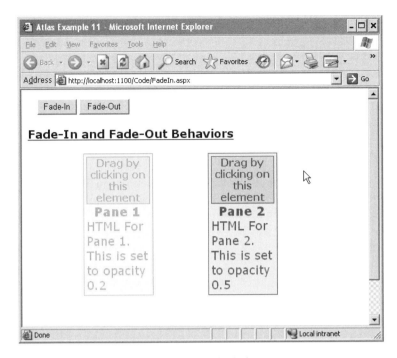

Figure 9-3. *The layer at the beginning of a fade-in*

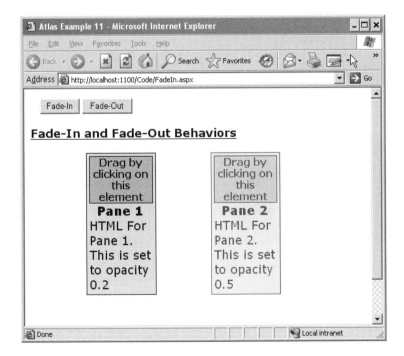

Figure 9-4. *The layer at the end of a fade-in*

You achieve this fade using Sys.UI.FadeAnimation. Tied to the button's OnClick event is the following JavaScript:

```
function FadeIn()
{
    var a = new Sys.UI.FadeAnimation();
    a.set_target(Sys.Application.findObject('Description'));
    a.set_effect(Sys.UI.FadeEffect.FadeIn);
    a.play();
}
```

Here an instance of a new Sys.UI.FadeAnimation is created and gets tied to the Description object. The effect is set to Sys.UI.FadeEffect.FadeIn, and when the play method is called, the animation trips, and the layer fades in. In a similar manner, you can fade out a layer using Sys.UI.FadeEffect.FadeOut like this:

```
function FadeOut()
{
    var a = new Sys.UI.FadeAnimation();
    a.set_target(Sys.Application.findObject('Description2'));
    a.set_effect(Sys.UI.FadeEffect.FadeOut);
    a.play();
}
```

You can see the effect of this in Figure 9-5 and Figure 9-6.

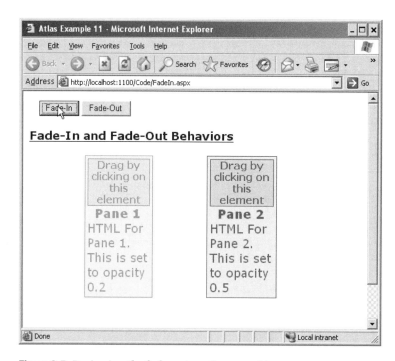

Figure 9-5. *Beginning the fade-out on the second layer*

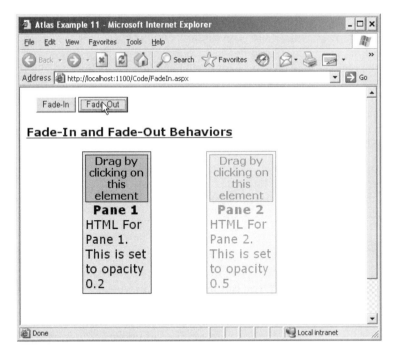

Figure 9-6. *Continuing the fade-out on the second layer*

You can also set up your animation using Atlas Script. In this case, you create an abstract animation control in Atlas Script and tie that control to the area you want to animate. Then you can, for example, attach an action to a button that triggers the animation.

Considering the previous example, the markup for the Fade-In button will look like this:

```
<input id="btnFadeIn" type="button" value="Fade-In" />
```

The important thing to note is its ID, which is btnFadeIn. This is what you will use to reference it in Atlas Script.

Next, you create the animation control. Within your Atlas Script controls declaration, you will have markup like this:

```
<fadeAnimation id="thefadeAnimation"
        target="Description" effect="FadeIn" />
```

The FadeAnimation controls description uses the attributes shown in Table 9-1.

Table 9-1. *FadeAnimation Attributes*

Attribute Name	Description
ID	The identity for this animation, used by other controls to trigger actions on this control.
Target	The page element to which to apply the animation.
Effect	Can be FadeIn or FadeOut. Defines how the fade animation runs. FadeIn takes it from Invisible to Visible; FadeOut does the opposite.

In this case, you can see that the animation is called thefadeAnimation, it is set to target the <div> element on the HTML page that is called Description, and the effect that will be used to animate it is FadeIn.

You can then trigger the animation to take place upon clicking the Fade-In button using an <invokeMethod> on its <click> action like this:

```
<button id="btnFadeIn">
  <click>
    <invokeMethod target="thefadeAnimation" method="play" />
  </click>
</button>
```

Then when you click the button, you get the same behavior as earlier.

Using Length Animations

Another animation that you can use is the length animation, which changes the state of a property between a start and an end value that you can specify. You can typically use this to animate the setting of the width or height of a control that uses them.

However, because it simply sets the property of a control to the numeric value between the start value and the end value, it can also perform countups or countdowns if applied to the text property of a control.

Table 9-2 lists the properties of the animation.

Table 9-2. *LengthAnimation Properties*

Property Name	Description
Target	Specifies the target control for the animation.
Property	Specifies which property will be the target for the animation.
StartValue	Specifies the start value for animation.
EndValue	Specifies the end value for animation.
Unit	Text specifying the unit to use. Examples are px for pixels or % for percentage.
Duration	Specifies the duration (in seconds) that it should take to play the animation.

You can see the length animation in action in Figure 9-7, Figure 9-8, and Figure 9-9. Figure 9-7 shows the application before the animation begins, Figure 9-8 shows the animation as it is in progress and the image is growing, and Figure 9-9 shows the completed animation.

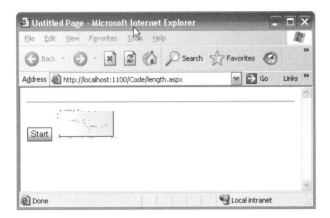

Figure 9-7. *Beginning the animation*

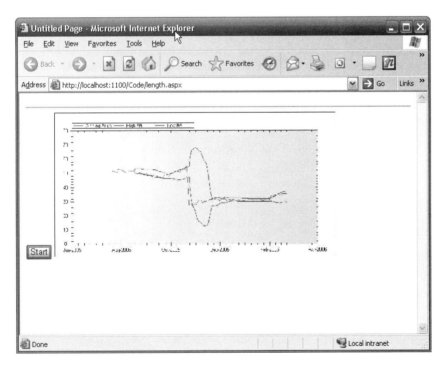

Figure 9-8. *The animation as it progresses*

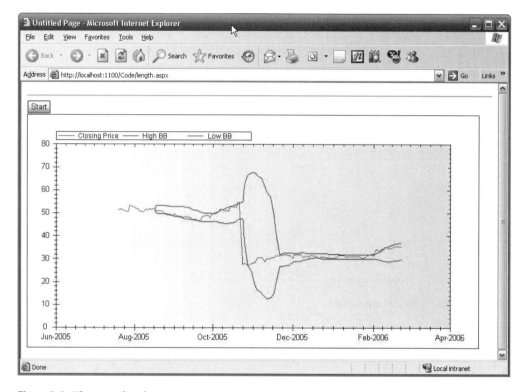

Figure 9-9. *The completed animation*

In this case, the animation is set to change the width property of the image. Let's see how this works.

First, here is the markup that defines the page, including the image:

```
<form id="form1" runat="server">
<div>
<atlas:ScriptManager ID="ScriptManager1" runat="server"
                     EnablePartialRendering="True">
  <Scripts>
    <atlas:ScriptReference ScriptName="AtlasUIGlitz" />
  </Scripts>
</atlas:ScriptManager>

<input type="button" id="startButton" value="Start"/>
<img id="i" src="sample.jpg" width="100" />

</div>
</form>
```

As you can see, this simply creates a button using the `<input>` tag and an image using the `<img>` tag. The initial state of the image is set to have the width be 100.

Next comes the Atlas Script that defines these controls and specifies the animation, tying its launch to the click action of the button:

```
<script type="text/xml-script">
<page xmlns:demo="demo">
  <components>
    <image id="i" />

    <lengthAnimation id="l"
      target="i" property="width"
      startValue="100" endValue="800"
      duration="30" />

    <button id="startButton">
      <click>
        <invokeMethod target="l" method="play" />
      </click>
    </button>
  </components>
</page>
</script>
```

Here you create an instance of a Sys.UI.Image control using the <image> tag and point it at the underlying HTML element called i.

Next you define the animation. Give the ID l and target it at i. The property you are specifying to change on the animation is width. The default unit on the lengthAnimation property is px, so the animation will change the width property to a number of pixels.

You define this number by specifying startValue and endValue. In this case, set startValue to 100, and set endValue to 800. Finally, set the duration to 30. This means the values 100px–800px will be sent to the width property of the image over a duration of 30 seconds. Changing the duration to a smaller value will mean that the image will grow to its final size more quickly, and changing it to a larger value will mean that it grows more slowly!

Additionally, the animation is smart enough to know that if startValue is greater than endValue, the animation will play backward, reducing the text from startValue to endValue, and in a case like this, the image will shrink in size over the specified duration.

Using Number Animations

Another animation provided by the AtlasUIGlitz framework is the number animation. This is similar to the length animation in that it provides an animation between a start value and an end value over a specified duration.

An important difference with the number animation is that it allows for fractional values as it goes through the animation. This can give you some nice effects for progress meters and other elements that may require numerics.

The NumberAnimation control supports the properties shown in Table 9-3.

Table 9-3. *Number Animation Properties*

Property Name	Description
Target	Specifies the target control for the animation.
Property	Specifies which property that will be the target for the animation.
StartValue	Specifies the start value for animation.
EndValue	Specifies the end value for animation.
IntegralValues	Boolean that specifies whether whole numbers will be presented. If true, then the animation will cycle through whole values. If false, then it will render fractional numbers.
Duration	Specifies the duration (in seconds) that it should take to play the animation.

You can see the animation in action in Figure 9-10, Figure 9-11, and Figure 9-12. This shows the animation causing a countdown from 30 to 1 with IntegralValues set to False, thus rendering fractional numbers.

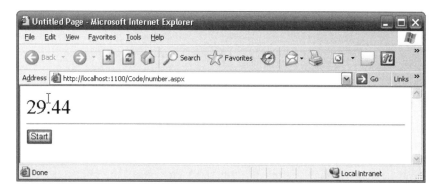

Figure 9-10. *The countdown animation has begun.*

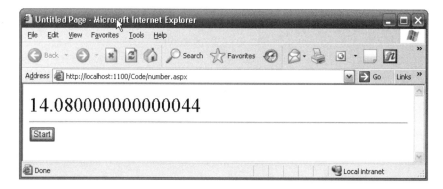

Figure 9-11. *The animation continues.*

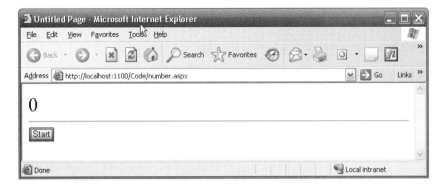

Figure 9-12. *The animation completes.*

Let's see how this works. Here is the markup that defines the page content:

```
<form id="form1" runat="server">
<div>
  <atlas:ScriptManager ID="ScriptManager1" runat="server"
                   EnablePartialRendering="True">
    <Scripts>
      <atlas:ScriptReference ScriptName="AtlasUIGlitz" />
    </Scripts>
  </atlas:ScriptManager>
  <span id="sampleLabel" style="font-size: 24pt"></span>
  <hr />
  <input type="button" id="startButton" value="Start"/>

</div>
</form>
```

As you can see, it is straightforward. It defines a <span> element called simpleLabel that will contain the text to be animated and the button that will trigger the action that invokes the animation.

The Atlas Script that defines the controls for this HTML, the animation, and the action to perform when the button is pressed is as follows:

```
<script type="text/xml-script">
<page xmlns:demo="demo">
  <components>
    <label id="sampleLabel" />

    <numberAnimation id="nAnimation"
      target="sampleLabel" property="text"
      startValue="30" endValue="0"
      integralValues="false"
      duration="30" />
```

```
      <button id="startButton">
        <click>
          <invokeMethod target="nAnimation" method="play" />
        </click>
      </button>
    </components>
  </page>
</script>
```

In this script, you can see that an Atlas Label control gets assigned to the `<span>` element called sampleLabel. The Label control has a text property, and if this is set, its contents will get loaded into the `<span>` element, thus rendering the text on the page.

You then set up the `<numberAnimation>` element, targeting this label. You specify the property on this label to target in the property attribute; it is the text property.

Then you specify the values to animate. You state to start at the value 30 and end at the value 0.

IntegralValues is set to false, so fractional values will be rendered (as you can see in Figures 9-10 through 9-12).

As such, a simple numeric progression is easy to implement and to tie to a web element using the NumberAnimation control.

Using Discrete Animations

Discrete animations are similar to length and number animations in that they will cycle through a range of values during a fixed duration. For both of these, you specify start and end values, and the Atlas framework calculates the interim values for the animation.

For example, you could specify a range of letters from *a* to *z* and cycle the animation through them, or you could specify a range of names or words to animate through.

Table 9-4 lists the properties that the DiscreteAnimation control supports.

Table 9-4. *DiscreteAnimation Properties*

Property Name	Description
Target	Specifies the target control for the animation.
Property	Specifies which property that will be the target for the animation.
Values	Specifies a range of values to cycle through when animating. This should be a comma-separated list of string values.

You can see the animation in action in Figure 9-13, Figure 9-14, and Figure 9-15. These show a discrete animation cycling the text of a label from values *a* through *z*.

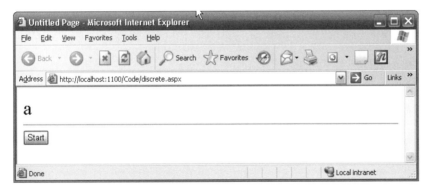

Figure 9-13. *Beginning the animation. The label reads* a.

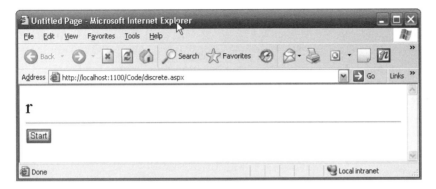

Figure 9-14. *Continuing the animation. The label now reads* r.

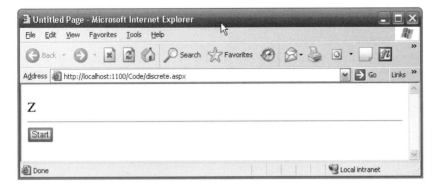

Figure 9-15. *The animation is finished. The label now reads* z.

Let's take a look at how this works. First, here is the markup defining the HTML:

```
<form id="form1" runat="server">
<div>
  <atlas:ScriptManager ID="ScriptManager1" runat="server"
                        EnablePartialRendering="True">
    <Scripts>
      <atlas:ScriptReference ScriptName="AtlasUIGlitz" />
    </Scripts>
  </atlas:ScriptManager>
  <span id="sampleLabel" style="font-size: 24pt">a</span>
  <hr />
  <input type="button" id="startButton" value="Start"/>

</div>
</form>
```

Here you define a `<span>` element called sampleLabel. This will be the target for the animation. The discrete animation works by changing a property on the target control through a series of predefined values. The `<span>` element can be represented by an Atlas Label control. This control exposes a text property so that when you change the text property of this control, the contents of the underlying `<span>` element get set to this text, and thus it is written to the page.

Here is the Atlas Script that defines this control, the animation, and the action to link to the button to trigger the animation effect:

```
<script type="text/xml-script">
  <page xmlns:demo="demo">
    <components>
      <label id="sampleLabel" />

      <discreteAnimation id="letterAnimation"
           target="sampleLabel" property="text"
           values="'a', 'b', 'c', 'd', 'e', 'f', 'g', 'h',
                   'i', 'j', 'k', 'l', 'm', 'n', 'o', 'p', 'q'
                   'r', 's', 't', 'u', 'v', 'w', 'x', 'y', 'z'"
           duration="3" />

      <button id="startButton">
        <click>
          <invokeMethod target="letterAnimation"
                        method="play" />
        </click>
      </button>
    </components>
  </page>
</script>
```

In this script, you can see that the Label control gets assigned to the `<span>` element by using the ID attribute and pointing it at the name of the `<span>` element, which in this case is sampleLabel.

Next you set up the `<discreteAnimation>` control by pointing it at the text property of the `<sampleLabel>` control using the property and target attributes, respectively.

The important property here to understand is the values property. You set this to a comma-separated list of the desired values, enclosed within a string. In this case, it is the full alphabet, but it can be anything; for example, to animate through the names Andrew, Bob and Claire, you would set it to the following:

```
" 'Andrew', 'Bob', 'Claire' "
```

The duration attribute specifies the time in seconds that it should take to cycle through the defined values.

Finally, a Button control points at the underlying `<input>` control that renders a button in HTML. It has an invoke method behavior associated with its click action that triggers the play method of the animation. Thus, clicking the button starts the animation and the behavior exhibited in Figures 9-13 to 9-15.

Summary

The AtlasUIGlitz library is a nice add-on library that provides a number of UI behaviors that you can use to make your user interfaces more attractive and, well, glitzy. The library offers two behaviors that you can manipulate: opacity and layout.

The former, opacity, allows you to set the alpha level of transparency/opacity of your page elements. You can create whizzy user interfaces that make the most of modern graphics cards and browsers to render complex UIs that have controls overlaid on each other, with the hidden controls visible through slight transparency on the overlaying controls, allowing the user to look "through" them.

The latter, layout, allows you to easily and explicitly place controls on the page. It allows you to set the top, left, height, and width properties of an element through properties of the behavior. This gives you fine-grained control over how your interface is laid out.

In addition, the AtlasUIGlitz library offers a number of animation effects that can be applied to controls on your page:

- The fade animation allows you to fade the opacity of a control in or out. You can use this to smoothly make controls appear or disappear or to provide a nice visual indicator of inactive controls by smoothly making them more transparent.

- Length animations allow you to map a range of numbers to a control's property where the framework automatically drives the value of the property from the start value to the end value and appends a text unit to the end, such as px allowing you to specify image, table, or other element's width and height properties through an animated range.

- Number animations are similar to length animations but don't append the text to the end and instead offer the facility to use fractional values. In this case, you can animate through a range of values that aren't limited to whole numbers.

- Discrete animations also allow you to change the value of a control's property automatically through a predefined range. You could, for example, automatically cycle the contents of a text field through the values *a* through *z* by specifying these as a list to a property on the animation and then triggering that animation.

From this chapter you have gleaned some great new tools to make your UIs more sophisticated and easy to use for your users. In the next chapter, you will look at another value-added client-side library that Atlas gives you—the Mapping library. This library allows you to instantly and easily add mapping and geocoding functionality to your applications that will update in an asynchronous, Ajax-like manner.

■ ■ ■

CHAPTER 10

Mapping with Atlas

Perhaps it is natural that a framework called Atlas has a built-in set of libraries for handling mapping functionality! In this chapter, you will look at this functionality and how you can use and leverage it in your own applications.

Seeing Some Mapping Functionality in Action

Mapping is a huge part of the new Windows Live Local web application, which you can use to look at what services are available at a particular location and have them all mapped out for you.

Figure 10-1 shows an example of this; you can see that the context of this map is Seattle, Washington; the image is zoomed in to the famous Pike Place Market; and the search term is *coffee*.

If you look at Figure 10-1, you'll see that two text boxes appear at the top of the page. You use the one on the right to set your current map context by searching for a location. So, for example, you could search for *Pike Street, Seattle, WA*. You use the text box on the left to search for the services you are interested in, such as *coffee* or *soccer*. The search results appear in the left pane, and their numbered icons appear on the map. These icons are called *pushpins*, and you'll see how to implement them in the "Using Pushpins" section, as well as how to use the same mapping libraries for your own applications.

Atlas incorporates mapping functionality via the script library called AtlasUIMap. This script library installs with Atlas; you can find it in the C:\Program Files\Microsoft ASP.NET\ Atlas\v2.0.50727\Atlas\ScriptLibrary directory. Previous releases of Atlas—prior to the Go Live license version issued in 2006 as the March Community Technology Preview (CTP)— included the scripts in your Visual Studio 2005 solution, so you would be able to find them there. If you cannot see them in your solution file, you'll be able to find them in the aforementioned directory.

Figure 10-1. *Using Windows Live Local*

Getting Started with Atlas Maps

To use Atlas maps on a page, you follow the typical procedure as when using client-side controls in Atlas. For more about this, see Chapters 3, 4, and 5. Typically you create an HTML page and place controls and <div> tags on this page. You give these controls and tags IDs, which you use to map the Atlas control to an underlying element.

So, to use an Atlas map on an area of your page, you would use some HTML like this:

```
<div id="MyMap" style="height:400px;width:400px; ">
</div>
```

Atlas map controls are called virtualEarthMap, and you can assign one to this <div> element using the following Atlas Script:

```
<virtualEarthMap id="MyMap" latitude="48"
                 longitude="-122" mapStyle="Road"
                 zoomLevel="9">
</virtualEarthMap>
```

The March CTP of Atlas has a minor bug that requires you to use a Virtualearth.net CSS script on the page; otherwise, you will have problems dragging and zooming the map. You can include this script in your page using the following tag in your HTML <head> section:

```
<link type="text/css" href=http://dev.virtualearth.net/standard/v2/MapControl.css
    rel="stylesheet" />
```

Listing 10-1 shows the complete code for a simple page that includes everything you need to display a simple Atlas map, including references and the necessary Atlas ScriptManager control.

Listing 10-1. *Simple Page Containing an Atlas-Based Map*

```
<%@ Page Language="C#" %>

<!DOCTYPE html PUBLIC "-//W3C//DTD XHTML 1.0 Transitional//EN"
    "http://www.w3.org/TR/xhtml1/DTD/xhtml1-transitional.dtd">
<html xmlns="http://www.w3.org/1999/xhtml">
<head runat="server">
    <title>Atlas Map of Seattle Area</title>
    <link type="text/css"
        href="http://dev.virtualearth.net/standard/v2/MapControl.css"
        rel="stylesheet" />
</head>

<body>
  <form id="form1" runat="server">
  <atlas:ScriptManager ID="ScriptManager1" runat="server" >
  <Scripts>
    <atlas:ScriptReference ScriptName="AtlasUIMap" />
  </Scripts>
  </atlas:ScriptManager>

  <div id="MyMap"
      style="height:400px;width:400px; ">
  </div>

  </form>

  <script type="text/xml-script">
  <page xmlns:script="http://schemas.microsoft.com/xml-script/2005">

  <components>
    <virtualEarthMap id="MyMap" latitude="48"
                    longitude="-122" mapStyle="Road"
                    zoomLevel="9">
```

```
        </virtualEarthMap>
      </components>
      </page>
      </script>
</body>
</html>
```

Figure 10-2 shows the results of running this page.

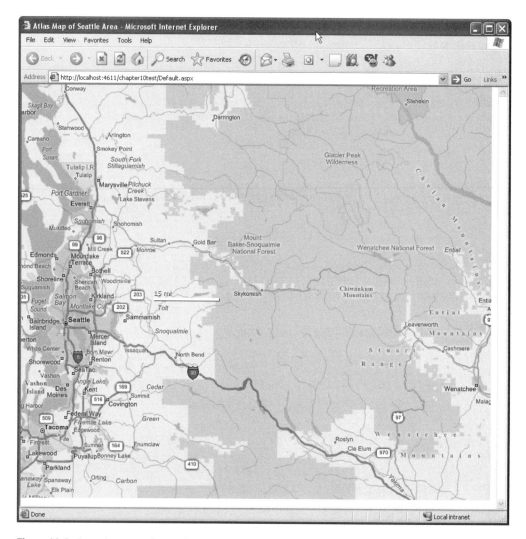

Figure 10-2. *Running your first Atlas UI map*

The virtualEarthMap control contains all the code necessary to handle mouse interaction. If you hold the mouse button down on the map, you can then drag the map. This demonstrates an important principle of Ajax and Atlas, namely, that asynchronous updates can improve the user experience. In this case, the map you are viewing consists of a number of tiles. As you are viewing the map surface, the tiles for the surrounding areas are downloaded and cached. If you drag the map around, another download for these tiles isn't necessary. However, if you drag really fast to see areas that are far away, you'll see the Atlas Script working to catch up, caching the tiles as it goes. See Figure 10-3 for an example of this.

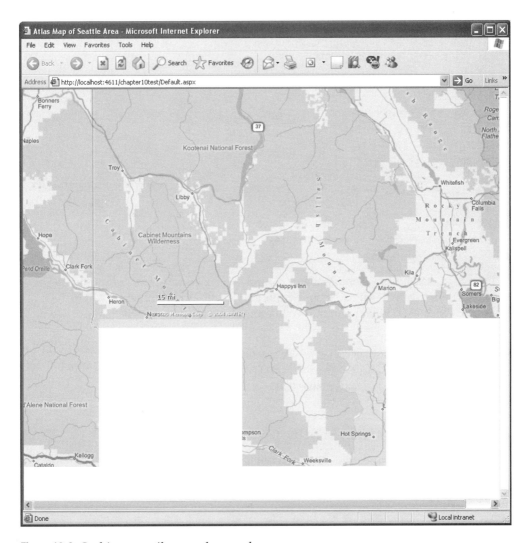

Figure 10-3. *Caching map tiles asynchronously*

If you look at an HTTP trace of what is happening as you run this application, you'll see the following. (I have removed a lot of this for brevity, but the full trace is available with the download for this book. It is called Chapter10sniff.txt.) Take note that the Microsoft Virtual Earth service implements the mapping functionality, returning the correct map tiles upon requests from this client library.

First the browser issues the initial request to a page:

```
#1   10:34:27.328   127.0.0.1:4611
GET /chapter10test/Default.aspx HTTP/1.1
Accept: */*
Accept-Language: en-us
Accept-Encoding: gzip, deflate
Connection: Keep-Alive
```

Then the server responds with this:

```
#2   10:34:27.390   127.0.0.1:4611
HTTP/1.1 200 OK
Server: ASP.NET Development Server/8.0.0.0
Date: Fri, 24 Mar 2006 18:34:27 GMT
X-AspNet-Version: 2.0.50727
Cache-Control: private
Content-Type: text/html; charset=utf-8
Content-Length: 1624
Connection: Close
<!DOCTYPE html PUBLIC "-//W3C//DTD XHTML 1.0 Transitional//EN"
    "http://www.w3.org/TR/xhtml1/DTD/xhtml1-transitional.dtd">
...
```

The page uses the Atlas ScriptManager control to manage the scripts, so another call is made to the server to download them. Scripts are web resources embedded within the Microsoft.Web.Atlas.dll binary, and thus WebResource.axd is called with the request:

```
#3   10:34:27.796   127.0.0.1:4611
GET /chapter10test/WebResource.axd?d=9VOZqrVZBFaNFGS19
FcxXx2zoT5SJYkcU2s4XaRKcMXB5bDsUzdwcKoRnoZ_LFO22lm
sieXK9Fsqq9E_Dfc8EzoHpAMm7Aed1y8IsODBeX81&t=6327821
66040000000 HTTP/1.1
Accept: */*
Referer: http://localhost:4611/chapter10test/Default.aspx
```

The server then responds with the JavaScript libraries:

```
#4   10:34:27.796   127.0.0.1:4611
HTTP/1.1 200 OK
...
```

After this, the CSS file is downloaded, followed by the AtlasUIMap.js file. Note that this file isn't a default script managed by the Atlas ScriptManager control—it is instead requested using the <Scripts> tag within <atlas:ScriptManager> and thus is downloaded later.

Once the page has completed downloading, the map control kicks in and starts making the asynchronous requests for the map tiles using XMLHttpRequest.

You can see this here; this is the request, issued by the map control:

```
#11   10:34:28.656   65.55.241.30:80
GET /tiles/r021230000.png?g=15 HTTP/1.1
Accept: */*
Referer: http://localhost:4611/chapter10test/Default.aspx
Accept-Language: en-us
Accept-Encoding: gzip, deflate
User-Agent: Mozilla/4.0 (compatible; MSIE 6.0; Windows NT 5.1; SV1; .
NET CLR 2.0.50727; WinFX RunTime 3.0.50727)

Host: r0.ortho.tiles.virtualearth.net

Connection: Keep-Alive
```

This is the response from the Virtual Earth Map server:

```
#12   10:34:28.859   65.55.241.30:80
HTTP/1.1 200 OK
Content-Length: 17055
Content-Type: image/png
Expires: Sat, 24 Mar 2007 01:39:58 GMT
Server: Microsoft-IIS/6.0

Srv: 31300
Date: Fri, 24 Mar 2006 18:34:28 GMT
```

As you pan around the map, you see the same functionality—the images being requested, downloaded, and cached asynchronously.

In addition to panning around the map, you can zoom in and out because Atlas also caches images when you zoom, providing what is effectively a smart multilevel cache of the current map context. In other words, Atlas looks at the current context of the map and caches the area outside the current view in the current zoom context as well as a zoom-in context and a zoom-out context.

If you have a mouse with a wheel, you can roll the wheel to zoom in and out. You can see this for the current application in Figure 10-4.

Now that you've gotten a feel for the functionality of the map, you'll see some of the programmatic features that are available to application developers when using the map.

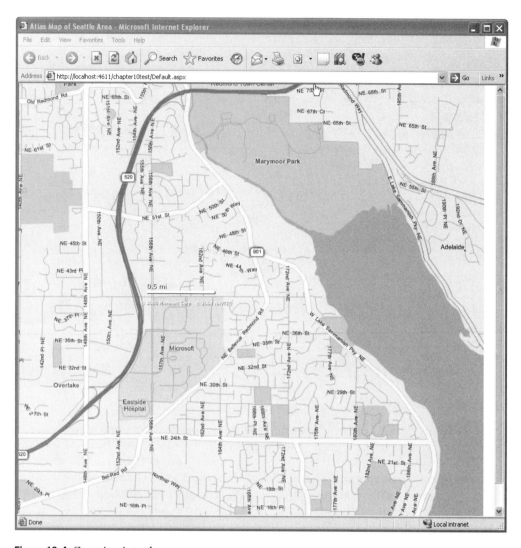

Figure 10-4. *Zooming into the map*

Programming the Map Control

In the previous section, you saw how to create a simple page that hosts the Atlas map control, which probably whetted your appetite for some juicy APIs that you can use to finely control the map.

Setting Longitude and Latitude

Places on a map have a latitude and a longitude. These are values that vary from –180 to +180, respectively. Using these values, you can calculate and locate any position in the world. Longitude determines how far east or west a location is, and latitude determines how far north or south a location is.

So, to determine any location, you need only these two values. Locations at a latitude of 0 are on the equator, locations with a latitude of +180 are at the North Pole, and locations with a latitude of –180 are at the South Pole. Locations with a longitude of 0 are either directly north or directly south of the Royal Observatory in Greenwich (a suburb of London, England), with negative values being to the west and positive values being to the east.

So, if you look at the map shown in Figure 10-1, you will see that it is specified with a latitude of 48 (48 degrees north of the equator) and a longitude of –122 (122 degrees west of Greenwich, England), which brings you to the Seattle area:

```
<virtualEarthMap id="MyMap" latitude="48"
                 longitude="-122" mapStyle="Road"
                 zoomLevel="9" />
```

You don't have to use whole numbers when specifying longitude and latitude, because it's a big world and you may want some fine-grained control over locations. The Atlas control uses the JavaScript Number type, which is a 64-bit floating-point value. So, you can quite happily control your location like this:

```
<virtualEarthMap id="MyMap" latitude="47.7512121212"
                 longitude="-122.43234" mapStyle="Road"
                 zoomLevel="9" />
```

You can see this in Figure 10-5.

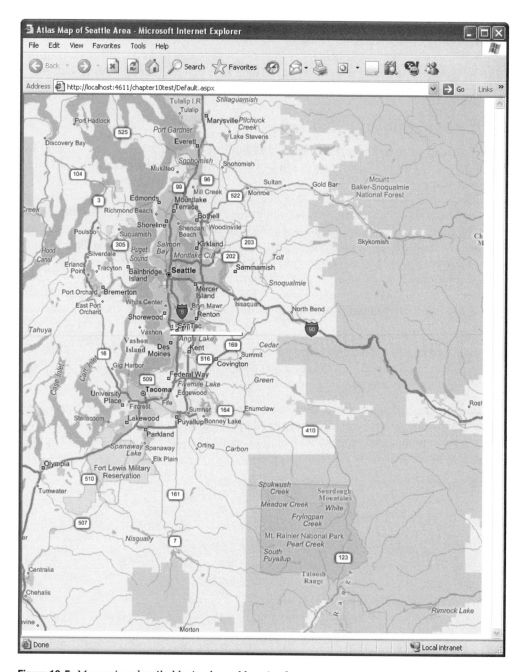

Figure 10-5. *Map using detailed latitude and longitude*

Setting the Zoom Level

You can set the zoom level of a map using the ZoomLevel property. This property can take an integer value from 0, which corresponds to the map view from 5,000 miles altitude, to 19, which corresponds to the map view from 30 yards altitude. Please note that not all zoom levels are available for all locations in the world. However, the maximum zoom level is available for all U.S. mainland locations.

Using the following definition for the map, you will see the map shown in Figure 10-6:

```
<virtualEarthMap id="MyMap" latitude="47.7512121212"
                 longitude="-122.43234" mapStyle="Road"
                 zoomLevel="0" />
```

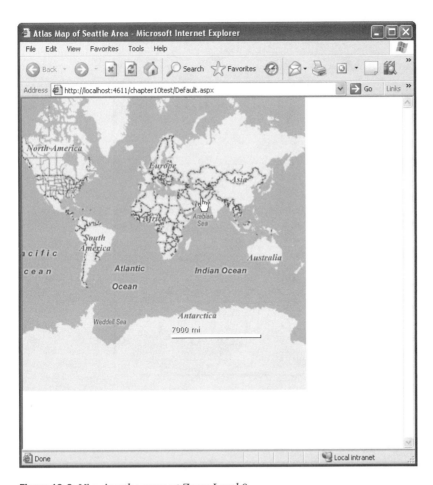

Figure 10-6. *Viewing the map at ZoomLevel 0*

Changing the ZoomLevel property to 12, as shown here, will produce the map shown in Figure 10-7:

```
<virtualEarthMap id="MyMap" latitude="47.7512121212"
                 longitude="-122.43234" mapStyle="Road"
                 zoomLevel="12" />
```

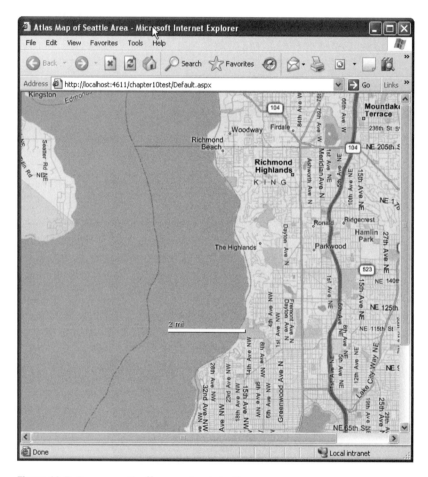

Figure 10-7. *Programatically zooming into the map*

Choosing a Map Type

In addition to setting the location of the map, you can also specify the map type. Three types are available:

Road: This gives the typical road-type map. All the examples used so far in this chapter use this type.

Aerial: This gives you a photograph of the location from above.

Hybrid: This gives you a combination of the previous two—an aerial photograph of the location with roads, names, and locations superimposed on it.

You set the type using the mapStyle property attribute. In all the previous sections of this chapter, this attribute was set to Road, and as such, all the maps so far in this chapter have been road maps.

Here's an example of how to specify an aerial map:

```
<virtualEarthMap id="MyMap" latitude="47.69"
                 longitude="-122.08" mapStyle="Aerial"
                 zoomLevel="16" />
```

You can see the map in Figure 10-8.

Figure 10-8. *An aerial map of the location from Figure 10-7*

Specifying this as a hybrid map is also straightforward. Here's the script:

```
<virtualEarthMap id="MyMap" latitude="47.69"
                 longitude="-122.08" mapStyle="Hybrid"
                 zoomLevel="16" />
```

You can see the results in Figure 10-9.

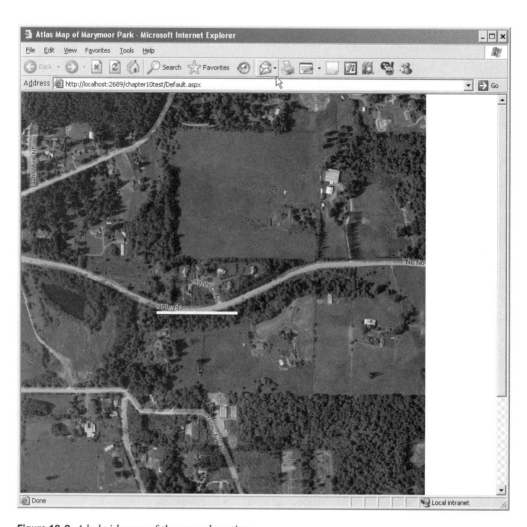

Figure 10-9. *A hybrid map of the same location*

Panning to a Location

You can programmatically use the PanTo method of the map control to create a button that, when clicked, will pan the map to a location specified in longitude and latitude. You cannot set the zoom level with this method, so you will be panning across the current zoom level.

The following is the Atlas Script that invokes this method. This uses an HTML `<input>` control called GoHome on the page.

```
<button id="GoHome">
 <click>
  <invokeMethod target="MyMap" method="panTo">
    <parameters longitude="-122.08" latitude="47.69" />
  </invokeMethod>
 </click>
</button>
```

In Atlas, the button component has a `<click>` behavior that can be used to invoke a method on it or on any other named control. In this case, the invokeMethod is configured for the MyMap control, which is the map control you've been using throughout this chapter. The code specifies the PanTo method, which accepts two parameters (longitude and latitude). These are specified in the `<parameters>` child tag as attributes.

Thus, when you click the button, the map will pan to the specified coordinates.

So, when viewing another location—for example, the Kennedy Space Center that you can see in Figure 10-10—if you click the GoHome button and invoke the PanTo method as specified earlier, you will be taken directly to the specified coordinates, in this case the coordinates near Seattle, as shown in Figure 10-11.

Figure 10-10. *Viewing the Kennedy Space Center*

Figure 10-11. *The results of calling the PanTo method*

Panning by an Amount

In addition to panning to a particular location, you can also pan relative to the current location by a number of pixels. It takes two parameters, deltaX and deltaY, with which you specify the direction.

For deltaX, negative values pan to the left of the map, and positive values pan to the right.

For deltaY, negative values pan toward the bottom of the map, and positive ones pan to the top.

Here's the Atlas Script that manages two buttons and invokes this method to pan the map left or right by 100 pixels each way:

```
<components>
<virtualEarthMap id="MyMap" latitude="47.7512121212"
                 longitude="-122.43234" mapStyle="Hybrid"
                 width="400px" height="400px"
                 zoomLevel="12" />

<button id="GoLeft">
    <click>
      <invokeMethod target="MyMap" method="panBy">
       <parameters deltaX="-100" deltaY="0" />
      </invokeMethod>
    </click>
</button>
<button id="GoRight">
    <click>
      <invokeMethod target="MyMap" method="panBy">
       <parameters deltaX="100" deltaY="0" />
      </invokeMethod>
    </click>
</button>
</components>
```

Using Pushpins

Maps are all very nice, but without any kind of attribution and labeling, they lose their usefulness after a while. Fortunately, Atlas maps support graphical pushpins that allow you to highlight specific locations on the map.

Figure 10-12 shows an example of a map containing four pushpins.

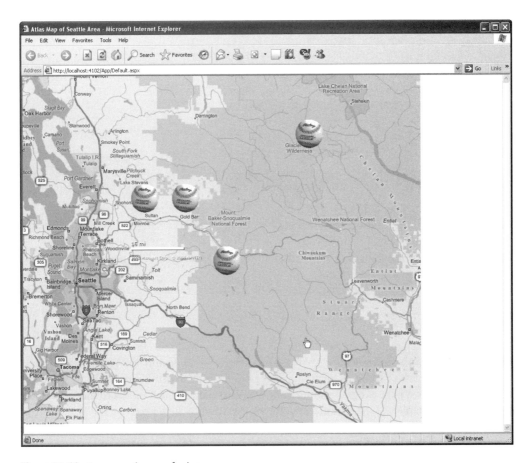

Figure 10-12. *A map using pushpins*

This map uses four pushpins, which are transparent GIFs of a baseball, specified based on their longitude and latitude.

Here is how you implement this using Atlas Script:

```
<script type="text/xml-script">
  <page xmlns:script="http://schemas.microsoft.com/xml-script/2005">

  <components>
    <virtualEarthMap id="MyMap" latitude="48"
                     longitude="-122" mapStyle="Road"
                     zoomLevel="9">
      <pushpins>
        <pushpin id="1" latitude="48" longitude="-122"
                 imageURL="images/bb.gif" />
```

```
            <pushpin id="2" latitude="48.25" longitude="-121"
                    imageURL="images/bb.gif" />
            <pushpin id="3" latitude="47.75" longitude="-121.5"
                    imageURL="images/bb.gif" />
            <pushpin id="4" latitude="48" longitude="-121.75"
                    imageURL="images/bb.gif" />
        </pushpins>
        </virtualEarthMap>
    </components>
    </page>
    </script>
```

In this case, the map contains a child tag, `<pushpins>`, that contains a list of `<pushpin>` tags. Each of these defines a single pushpin.

Defining a pushpin is straightforward—you need only to give it a latitude, a longitude, and the URL of an image. Then, at render time the specified image will be placed on the map at the specified location.

Summary

In this chapter, you looked at the Atlas libraries for mapping and how you can use them to build your own mapping applications. You looked at how to create and invoke an Atlas map on a page and how you can set its location using latitude and longitude. You looked at how to zoom in and out of a page programmatically and how to use its object model to move the map pane from place to place. Finally, you learned how to annotate the map using the built-in pushpin technology.

With all this in your toolbox, you can now start building your own mapping applications.

CHAPTER 11

■■■

Building a Sample Application with ASP.NET and Atlas

Throughout this book, you've been exploring the technologies underpinning Atlas, including the client-side libraries that enable the encapsulation of HTML and JavaScript, the object-oriented controls, the addition of animation and mapping functionality, and the server-side enabling of asynchronous update functionality through the use of server-side ASP.NET controls.

In this chapter, you'll go through, in detail, what it takes to build an application that makes the most of these features to deliver a real-world application. The application you will build will be a financial research tool that delivers stock quotes, extended stock information, and some price history analytics. This is the information that is typically used in *technical analysis* stock trading. Stock traders use a number of methodologies to determine a good buying or selling price of a stock, including *fundamental analysis* where you look at company fundamentals such as dividends, profits, earnings per share, gross sales, and more. This is typically a good methodology when investing in a company for medium- to long-term investments. Day traders, who are looking for a quick in and out, typically use technical analyses where they want to look at the momentum of the stock based on how it has performed in similar situations recently. The closing price for a stock over time is called the *price history*, and by applying various mathematical transforms to it, a day trader can guess where it is going to go. It's an inexact science, but when carefully applied, it can be effective.

In this chapter, you'll be building a Bollinger band–based analysis of price history and delivering it in an Atlas application. You'll also see how technical traders use this to determine potential times to get in and out of a stock. This should not be construed as investment advice; it is provided for informational use only and as a demonstration of the ASP.NET technology.

Figure 11-1 shows the application.

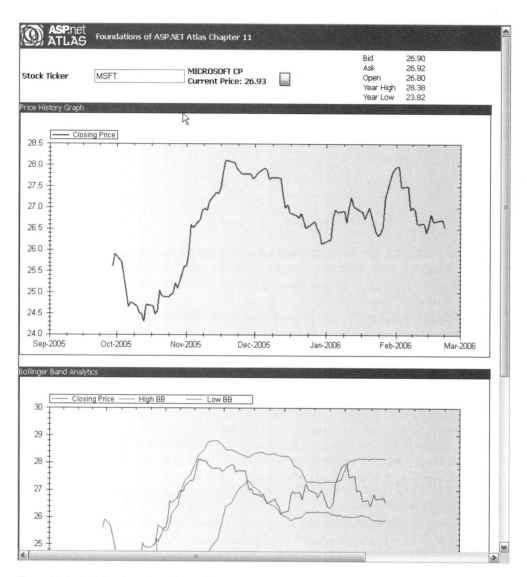

Figure 11-1. *An Atlas-based stock application*

Understanding the Application Architecture

The application is built as a typical *n*-tier application comprising a resource tier that contains the back-end resources. In this case, the resources are the Company Information web service (courtesy of Flash-db.com) and the Price History web service that provides comma-separated values (CSV) over HTTP from Yahoo. You can see the architecture in Figure 11-2.

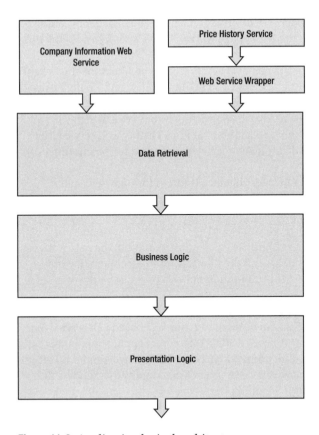

Figure 11-2. *Application logical architecture*

In a multitiered architecture like this, the resource tier is where the information that drives your service comes from. In many applications, and this one is no exception, the information is read-only—you are simply presenting the resources to the end user. However, rarely are the raw resources presented. Some value has to be added to show how you visually present them and also how you enhance them for presentation using business logic. Many applications blur the distinction between business logic and presentation logic, but it is important to distinguish these, and indeed, when using Atlas, the ability to distinguish them becomes a lot easier.

This is because before Ajax and Atlas, a developer would have to make a full-page refresh whenever the user interacted with the page. Then, with the advent of DHTML, they could make a decision—for a simple interaction and for a simple business logic, it might be easier not to do it on the server but instead to do it using a script on the page. For example, if the current price for the stock is on the page, the current earnings are known to the page, and the user wants to display the profit/earnings (P/E) ratio (which divides the former by the latter), why not just calculate it using an on-page JavaScript and then render it in a `<div>` element instead of performing yet another round-trip to the server and producing a "blink" as the page refreshes?

This can quickly lead to a maintenance nightmare and is a common problem that has been solved by asynchronous updates. Now, even though in the previous scenario you may incur another request to the server, the packet of information will be a lot smaller because you are just going to update part of the page; the entire page will not "flash" as it refreshes the user interface with the update.

Beneath the resource tier comes the data retrieval tier. In a clean architecture, this is kept separate from the logic so that if data sources change, you do not need to get into the business logic plumbing and rip it out. It should provide a clean interface to the data layer. Visual Studio 2005 offers you the facility to create a proxy to an existing web service, which you can use to implement a data retrieval tier. In this application, the Price History web service from Yahoo provides CSV over HTTP, so you will implement a web service that wraps this functionality and can easily be proxied.

The business logic tier is where you add value to your resources through aggregation, integration, and calculation. For example, in the case of calculating the P/E discussed earlier, with price information coming from one resource and earnings from another, instead of integrating and calculating these on the page level, you would aggregate the information in the business logic tier where the function performing the calculation would call the data retrieval tier to get the information from both resources and then perform the calculation. It would then provide the resultant information to the presentation tier as a response to the original request for the P/E analytic.

The presentation tier is typically server-side logic that provides the markup and/or graphics that will get rendered in the browser. This can be anything from a C-based CGI service that generates raw HTML to an advanced control-based ASP.NET 2.0 server application. In this case, the example will use a variety of technologies, from ASP.NET controls that will render HTML that is generated by server-side C# code to advanced graphics functionality that renders the time series chart (you can see these charts in Figure 11-1).

Finally, what appears to the user is the output of this presentation tier, and it is a document that contains HTML, graphics, JavaScript, style sheets, and anything else the browser needs to render.

As I show how to construct the application, you'll see each of these tiers in a little more detail.

Creating the Company Information Pane

Flash-db.com provides several hosted web services free of charge. One of these services is the excellent Company Information Web service. This provides basic and extended stock price information, as well as the name of the company associated with a stock ticker. Accessing this from a Visual Studio 2005 application is straightforward. The WSDL for the web service is hosted at the following location:

```
http://www.flash-db.com/services/ws/companyInfo.wsdl
```

To create a proxy to this, right-click your project in Solution Explorer, and select Add Web Reference (see Figure 11-3).

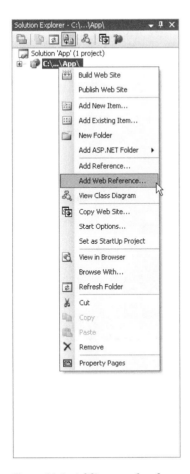

Figure 11-3. *Adding a web reference*

This will present a dialog box in which you specify the WSDL of the service you are referencing (see Figure 11-4).

When you enter a valid WSDL here, the description pane will update with the supported functions on the web service, as well as the services that are available to this WSDL (multiple services can be published to a single WSDL). In the Web Reference Name field, you should enter a friendly name, because this is the name that will be generated for the proxy that talks to the web service on your behalf.

The Company Information web service is used in the application to present the name of the company as well as the current price information (see Figure 11-5).

Additionally, when the button to the right of the current price is clicked, some extended stock price information appears. This demonstrates a partial update of the page. When running it, you will see that this segment updates without incurring a full-page refresh and associated "blink." It also provides a status that the application is loading while the asynchronous update is taking place (see Figure 11-6).

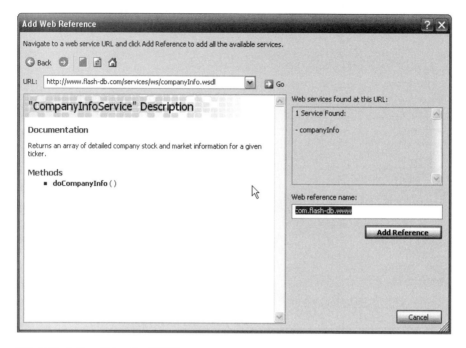

Figure 11-4. *Specifying the WSDL*

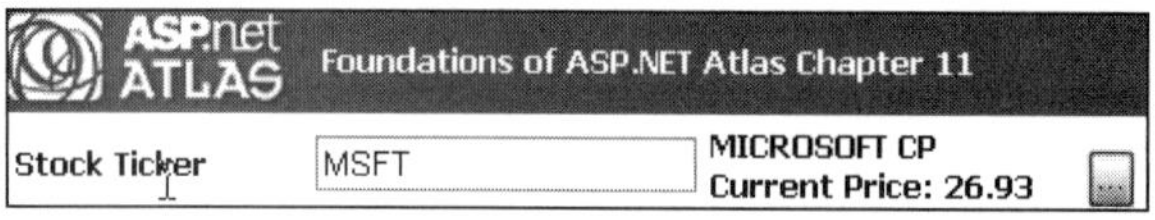

Figure 11-5. *The company and current price information*

Figure 11-6. *The progress messages during the asynchronous update*

Once the update is complete, the extended price information appears, as shown in Figure 11-7.

Figure 11-7. *Showing the extended price information*

The extended price information includes the bid and ask prices. These are, respectively, the current price that is being bid on the stock by prospective buyers and the one that is being asked for by sellers. When you make a purchase at the current market price, it will usually be between these two values, provided you are buying a large amount of shares in the stock. It also provides the opening price for the day, as well as the year's high and low. As you can see in Figure 11-7, Microsoft stock was quoted at 26.93, but pressure is moving it downward (the ask price and the bid price are both lower than this); however, it is up on its opening price of 26.80.

Now let's take a look at the code that implements this.

Figure 11-8 shows the ASP.NET web form that contains the server-side controls used to implement this functionality.

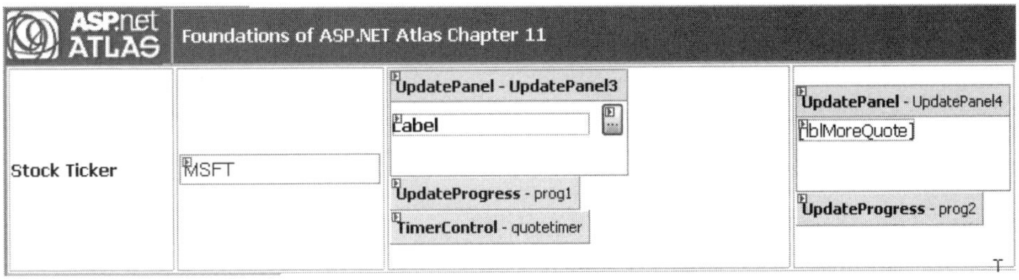

Figure 11-8. *The ASP.NET designer view of the company information*

As you can see in Figure 11-8, the application uses two UpdatePanel controls. Each of these contains a label. Each has an associated UpdateProgress control. The ScriptManager control on the page has Enable Partial Rendering set to true, meaning that updates to these UpdatePanel controls will not incur a full-page refresh. Finally, a timer control on the left triggers a timed update to the basic quote information every minute. Listing 11-1 shows the markup for these controls.

Listing 11-1. *Markup for the UpdatePanel Controls*

```
<table width="100%" cellpadding="2" style="border-width: 0">
<tr>
  <td style="width: 117px" class="style1">
    <strong>Stock Ticker</strong>
  </td>
  <td style="width: 133px">
    <asp:TextBox ID="TextBox1" runat="server"
        OnTextChanged="TextBox1_TextChanged">MSFT
    </asp:TextBox>
  </td>
  <td class="style1" style="width: 289px">
  <strong>
    <atlas:UpdatePanel ID="UpdatePanel3" runat="server">
      <ContentTemplate>
```

```
                <asp:Label ID="lblQuote" runat="server"
                            Text="Label" Width="144px">
                </asp:Label>
                <asp:Button ID="btnMore" runat="server"
                            Text="..." OnClick="btnMore_Click"
                            CausesValidation="False" />
            </ContentTemplate>
        </atlas:UpdatePanel>

        <atlas:UpdateProgress runat="server" ID="prog1">
            <ProgressTemplate>
                Loading...
            </ProgressTemplate>
        </atlas:UpdateProgress>

        <atlas:TimerControl runat="server"
                            Interval="60000"
                            ID="quotetimer"
                            OnTick="quoteTimer_tick" />
        </strong>
        </td>
        <td class="style1" style="width: 147px">
          <atlas:UpdatePanel ID="UpdatePanel4" runat="server">
            <ContentTemplate>
              <asp:Label ID="lblMoreQuote" runat="server">
              </asp:Label>
            </ContentTemplate>
          </atlas:UpdatePanel>
          <atlas:UpdateProgress runat="server" ID="prog2">
            <ProgressTemplate>
              Loading...
            </ProgressTemplate>
          </atlas:UpdateProgress>
        </td>
      </tr>
</table>
```

The first UpdatePanel control (called UpdatePanel3) contains a Label control and a Button control. The Label control will contain the company name and current stock price, as you saw in Figure 11-6 and Figure 11-7. This gets updated whenever you enter a new stock ticker in the text box, and you'll see from the markup that this fires an event, called TextBox1_TextChanged, whenever the text changes.

The code for this event is simple—it calls the DoUpdate() function:

```
protected void TextBox1_TextChanged(object sender, EventArgs e)
{
    DoUpdate();
}
```

This DoUpdate() function is as follows:

```
private void DoUpdate()
{
    GetCompanyInfo(TextBox1.Text);

    lblPH.Text = GetPriceHistoryText(TextBox1.Text);

    lblPHGraph.Text = "<img src='PH.aspx?ticker="
                    + TextBox1.Text
                    + "&days=100' />";

    lblAnalyticGraph.Text = "<img src='PHBB.aspx?ticker="
                    + TextBox1.Text
                    + "&days=100' />";

    lblMoreQuote.Text = "";
}
```

This function updates the company information pane as well as the price history text and graphs. In what you are exploring here—the company information—the first line is the most important; it's a call to the helper function called GetCompanyInfo.

Here's what this function looks like:

```
private void GetCompanyInfo(string strTicker)
{
    companyInfo.CompanyInfoService svc =
        new companyInfo.CompanyInfoService();

    companyInfo.CompanyInfoResult rslt =
        svc.doCompanyInfo("anything", "anything", strTicker);

    lblQuote.Text = rslt.company
                    + " Current Price: "
                    + rslt.lastPrice;

}
```

The proxy to the Flash-db.com web service is called companyInfo. An instance of this proxy is first created, called svc. This exposes an object of type CompanyInfoResult that is used to store the returned information from the service. The second line creates an instance of this type, called rslt, into which the results of a doCompanyInfo web method call are loaded. This web method takes three parameters; the first two are user name and password. The web service is open, so you can put anything in for the user name and password parameters. The third parameter is the ticker for which you are seeking the company information.

The company name (rslt.company) is then appended to a string containing text (Current Price:), which in turn is appended to the last traded price for the stock (rslt.lastPrice). This is then assigned to the text property of lblQuote.

If you look back at the markup in Listing 11-1, you'll see that lblQuote is contained within the UpdatePanel control's <ContentTemplate> setting. Because the ScriptManager control has enabled partial rendering and because the label is within the UpdatePanel control, this enables the Ajax-style update of the page whenever lblQuote has its text property changed.

You can see that there is no explicit coding for a partial-page update. Everything is handled under the hood by the Atlas runtime. You concentrate on building your application, and by wrapping standard ASP.NET controls with an <UpdatePanel>, you can enable the asynchronous functionality.

You'll now see what happens when you click the ellipsis button in this page to render the extended price information.

You can see from the markup that the button is called btnMore and that it has a click event handler called btnMore_Click. Here's a snippet from the markup as a reminder:

```
<asp:Button ID="btnMore" runat="server"
               Text="..." OnClick="btnMore_Click"
               CausesValidation="False" />
```

This btnMore_Click event handler looks like this:

```
protected void btnMore_Click(object sender, EventArgs e)
{
    GetExtendedQuote(TextBox1.Text);
}
```

It simply calls a helper function, passing it the contents of the text box containing the ticker information entered by the user.

This function looks like this:

```
private void GetExtendedQuote(string strTicker)
{
  companyInfo.CompanyInfoService svc = new
    companyInfo.CompanyInfoService();
  companyInfo.CompanyInfoResult rslt =
    svc.doCompanyInfo("anything", "anything", strTicker);
  StringBuilder theHTML = new StringBuilder();
  theHTML.Append("<table width='100%' cellspacing='0'
                  cellpadding='0' style='border-width: 0'>");
  theHTML.Append("<tr><td  width='40%'>");
  theHTML.Append("Bid ");
  theHTML.Append("</td><td  width='40%'>");
  theHTML.Append(rslt.bid);
  theHTML.Append("</td></tr>");

  theHTML.Append("<tr><td  width='40%'>");
  theHTML.Append("Ask ");
  theHTML.Append("</td><td  width='40%'>");
  theHTML.Append(rslt.ask);
  theHTML.Append("</td></tr>");
```

```
theHTML.Append("<tr><td  width='40%'>");
theHTML.Append("Open ");
theHTML.Append("</td><td  width='40%'>");
theHTML.Append(rslt.open);
theHTML.Append("</td></tr>");

theHTML.Append("<tr><td  width='40%'>");
theHTML.Append("Year High ");
theHTML.Append("</td><td  width='40%'>");
theHTML.Append(rslt.yearHigh);
theHTML.Append("</td></tr>");

theHTML.Append("<tr><td  width='40%'>");
theHTML.Append("Year Low ");
theHTML.Append("</td><td  width='40%'>");
theHTML.Append(rslt.yearLow);
theHTML.Append("</td></tr>");

theHTML.Append("</table>");
lblMoreQuote.Text = theHTML.ToString();


}
```

This function is similar to what you saw earlier. It creates an instance of the proxy to the Flash-db.com web service and an instance of the object type that contains the results to the doCompanyInfo() web method call. It then generates HTML for a table using a StringBuilder control and places this HTML into the Text property of the lblMoreQuote control.

In a similar manner to earlier, because this control is contained within the content template of an UpdatePanel control, the refreshing of this information on the page is handled asynchronously; in addition, because it is using Ajax techniques through the underlying Atlas mechanisms, the page will not blink as the update is received.

In both cases, an <UpdateProgress> control is used. Here's an example:

```
<atlas:UpdateProgress runat="server" ID="prog2">
  <ProgressTemplate>
    Loading...
  </ProgressTemplate>
</atlas:UpdateProgress>
```

This provides the specification for what is displayed as the asynchronous update is taking place. It can contain flat text (as in this case) or HTML, so you could, for example, have an animated GIF showing the progress through a blinking light or similar and then embed that on the page using an <img> tag within the ProgressTemplate.

Creating the Price History Pane

The price history pane on the page renders the 100-day price history (the closing price for the stock over the past 100 days) in a simple text table. You can see it in Figure 11-9.

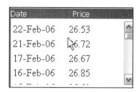

Figure 11-9. *The price history pane*

This information is ultimately sourced from Yahoo as CSV over HTTP. This CSV file is returned from a call to the iFinance server at Yahoo using a URL call like this:

```
http://ichart.finance.yahoo.com/table.csv?s=MSFT&d=2
        &e=4&f=2006&g=d&a=2&b=13&c=1986&ignore=.csv
```

This returns a CSV file whose format is like this:

```
Date,Open,High,Low,Close,Volume,Adj. Close*
3-Mar-06,26.81,27.16,26.74,26.93,45218800,26.93
2-Mar-06,27.02,27.10,26.90,26.97,41850300,26.97
1-Mar-06,26.98,27.20,26.95,27.14,53061200,27.14
28-Feb-06,26.95,27.30,26.87,26.87,65036100,26.87
```

Each data item is separated by a comma, and each line is separated by a carriage return. To make this data easier to consume by the data retrieval and business logic tiers, a web service consumes this HTTP service and exposes it as a structured DataTable. You'll see this in the next section.

Creating the Wrapper Web Service

This web service will provide a web method that makes a call to the Yahoo iFinance server on your behalf, takes the CSV that is returned from it, and serializes it as a DataTable. It is designed to be consumed by a .NET-based client, so using a DataTable object works nicely. If you want to expose a web service that is easily interoperable with other platforms, you should serialize the returned data using straight XML that can be parsed on the client side.

Here is the code for the web method:

```
[WebMethod]
public DataTable GetFullPriceHistory(string strTicker, int nDays)
  {
    WebClient client = new WebClient();
    StringBuilder strURI = new
        StringBuilder("http://ichart.finance.yahoo.com/table.csv?s=");
    strURI.Append(strTicker);
```

```
  strURI.Append("&d=1&e=22&f=2006&g=d&a=8&b=28&c=1989&ignore=.csv");
  Stream data = client.OpenRead(strURI.ToString());
  StreamReader reader = new StreamReader(data);
  string s = reader.ReadToEnd();
  DataTable theTable = CsvParser.Parse(s);
  if (nDays > 0)
  {
    int i = nDays + 1;
    while (theTable.Rows.Count > i)
    {
      theTable.Rows.RemoveAt(i);
    }
  }
  data.Close();
  reader.Close();
  return theTable;
}
```

This makes the connection to the Yahoo server by using an object derived from the WebClient class. To use this, you use its OpenRead method, which is pointed at a URI. This returns a stream, which can be read by a StreamReader. The contents of this can be parsed into a string using a CsvParser abstract helper class.

This helper class provides the parsing functionality that reads the CSV information and returns it as a DataTable. The download for this book includes a version of this class that was derived from one published in the excellent blog from Andreas Knab at http://knab.ws/blog/.

The call to the Yahoo iFinance server provides the entire price history for the stock, which can be thousands of days worth of information. It provides an additional layer that allows you to crop this data to the specified number of days. It does this by iterating through the DataTable and removing rows beyond what you are interested in. So if you want to pull 100 days worth of data, you remove all rows beyond number 100.

That's about it. This web method is present in a web service called DataTier.

Consuming the Web Service

Figure 11-10 shows the design for the price history pane.

Figure 11-10. *Designing the price history pane*

As you can see from Figure 11-10, it contains a simple HTML table that contains the headers for the table. Then, under this an UpdatePanel control is placed, which contains a single label. This label will be loaded with the HTML for the rest of the table, as you will see in a moment. Although it isn't visible in the designer, this is contained within an ASP.NET Panel control that allows you to put this in a fixed dimension area with scrollbars that allow you to scroll through the data. This has two benefits. First, the header fields for the data and price will not scroll off the screen. Second, if the table has several hundred rows and is not contained in a scrollable pane like this, then it will dominate the UI, and you will need to scroll way down in the browser to see the rest of the page content.

You can see it in action using the scrollbars in Figure 11-11.

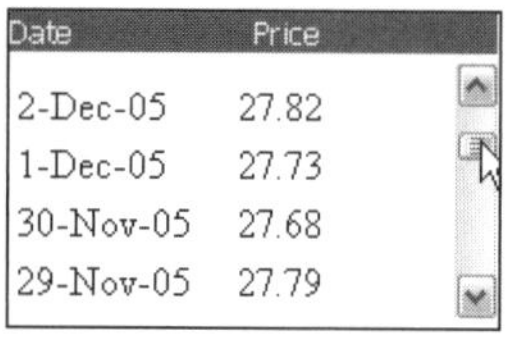

Figure 11-11. *The price history text pane in action with a scrollbar*

Let's take a look at the markup that is used to implement this:

```
<li id="PHItem">
 <div id="PHDiv">
  <table cellspacing='0' cellpadding='0'
        class='style1' style='border-width: 0'>
   <tr class='style2'>
    <td style='background-color: #1077ad; '
        width="100px">
        Date</td>
    <td style='background-color: #1077ad; '
        width="100px">
        Price</td>
   </tr>
  </table>
 </div>
 <div id="PHContents">
  <atlas:UpdatePanel ID="THTextPanel" runat="server">
   <ContentTemplate>
    <asp:Panel ID="Panel1" runat="Server"
               ScrollBars="auto" Width="200px"
               Height="100px">
     <asp:Label ID="lblPH" runat="server" Text=""></asp:Label>
    </asp:Panel>
   </ContentTemplate>
  </atlas:UpdatePanel>
```

```
<atlas:UpdateProgress runat="server" ID="Prog3">
  <ProgressTemplate>
    Loading...
  </ProgressTemplate>
</atlas:UpdateProgress>
</div>
</li>
```

At the top of this listing you can see the table that contains the header cells. This is implemented as a separate table so that it doesn't scroll off the screen when you scroll through the data, effectively locking the titles. At the top is an `<li>` tag, indicating this is an item in an HTML list. This is used for drag-and-drop functionality, which you will see later in the "Using Atlas Client Controls for an Enhanced UI" section.

Further down in the markup you can see the UpdatePanel control that contains two controls in its content template. These are an `<asp:Panel>` control and an `<asp:Label>` control called lblPH. The latter is contained within the former, meaning that the panel creates the scroll pane area for the contents of the label. You can see that the panel is specified as being 200 pixels wide and 100 pixels high. Anything that appears outside this will generate scrollbars on the panel.

Earlier, when looking at the company and extended quote information, you saw a function called DoUpdate. Let's look at this function again:

```
private void DoUpdate()
{
  lblPH.Text = GetPriceHistoryText(TextBox1.Text);

  GetCompanyInfo(TextBox1.Text);

  lblPHGraph.Text =
    "<img src='PH.aspx?ticker=" + TextBox1.Text + "&days=100' />";

  lblAnalyticGraph.Text =
    "<img src='PHBB.aspx?ticker=" + TextBox1.Text + "&days=100' />";

  lblMoreQuote.Text = "";
}
```

The first line sets the value of lblPH. Setting this value triggers the partial update because this control is embedded within the content template of the UpdatePanel control.

So when the user enters a new ticker and changes the contents of the text box, this function is called. The new value for lblPH.Text is then set to the response from GetPriceHistoryText when the value of the text box is passed to it.

Let's take a look at this function and see what it does:

```
private String GetPriceHistoryText(string strTicker)
{
  DataTier theData = new DataTier();
  DataTable theTable =
    theData.GetFullPriceHistory(strTicker, 300);
  StringBuilder theHTML = new StringBuilder();
  theHTML.Append("<table>");
  int nRows = theTable.Rows.Count;
  for (int i = 1; i < nRows; i++)
  {
    theHTML.Append("<tr><td width='100px'>");
    theHTML.Append(theTable.Rows[i].ItemArray[0].ToString());
    theHTML.Append("</td><td width='100px'>");
    theHTML.Append(theTable.Rows[i].ItemArray[1].ToString());
    theHTML.Append("</td></tr>");
  }
  theHTML.Append("</table>");
  return theHTML.ToString();
}
```

At the top of the function, you can see where it creates a reference to the web service that wraps the Yahoo CSV service. It calls this, passing it the ticker and the value 300 and thus getting back a DataTable containing 300 days worth of data.

It then iterates through this DataTable and generates the HTML markup for a two-column table with 300 rows. Each row contains a day's worth of data with the date in the first column and the value in the second. These are derived from the ItemArray exposed by the Rows collection of a DataTable. It is zero-based, so the first column's contents are in .ItemArray[0], the next are in .ItemArray[1], and so on.

Generating the Price History Graph

You are no doubt familiar with seeing price history graphs on business TV shows on CNN or the Bloomberg channel. Figure 11-12, Figure 11-13, and Figure 11-14 show the price history charts for companies such as Microsoft (MSFT), Google (GOOG), and Starbucks (SBUX), respectively.

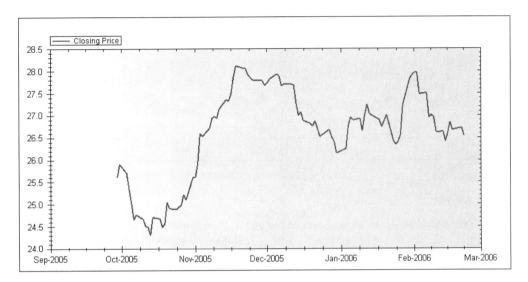

Figure 11-12. *300-day price history for MSFT*

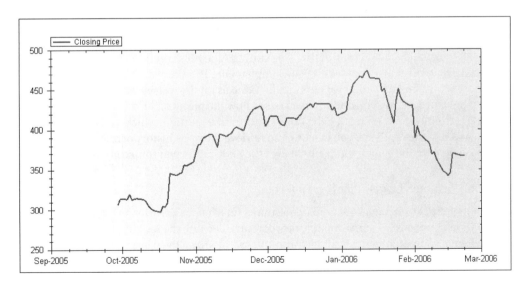

Figure 11-13. *300-day price history for GOOG*

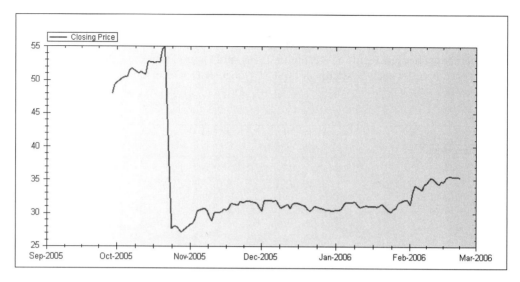

Figure 11-14. *300-day price history for SBUX*

These charts are useful in determining where a stock is going, what its recent trend is, and what its long-time trend is. Many stocks move between high and low values in what sometimes looks as a sine wave, and this is typically called its *trading envelope*. This is apparent in Figure 11-12, which shows a cycle from 26 to 28. It indicates that March 2006 may be a good time to purchase the stock because it is at the lower end of the trading envelope. This is no guarantee that the stock will not break from the trading envelope and fall far below 26. Also, typically when a stock breaks from its trading envelope, it tends to move quickly outside the trading range, which can lead to it rocketing either upward or downward. A more reliable methodology for using price history analysis is to use the Bollinger band method, which you will see in the "Generating Analytics" section later.

But, back to the technology—how is this implemented?

The resource and data retrieval tiers are the same as for the text-based price history pane you saw previously. If you've skipped ahead to see how the pretty pictures are drawn, it's a good idea to return to the "Creating the Price History Pane" section, which describes the DataTier web service and how you can use it to retrieve the price history of a stock.

To implement the charts, the example uses the ZedGraph open source library.

Using the ZedGraph Library Charting Engine

ZedGraph (http://zedgraph.org) is an open source set of classes, written in C#, that enable the creation of various 2D graphs of arbitrary datasets. Because the set is class-based, it has a high degree of programmatic flexibility, and you can modify almost every aspect of a graph including features such as scale ranges, scale types, step sizes, and so on, to be overridden from their defaults. It also allows for multirange, multitype, multiaxis graphs to be overlaid in a single chart. See Figure 11-15 for an example of a single chart that includes stacked bars, transparent overlays, and filled lines. It also includes legends and annotations.

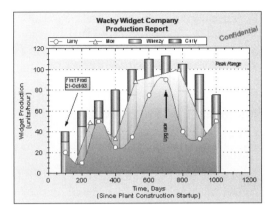

Figure 11-15. *Sample ZedGraph chart*

As such, ZedGraph makes an excellent choice for use in an Atlas-based project and is easy to implement in your applications. You simply make a reference to the ZedGraph.DLL in your solution and add the ZedGraph tools to your Toolbox in the standard way.

Drawing the Price History Graph with ZedGraph

To implement the price history graph, you can use a new web form. The download contains the web form in a file called PH.aspx. This web form contains a single ZedGraph control.

When you place a ZedGraph control from your Toolbox onto a Web form, it draws the default chart you saw in Figure 11-15. You can see the PH.aspx page in the web form designer in Figure 11-16.

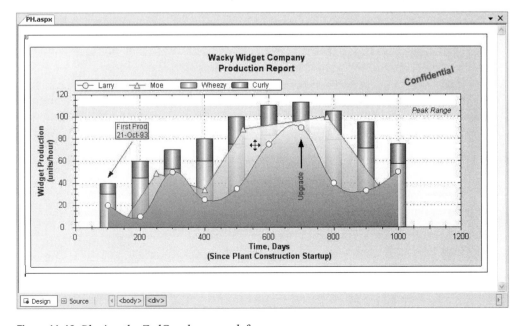

Figure 11-16. *Placing the ZedGraph on a web form*

The ZedGraph fires an event upon rendering, which occurs when the page is loaded or refreshed. This event is called RenderGraph.

In this case, the page is going to take two parameters, one for the ticker of the stock to be rendered and the other for the number of days to render. These will be used to make a call to the DataTier web service to get the DataTable back. The DataTable will then load the graph with the appropriate data.

Listing 11-2 shows the full code for the ZedGraphWeb1_RenderGraph event handler.

Listing 11-2. *Rendering the Graph*

```
protected void ZedGraphWeb1_RenderGraph(
   System.Drawing.Graphics g, ZedGraph.MasterPane mPane)
{
  int nDays = 0;
  int nRows = 0;
  GraphPane pane = mPane[0];
  PointPairList pt = new PointPairList();
  double nx;
  double ny;

  string days = (string)Page.Request.Params["days"];
  string ticker = (string)Page.Request.Params["ticker"];

  if (ticker != null)
  {
    ticker = ticker.Trim();
    DataTier theDataTier = new DataTier();
    if (days == null)
      nDays = 0;
    else
      nDays = Convert.ToInt32(days);

    DataTable dtTable =
      theDataTier.GetFullPriceHistory(ticker,nDays);
    nRows = dtTable.Rows.Count;


    for (int i = 1; i < nRows; i++)
    {
      ny = Convert.ToDouble(dtTable.Rows[i].ItemArray[1]);
      XDate tmpDate = new XDate(
        Convert.ToDateTime(dtTable.Rows[i].ItemArray[0]));
      nx = (double)tmpDate;
      pt.Add(nx, ny);
    }
```

```
    pane.XAxis.Type = AxisType.Date;
    pane.XAxis.GridDashOff = 0;
    LineItem priceCurve = pane.AddCurve(
      "Closing Price", pt, Color.SlateBlue,
      SymbolType.None);
    priceCurve.Line.Width = 2.0F;
    pane.AxisFill = new Fill(Color.White, Color.AntiqueWhite);
    pane.XAxis.MinGrace = 0;
    pane.XAxis.MaxGrace = 0;
    pane.YAxis.MinGrace = 0;
    pane.YAxis.MaxGrace = 0;
    pane.AxisChange(g);
  }
}
```

This event handler takes two parameters. The first is the base System.Drawing.Graphics object. To render the graph, right at the bottom of the event handler, the System.Drawing. Graphics object is passed to the AxisChange method of a ZedGraph pane to refresh and redraw the graph. The second parameter is a reference to the ZedGraph master pane, which is the collection of drawing surfaces that the ZedGraph exposes. Check out the ZedGraph documentation for information about how to use the panes to create different drawing surfaces. This graph will be a simple line chart that uses only one pane, which is the one at the zero index of this collection.

You refer to the pane with this line:

```
GraphPane pane = mPane[0];
```

The subsequent graphical operations will then be performed on this pane object.

To draw a line curve, it is a good idea to use the PointPairList collection that the ZedGraph library gives you. This allows you to create a single collection of data items that correspond to the X and Y values of a chart. The PointPairList supports many data types, including dates, so is perfect for the example's needs.

Once the input parameters (ticker and days) have been read in and sanitized, the DataTier service is called to return a DataTable containing the results of the query for that stock and the number of days of price history you want for it.

You then iterate through the DataTable and pull this information out like this:

```
for (int i = 1; i < nRows; i++)
    {
      ny = Convert.ToDouble(dtTable.Rows[i].ItemArray[1]);
      XDate tmpDate = new XDate(
        Convert.ToDateTime(dtTable.Rows[i].ItemArray[0]));
      nx = (double)tmpDate;
      pt.Add(nx, ny);
    }
```

The closing price for the stock should go on the Y axis, so it comes from .ItemArray[1] and is converted to a Double value. The original source from Yahoo, and the column on the DataTable, encodes the value as a string. This is retrieved and loaded into the ny variable.

The date for the closing price should go onto the X axis. This uses the XDate class (also part of the ZedGraph library), which is the data type used by ZedGraph to store dates in a chart and automatically generate axes from them. When using a PointPairList, you encode the XDate into a Double. You can see this being encoded in the variable nx.

Finally, you add the values for nx and ny to the PointPairList (called pt).

To finalize drawing the chart, you load the PointPairList, set the visual configuration of the chart, and trigger the AxisChange method, which refreshes it. First set the XAxis to be date encoded so that it recognizes the Doubles as dates:

```
pane.XAxis.Type = AxisType.Date;
```

Then load the PointPairList onto the chart. You do this using the AddCurve method of the pane. This method takes four parameters. The first is a string with the name of the data range. In this case, it is Closing Price. If you were superimposing data ranges on the chart (as in Figure 11-15), you would give them their distinct names here. The second parameter is the PointPairList. The third is the color for this range, which in this case is Color.SlateBlue, and the final parameter is the SymbolType used to indicate a point on the line. If you refer to Figure 11-15, you will see that some points are indicated with triangles or diamonds. You would specify these here. Because the graph has a lot of points, these would cause it to look cluttered, so you won't use a symbol type for this example.

```
LineItem priceCurve =
    pane.AddCurve("Closing Price", pt,
      Color.SlateBlue, SymbolType.None);
```

Next set the line width to 2 pixels to make the chart stand out a little more clearly, and fill the background for the pane with a graded fill between white and antique white:

```
priceCurve.Line.Width = 2.0F;
pane.AxisFill = new Fill(Color.White, Color.AntiqueWhite);
```

Finally, call the AxisChange event to render the graph:

```
pane.AxisChange(g);
```

This will draw the graph to the web form. Figure 11-17 shows this in action for the stock ticker SBUX with no date specified, thus showing the entire price history that Yahoo offers, going back to 1992.

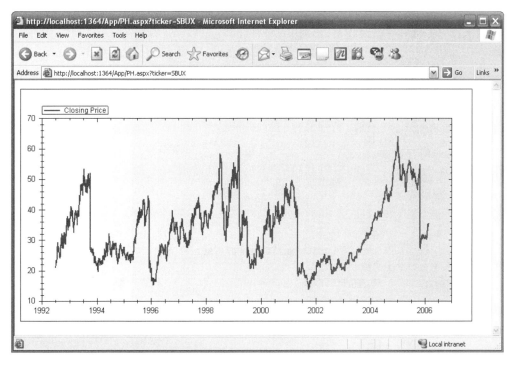

Figure 11-17. *The price history form in action*

Integrating with the Atlas Form

Integrating this with the Atlas-based web form you saw earlier and enabling it for asynchronous updates, Ajax style, is easy.

Figure 11-18 shows the designer for the web form.

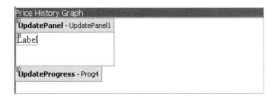

Figure 11-18. *The price history graph designer*

The UpdatePanel control contains a label, which is a server-side control that allows you to set its contents. You will be setting it to be an <img> tag and pointing the image source at the PH.aspx page so that it will return the graphic into the pane wrapped by the UpdatePanel control, thus achieving an asynchronous update.

Here's the markup:

```
<li id="PHGraph">
<div id="PHGraphDiv">
  <table width="400px" cellspacing="0"
         cellpadding="0" style="border-width: 0">
  <tr>
    <td style="background-color: #1077AD">
      <span class="style2">
      Price History Graph
      </span>
    </td>
  </tr>
  <tr>
    <td>
      <atlas:UpdatePanel ID="UpdatePanel1" runat="server">
        <ContentTemplate>
          <asp:Label ID="lblPHGraph"
                     runat="server"
                     Text="Label">
          </asp:Label>
        </ContentTemplate>
      </atlas:UpdatePanel>
      <atlas:UpdateProgress runat="server" ID="Prog4">
        <ProgressTemplate>
          Loading...
        </ProgressTemplate>
      </atlas:UpdateProgress>
    </td>
  </tr>
  </table>
</div>
</li>
```

The <li> tag denotes this section as being part of an HTML list. The drag-and-drop mechanism, which I'll discuss later in the "Using Atlas Client Controls for an Enhanced UI" section, uses this.

The markup defines a table with a header row containing the text *Price History Graph* and a second row containing the graph itself. The graph is implemented using a Label control, which is contained within the content template of an UpdatePanel control. The UpdatePanel control is contained within a <td> element, putting it within a cell in the table. The name of this Label control is lblPHGraph.

As you probably remember, the entire page update is triggered by the user changing the contents of the text box to select a new stock ticker. This calls the DoUpdate() function on the server.

Within this function, you'll find this line of C# code:

```
lblPHGraph.Text = "<img src='PH.aspx?ticker="
                  + TextBox1.Text +
                  "&days=100' />";
```

This sets the text of the label to contain the HTML markup for an image. The image uses the src attribute to call PH.aspx, and it passes the ticker that had been entered in the text box and the days=100 parameter to call for a 100-day price history graph. By setting it this way, the contents of the UpdatePanel change, which triggers an asynchronous update on the page. This update rerenders the image, providing a new chart. And of course it all happens with an Ajax-style asynchrony.

You can see it in action in Figure 11-19.

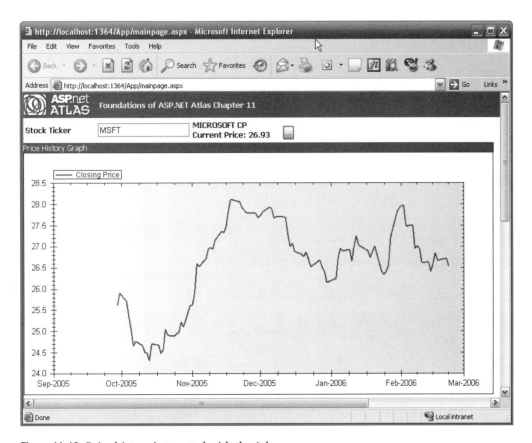

Figure 11-19. *Price history integrated with the Atlas page*

Generating an Analytics Graph

A methodology for determining good buy and sell prices for a stock comes from a technical analysis of the stock's trading envelope through the use of Bollinger bands. These bands are based on a calculation of the moving average of the stock—the moving average being the average price of the stock over a number of periods preceding the current one. For example, a 30-day moving average on any day is the average of closing prices for the stock over the previous 30-day period. Thus, today's average will be slightly different from yesterday's, which is slightly different from the day before; hence, it is called a *moving average*.

Bollinger bands are calculated from this value, with the "upper" band being the average over the preceding period plus two times the standard deviation and the "lower" band being the average over the preceding period minus two times the standard deviation. Figure 11-20, Figure 11-21, and Figure 11-22 show the price history overlaid with Bollinger bands for MSFT, GOOG, and SBUX.

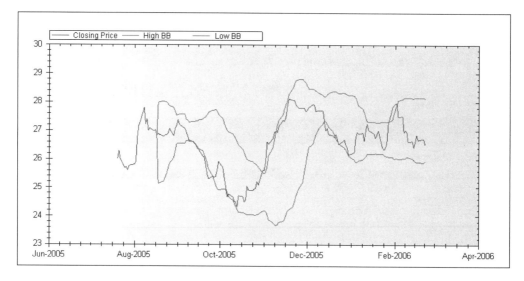

Figure 11-20. *Bollinger bands for MSFT over 150 days*

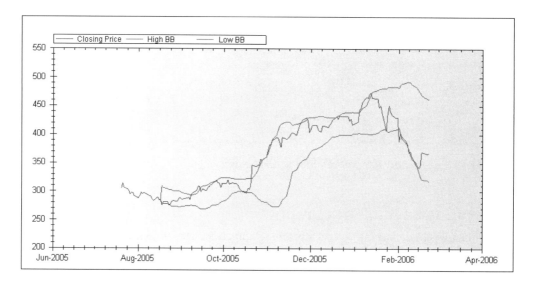

Figure 11-21. *Bollinger bands for GOOG over 150 days*

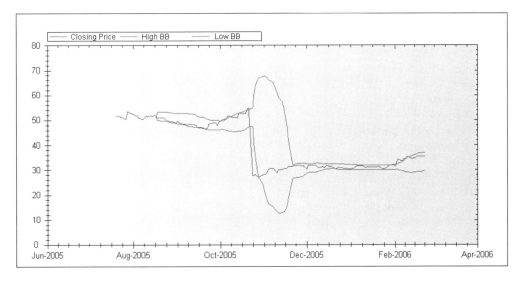

Figure 11-22. *Bollinger bands for SBUX over 150 days*

These bands are sometimes used to predict the value of a stock based on a projection of its future value based on its past behavior. A typical rule is to buy the stock when it penetrates the lower band moving upward or when it "bounces off" the lower band, and to sell it when it penetrates the upper band moving downward or when it bounces off the upper band.

Consider Figure 11-20; if a trader were using this technique, they would have bought MSFT stock in October 2005 at about 24 per share when it penetrated the lower line moving upward and would have sold it when it hit the top line about four weeks later at 25.50. More aggressive traders may have waited until the reverse trailing upper line caught up with the stock (this is called *momentum tracking*) and then sold it in mid-November at the point where it bounced off the upper line moving downward, selling at around 28 and making a nice profit.

It's a useful methodology for assessing the value of a stock, and as such this application includes a Bollinger band graph.

Implementation-wise it is identical to that used for the price history graph. A web form called PHBB.aspx hosts a ZedGraph control. This form accepts the stock ticker and number of days parameters in the same manner as earlier. Instead of adding a single curve to the chart, you add three curves: the price history, the upper Bollinger band, and the lower Bollinger band. Listing 11-3 shows the code to do all this.

Listing 11-3. *Generating Bollinger Band Analytics*

```
int nDays = 0;
int nRows = 0;
GraphPane pane = mPane[0];


string days = (string)Page.Request.Params["days"];
string ticker = (string)Page.Request.Params["ticker"];
```

```
if (ticker != null)
{
  ticker = ticker.Trim();
  DataTier theDataTier = new DataTier();
  if (days == null)
    nDays = 0;
  else
    nDays = Convert.ToInt32(days);

  DataTable dtTable = theDataTier.GetFullPriceHistory(ticker, nDays);
  nRows = dtTable.Rows.Count;
  double[] nx = new double[nRows-1];
  double[] ny = new double[nRows-1];
  double[] bbh = new double[nRows-1];
  double[] bbl = new double[nRows-1];
  double[] pht = new double[20];
  int nIndex = 0;
  for (int i = nRows-1; i > 0; i--)
  {
    ny[nIndex] = Convert.ToDouble(dtTable.Rows[i].ItemArray[1]);
    XDate tmpDate = new
        XDate(Convert.ToDateTime(dtTable.Rows[i].ItemArray[0]));
    nx[nIndex] = (double)tmpDate;
    if (nIndex > 20)
    {
      int x = 0;
      for (int n = nIndex - 20; n < nIndex; n++)
      {
        pht[x] = ny[n];
        x++;
      }
      bbh[nIndex] = GetAverage(pht)
          + (2 * GetStandardDeviation(pht));
      bbl[nIndex] = GetAverage(pht)
          - (2 * GetStandardDeviation(pht));

    }
    else
    {
      bbh[nIndex] = ny[nIndex];
      bbl[nIndex] = ny[nIndex];
    }
    nIndex++;
  }
  pane.XAxis.Type = AxisType.Date;
  pane.XAxis.GridDashOff = 0;
  pane.AddCurve("Closing Price", nx,
      ny, Color.SlateBlue, SymbolType.None);
```

```
pane.AddCurve("High BB", nx,
    bbh, Color.Red, SymbolType.None);

pane.AddCurve("Low BB", nx,
    bbl, Color.Red, SymbolType.None);

pane.AxisFill = new Fill(Color.White, Color.AntiqueWhite);
Axis.Default.MinGrace = 0;
Axis.Default.MaxGrace = 0;
pane.AxisChange(g);
```

The GetAverage and GetStandardDeviation helper functions that the application uses are as follows:

```
public double GetAverage(double[] num)
{
  double sum = 0.0;
  for (int i = 0; i < num.Length; i++)
  {
    sum += num[i];
  }
  double avg = sum / System.Convert.ToDouble(num.Length);

  return avg;
}


public double GetStandardDeviation(double[] num)
{
  double Sum = 0.0, SumOfSqrs = 0.0;
  for (int i = 0; i < num.Length; i++)
  {
    Sum += num[i];
    SumOfSqrs += Math.Pow(num[i], 2);
  }
  double topSum = (num.Length * SumOfSqrs) - (Math.Pow(Sum, 2));
  double n = (double)num.Length;
  return Math.Sqrt(topSum / (n * (n - 1)));
}
```

To integrate this with the Atlas-based form, allowing for asynchronous updates, the process is the same as you saw for the price history graph. A Label control (called lblAnalyticGraph) is embedded within an UpdatePanel control. When the user types a new ticker value into the text box, the DoUpdate() function is called on the server side. This function contains the following C# code:

```
lblAnalyticGraph.Text =
    "<img src='PHBB.aspx?ticker="
    + TextBox1.Text
    + "&days=100' />";
```

This changes the text for the label, which triggers the asynchronous update. The text, in the same way as earlier, is an HTML `<img>` tag, pointing the image source at the PHBB.aspx page to generate the graphic. This gives an asynchronous update to the Bollinger bands chart. You can see it in action in Figure 11-23.

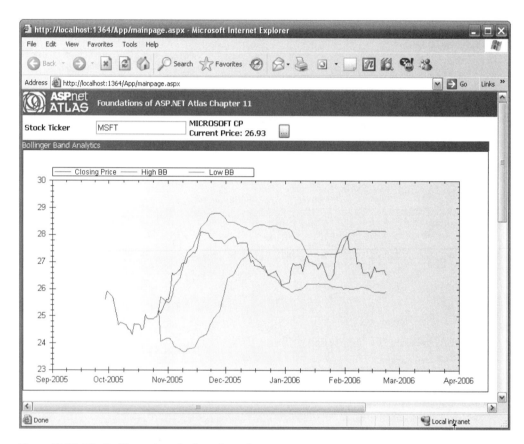

Figure 11-23. *The Bollinger bands chart in action*

Using Atlas Client Controls for an Enhanced UI

This application implements some Atlas client controls and associated behaviors to empower a drag-and-drop functionality. Figure 11-24 shows the price history graph being dragged over the Bollinger band analytics graph. You can drag and drop the three panes (the two graphs plus the price history text pane) around the page and arrange them vertically.

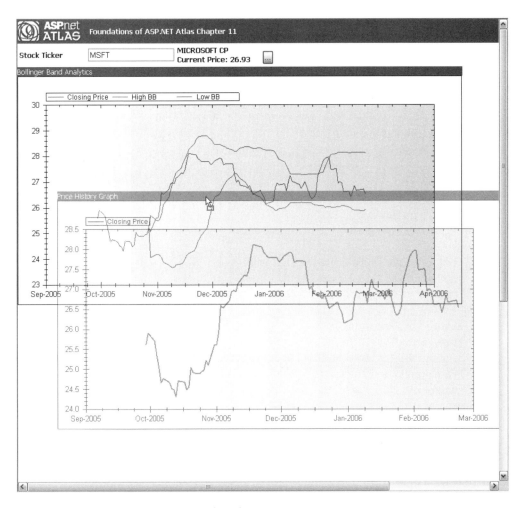

Figure 11-24. *Dragging one chart over the other*

You can see that while you are dragging one item over the other, the dragged item becomes partially transparent. All this functionality is provided in the Atlas libraries. You'll see how it is done as you dissect the code.

First, let's look at the Atlas Script that is on this page:

```
<script type="text/xml-script">
  <page xmlns:script="http://schemas.microsoft.com/xml-script/2005">
    <components>
      <control id="MasterList">
        <behaviors>
          <dragDropList dataType="HTML"
                        acceptedDataTypes="'HTML'"
                        dragMode="Move">
```

```
            <dropCueTemplate>
              <template layoutElement="dropCueTemplate" />
            </dropCueTemplate>
          </dragDropList>
        </behaviors>
      </control>

      <control id="PHItem">
        <behaviors>
          <draggableListItem handle="PHDiv" />
        </behaviors>
      </control>

      <control id="PHGraph">
        <behaviors>
          <draggableListItem handle="PHGraphDiv" />
        </behaviors>
      </control>

      <control id="PHAnalytic">
        <behaviors>
          <draggableListItem handle="PHAnalyticDiv" />
        </behaviors>
      </control>
    </components>

  </page>
</script>
```

When using Atlas Script, you define controls, behaviors, and actions using an XML document. You can see a lot more detail about it in Chapter 5.

This script defines four Atlas controls. Each control is associated with an underlying HTML element.

The first—MasterList—is an HTML list element. Each of the three panes is defined within a list element (<li> tag). This allows the panes to be dragged and dropped and locked into portions of the page. It's a three-item HTML list, and when you drag and drop the items, you simply rearrange how the elements are represented on the list.

You associate the <dragdropList> behavior with this element to turn it into a list where the items can be rearranged using drag and drop. The Atlas Script that provides this is as follows:

```
<dragDropList dataType="HTML"
                  acceptedDataTypes="'HTML'"
                  dragMode="Move">
        <dropCueTemplate>
          <template layoutElement="dropCueTemplate" />
        </dropCueTemplate>
      </dragDropList>
```

This defines the behavior and specifies it as having an HTML type, accepting HTML data being dropped on it. It also specifies a dropCuetemplate, which points at a page element that will render status and debug information while you are dragging an element around the page. You can see the dropCueTemplate in action in Figure 11-25.

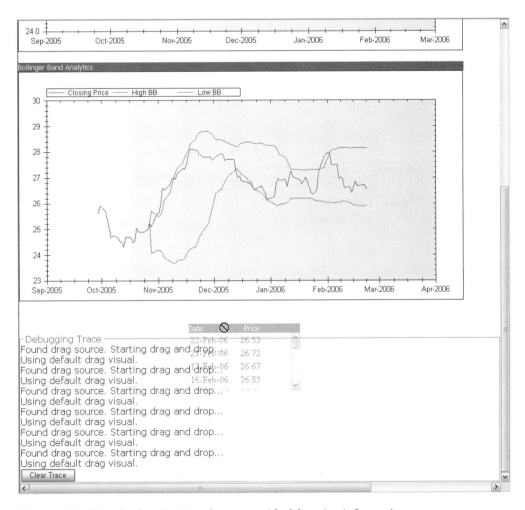

Figure 11-25. *Using the dropCueTemplate to provide debugging information*

Each of the three panes is a list item (`<li>` tag), and each one contains a table header, implemented as an HTML table contained within a `<div>` element. If you look at the Atlas Script, the list item is associated with a control, and the `<div>` element wrapping the corresponding table header within the list item is given the handle of a draggableListItem.

So if you look at the following HTML:

```
<li id="PHItem">
<div id="PHDiv">
  <table cellspacing='0' cellpadding='0'
         class='style1' style='border-width: 0'>
  <tr class='style2'>
    <td style='background-color: #1077ad; ' width="100px">Date</td>
    <td style='background-color: #1077ad; ' width="100px">Price</td>
  </tr>
  </table>
</div>
<div id="PHContents">
  <atlas:UpdatePanel ID="THTextPanel" runat="server">
   <ContentTemplate>
    <asp:Panel ID="Panel1" runat="Server"
                ScrollBars="auto" Width="200px"
                Height="100px">
      <asp:Label ID="lblPH" runat="server" Text="">
      </asp:Label>
    </asp:Panel>
   </ContentTemplate>
  </atlas:UpdatePanel>
  <atlas:UpdateProgress runat="server" ID="Prog3">
    <ProgressTemplate>
      Loading...
    </ProgressTemplate>
  </atlas:UpdateProgress>
</div>
</li>
```

and then examine the Atlas Script associated with it:

```
<control id="PHItem">
  <behaviors>
    <draggableListItem handle="PHDiv" />
  </behaviors>
</control>
```

you can see that the control gets mapped to the list item containing the entire table. The title for the table or graph is then assigned as the handle for the <draggableListItem> behavior. Thus, when you hold the mouse down on the title bar of any of the controls, you'll be able to drag them around the screen as you saw earlier. When you drop them, they will "snap" into place in the nearest available slot on the list. Thus, when you drag one control over another and drop it, it will snap into place either above or below the control depending on where the mouse was when you released the mouse button.

Summary

This chapter covered a typical real-world ASP.NET application and showed how you could drastically enhance it using the Atlas server and client libraries. It demonstrated a full *n*-tier architecture, with diverse resource tiers exposed via web services; a data retrieval layer that abstracted the complexity of talking to the resources; a business logic tier that applied business logic such as the calculation of financial analytics; and a presentation tier that implemented the presentation logic. The code that was written to implement this functionality was straight ASP.NET and C#.

You then enhanced this application using Atlas server-side controls. You used UpdatePanel controls throughout to wrap the different page panes that get updated to provide partial asynchronous page updates. A button on the page provided a drill down into some more advanced data, and this demonstrated how you could add an update to the page without triggering a full-page refresh and the associated "blink."

The example showed how to embed graphics—generated using a third-party control, the open source ZedGraph—within the page by hosting them on external pages and generating the HTML markup that would reference them on the main page. This HTML was embedded within an UpdatePanel, so again it didn't cause a full-page refresh when the graphic was downloaded and rendered on the page.

The example implemented two graphics: the first was a basic line graph containing the price history of the stock, and the second was a compound line graph containing three lines (the price history, the lower Bollinger band, and the upper Bollinger band).

Finally, you added some Atlas Script to the page that provided some typical Web 2.0 functionality where the user can set their preferences for the page by dragging and dropping its contents into their preferred layout.

With that, this book is now complete. I hope you have enjoyed learning about the *Foundations of Atlas*, including the tour of the philosophy of developing Ajax-style applications and the unique and powerful approach to this that ASP.NET Atlas gives you. You looked through how JavaScript has become object oriented when using Atlas client libraries; how to use Atlas Script, an XML variant that allows for powerful page-level functions to be declaratively developed; how to use server-side controls that empower asynchronous functionality with as little intrusion on your existing code as possible; and how to use the various value-added libraries that Atlas give you for UI glitz, animation, and mapping. Finally, in this chapter you looked at a real-world application and how you would implement it as an Ajax application quickly, simply, and powerfully using Atlas.

Welcome to the world of Web 2.0!

Index

You Need the Companion eBook

Your purchase of this book entitles you to buy the companion PDF-version eBook for only $10. Take the weightless companion with you anywhere.

We believe this Apress title will prove so indispensable that you'll want to carry it with you everywhere, which is why we are offering the companion eBook (in PDF format) for $10 to customers who purchase this book now. Convenient and fully searchable, the PDF version of any content-rich, page-heavy Apress book makes a valuable addition to your programming library. You can easily find and copy code—or perform examples by quickly toggling between instructions and the application. Even simultaneously tackling a donut, diet soda, and complex code becomes simplified with hands-free eBooks!

Once you purchase your book, getting the $10 companion eBook is simple:

➊ Visit **www.apress.com/promo/tendollars/**.

➋ Complete a basic registration form to receive a randomly generated question about this title.

➌ Answer the question correctly in 60 seconds, and you will receive a promotional code to redeem for the $10.00 eBook.

2560 Ninth Street • Suite 219 • Berkeley, CA 94710

eBookshop

Offer valid through 11/29/2006.